THE
ALCOHOLIC
SELF

SOCIOLOGICAL OBSERVATIONS

Series Editor: **JOHN M. JOHNSON,** Arizona State University

"This series seeks its inspiration primarily from its subject matter and the nature of its observational setting. It draws on all academic disciplines and a wide variety of theoretical and methodological perspectives. The series has a commitment to substantive problems and issues and favors research and analysis which seek to blend actual observations of human actions in daily life with broader theoretical, comparative, and historical perspectives. SOCIOLOGICAL OBSERVATIONS aims to use all of our available intellectual resources to better understand all facets of human experience and the nature of our society."

—John M. Johnson

THE ALCOHOLIC SELF

Norman K. Denzin

SAGE PUBLICATIONS
The Publishers of Professional Social Science
Newbury Park Beverly Hills London New Delhi

For information address:

SAGE Publications, Inc.
2111 West Hillcrest Drive
Newbury Park, California 91320

SAGE Publications Inc.   SAGE Publications Ltd.
275 South Beverly Drive   28 Banner Street
Beverly Hills   London EC1Y 8QE
California 90212   England

SAGE PUBLICATIONS India Pvt. Ltd.
M-32 Market
Greater Kailash I
New Delhi 110 048 India

Printed in the United States of America

Library of Congress Cataloging-in-Publication Data

Main entry under title:

Denzin, Norman K.
   The alcoholic self.

   (Sociological observations ; v. 18)
   Bibliography: p.
   Includes index.
   1. Alcoholics—Psychology.   2. Alcoholism.   I. Title.
II. Series.   [DNLM: 1. Alcoholism.   WM 274 D4171]
HV5045.D46   1986   616.86′1′0019   85-30744
ISBN 0-8039-2744-4
ISBN 0-8039-2745-2 (pbk.)

FIRST PRINTING

Contents

Acknowledgment

I would like to thank Carl Kingery for suggesting this project, Katherine Ryan for her insights throughout, and John Johnson for his assistance and aid in conceptualizing this volume and its companion *The Recovering Alcoholic.*

Self-consciousness withdrawn into the inmost retreats of its being . . . Doubled, divided and at variance with itself. . . . It lives in dread of action and existence . . . it is a hollow object which it fills with the feeling of emptiness [Hegel, 1931: 251].

Alcohol:	a colorless volatile flammable liquid, C_2H_5OH, synthesized or obtained by fermentation of sugars and starches, and widely used, either pure or denatured, as a solvent, in drugs, cleaning solutions, explosives, and intoxicating beverages.
Alcoholic:	a person who drinks alcoholic liquors habitually and to excess, or who suffers from alcoholism.
Alcoholism:	a chronic pathological condition, chiefly of the nervous and gastroenteric systems, caused by habitual excessive alcoholic consumption . . . temporary mental disturbance, muscular inco-ordination, and paresis caused by excessive alcoholic consumption. [*American Heritage Dictionary of the English Language.*]
Disease:	*(dis-ease)* "uneasiness (in this sense often written dis-ease); a disorder or want in health or body; an ailment: cause of pain—to make uneasy. [*Chambers 20th Century Dictionary*, 1983: 356].

(Anonymous Alcoholic): "When I drink I can't predict my behavior."

Foreword

Arizona State University, Tempe

Who could have anticipated that a study of drunks could have produced such a profound analysis of American white male culture, and what it means to be alive in America in the latter part of the twentieth century? What we are about to read in the following pages of Norman K.Denzin's book is an extraordinary analysis of alcoholism and alcoholics, one that is grounded in the recognition of the truth of each alcoholic's life. But it is also much more than that. It is a statement about white male culture and American social structure. In its pages, one finds the evidence of vast social and spiritual poverty as well as hopefulness about the possibilities for regeneration. In its pages, one will find the stories of how Denzin joined with many others in a search for their souls, and how one comes to recognize the existence of a spiritual power that transcends the individual. There is much more than this, too. But this book, like all other books, will gain its meaning for the reader based perhaps not so much on what Denzin says in its pages, but on how the life experiences of the reader have led to a certain stage of growth and development that allows for one, rather than another, interpretation of its contents. This is as it should be.

That we should find grand things in small and unexpected places is a noble part of the sociological tradition. So in this respect, Denzin's book stands shoulder to shoulder with some of our classics. In Emile Durkheim's *Suicide,* we learned how the seemingly most individual and private act of taking of one's life told us much about the nature of social cohesion and group integration. Max Weber's studies told us how the otherworldly asceticism of Calvinism created the ethic for material accumulation, so prevalent in Western societies. Robert Merton has told us about how the seemingly most obscure acts of rule violation tell us about the goals of American culture. From Kingsley Davis, we learn how the history of prostitution tells us much about the stability and integration of family life. From the works of Jack Douglas, we have learned about the interdependencies of deviance and respectability, and how the creation of social rules contains the seeds and possibilities of their violations for social actors. In the works of Erving Goffman, we were surprised to learn how mental hospitals and other total institutions could enlighten us about normality and the taken-for-granted and unseen rules by which it is presented and seen by others. These works, as well as many others in the social science traditions, began in small places, but partly transcended their space and time because they bridged the gap between the lived experiences of individuals and the social contexts in which they search for their truth. Denzin's book creates such a bridge, and from its edifice even those of us who do not drink will be much enlightened about what it means to be alive in our time.

The Alcoholic Self can be read in many ways. The most straightforward way, perhaps, is to learn about the substance of alcoholism, alcoholic experience, the alcoholic self, and the seeds of its regeneration. In this way, Denzin's book has much to say to us. This is a phenomenological analysis, which stems from the fact that many individuals shared their lives with Denzin in his search for truth. His goal is to articulate the inner structure and the inner experience of alcoholism. He recognizes each alcoholic as a universal singular, and the truth contained in each individual's experience with alcohol. Using alcohol is part of the experience of being a normal American at this point in time, and is associated by individuals with their selfhood, freedom, and locations in the status order. The story of alcoholism, then, is a story about a relationship between individuals and social structure. From Denzin's view, this relationship involves a dis-ease of time, a dis-ease of self, and dis-ease of emotionality for those who experience it in daily life. Alcoholics use alcohol in an attempt to make peace with their sense of the relationship between past, present, and future. The alcoholics' path is a mistaken one, but their problem is one that concerns all of the rest of us, too, and so in their search we may all learn more about our own path, to the extent that our own individual experiences have led us to recognize the problem. Alcoholism involves, for alcoholic subjects, a dis-ease of emotionality. Alcoholics use alcohol to make some peace with their negative emotions, guilts, fears, and resentments. They seek to control these, as do most of the rest of us. They are mistaken in their path, but in their search we learn more about own own guilts and fears, and how it is that, in recognizing them for what they are, we recognize more about the divine essence of life itself. Alcoholism involves a dis-ease of self, and experienced separation between the alcoholic subject and the place of alcohol in the social and spiritual order. Alcoholics use alcohol to gain, recognize, and assert their power in the world, their attempt to live an authentic existence with others. Alcoholics seek self-control. Each believes that he or she is in control of the world that surrounds the self, and in this control is experienced a sense of pride by the alcoholic subject, which leads him or her to take the next drink, even when the individual knows that he or she will probably lose control of self. It is this pride in self that ties the alcoholic to a competitive relationship with alcohol. The path is a mistaken one, but from the alcoholic's search, we learn more about our own, and our universal concerns to grapple with these questions. Finally, we find in Denzin's book the story about how the spiritual poverty of alcoholism contains the seeds for its own recovery, which begins with an alcoholic's surrender to his or her self-pride, bad faith, and imaginary ideals. In this surrender, we learn about how alcoholics achieve a more true and authentic sense of their rightful and legitimate power as individuals, and their rightful place in the social and spiritual world. The second volume of Denzin's search, *The Recovering Alcoholic,* tells us much more about this process of personal and spiritual regeneration.

Another way this book can be read is as a statement about American male culture in the latter part of the twentieth century. The values of alcoholics, whether they be men or women, are those that are found to be ingrained in white male culture. We all know, recognize, and value them: individuality, control, responsibility, identification with one's social roles, and the power to achieve social success as defined in this culture at this point in time. Denzin's focus is the alcoholic subject and the experience of alcoholism, but in this focus we find illuminated these larger structures and the processes of male culture. In this respect, the book is at once phenomenological and structural, thus bridging the frequently observed gap between different layers of social understanding Denzin writes:

> To study the active alcoholic, then, is to hold a mirror up to one side of society; that side which is taken-for-granted and driven deep inside the selves of ordinary men and women. To study recovery is to examine another side of society; that side which makes problematic what others take-for-granted. This is what the recovering alcoholic accomplishes. In his or her actions, the alcoholic subject reveals to the rest of us how we might become something other than we now are. In studying the alcoholic we study ourselves.

A final way to read this book is as a story about how Denzin joined with many others in a search for their souls. Western rationality guides individuals to separate the knowing subject from the objects of its knowledge, and denies to individuals a recognition of their divine and universal being in self. All of our speech in daily life is animated by our confusions in making this recognition. All readers of this book share this animus with Denzin and his alcoholic subjects. We read this book because we are still trying to use our rationality and our intellect to understand that which cannot be understood solely through rationality and intellect. We read it because we all desire to be in better touch with the deep wellsprings of our desires and our emotions.

Preface

The alcoholic self is the topic of this book. The alcoholic self is divided against itself, trapped within the negative emotions that alcoholism produces. The rather enormous literature on alcoholism does not contain any seriously sustained consideration of the lived experiences of the active alcoholic who lives an alcoholic self on a daily basis. This book, the first of three volumes on alcoholism in American society, represents an attempt to fill this void. (The second part of this study is titled *The Recovering Alcoholic;* the third part is titled *Treating Alcoholism,* and is intended for practitioners in the field of alcoholism.)

My point of departure is the active, problem drinker who comes to be defined as "alcoholic." Throughout this study I employ the lay definition of alcoholism. An alcoholic is a person who defines him- or herself as an alcoholic. To this definition I add two features. First, the alcoholic has lost control over drinking. Once an alcoholic starts drinking he or she is unable to stop and will continue drinking until intoxicated. Second, the alcoholic is unable to abstain from drinking. These two criteria were present in the life stories of every alcoholic I observed in this investigation. They are the same criteria employed by Jellinek (1960).

I understand alcoholism to be a dis-ease of conduct that is emotional, interactional, temporal, and relational. Alcoholism is rooted in the self-definitions and self-feelings of the alcoholic. The term *alcoholism* references, then, a twofold phenomenon. First, excessive, addictive drinking is at the heart of alcoholism. Second, drinking masks underlying interactional processes embedded in the self of the drinker. These processes structure the lived experiences of the alcoholic. Alcohol is used as an anesthetic to escape from deep problematics of self, including a basic uneasiness with living in the world without the aid of a drug. For alcoholics these underlying processes become distorted as alcoholism takes over their lives. The alcoholic is trapped in a vicious circle of addictive drinking. The self the alcoholic drank to escape remains buried inside the lived experiences that alcoholism produces. Alcohol has produced an alcoholically divided self.

This book reflects a dissatisfaction with current behavioral, cognitive, structural, and psychoanalytic theories of alcoholism. The literature concerned with these theories offers very few insights into the phenomenon of alcoholism as a form of lived experience that traps the individual in a self-destructive cycle of existence. My intentions are to present the inner side of alcoholism, as seen from the point of view of the active, drinking alcoholic.

The alcoholic subject is a mirror to the larger society. This individuality compresses into a single lifetime the tensions, the contradictions, and the conflicts that flow through the "social bodies" of a drinking culture. American culture, alternatively permissive and then prohibitive in its attitudes toward alcohol and drinking, "scripts" subjectivity and selfhood in the consumption of alcohol and other drugs. Nearly crushed and destroyed by alcohol consumption, the alcoholic suffers that dis-ease of conduct modern society chooses to call "alcoholism."

The alcoholic, recovering or still drinking, sheds light on the structures of everyday life that are taken for granted. This individual brings into vivid focus what it means to be a "normal" interactant in everyday situations. The alcoholic takes to the point of near self-destruction commonplace assumptions regarding alcohol, drinking, selfhood, emotionality, altered states of consciousness, and social relations with others.

This work is an elaboration of my earlier study, *On Understanding Emotion* (1984a), which offered a phenomenological analysis of emotionality as a facet of lived experience. This volume applies that perspective to the experiences of the active alcoholic. I assume that alcoholism is a form of self-experience in which negative emotions divide the self into warring inner factions that are fueled and distorted by alcohol and intoxication.

This book (and its companions) is directed to three audiences. First, it is addressed to social theorists who are concerned with the problematic of the vanishing subject in modern society. The alcoholic is an example of the loss of subjectivity that many postmodern, structuralist theories have anticipated. Second, it is directed to psychologists and social psychologists who are concerned with alcoholism as a form of individual pathology and social deviance. Third, this work is aimed at those researchers and practitioners in the field of alcoholism who confront the realities of active alcoholism on a daily basis. At the same time, it is intended for alcoholics, who may find familiar pictures of themselves in these pages.

CONTENTS AND ORGANIZATION

This work is divided into eight chapters. In Chapter 1, I discuss alcohol use and drinking in American society, situate my study within the alcoholism literature, present the Six Theses of Alcoholism, and discuss my empirical materials. Chapter 2 critically examines current scientific theories of alcoholism and alcoholics. I give special attention to Gregory Bateson's theory of alcoholism, which he calls "cybernetics of self." Chapter 2 presents what I hope is a definitive critique of radical behavioral approaches to alcoholism and its treatment.

Chapter 3 is a study of the theory of alcoholism and alcoholics that Alcoholics Anonymous offers to the active (and recovering) alcoholic. Chapter 4 presents a phenomenological analysis of the lay theory of drinking, problem drinking, alcoholism, and alcoholics. It examines the arguments the problem drinker constructs so as to continue drinking.

Chapter 5 sets out in detail the Six Theses of Alcoholism. These are interpretive positions that examine, from different angles, the inner structures of experience surrounding alcoholism. I focus on temporality, social relationships, emotionality, bad faith or denial, self-control, and the process of surrender. Chapter 6, the "Alcoholically Divided Self," studies the alcoholic self as a structure of negative experience. I examine the negative emotions—anger, fear, hate, resentment—that characterize the alcoholic situation. I also devote considerable attention to the relationship between alcohol and violence. Finally, I take the alcoholic through the stages of self-collapse and surrender that accompany the final stages of active, alcoholic drinking.

Chapter 7 speaks in compressed detail (because the topic is elaborated at length in the next book in this series, *The Recovering Alcoholic*) to the recovering alcoholic self. I examine the main structures of experience that must be confronted if recovery is to occur. Chapter 8 offers a set of reflections on self, temporality, and alcoholism. I suggest that in studying the alcoholic we study ourselves. Active or recovering, the alcoholic reveals to each of us how we might become more than we currently are, or considerably less than we now take for granted.

Throughout this book, I have tried to use nonsexist language. At times, however, the multiple use of "he or she" and "his or her" in a sentence has resulted in awkwardness. Therefore, at times the male or female pronouns and possessives are used exclusively in a passage. I have tried to use them equally often in order to convey the existence of alcoholism in both women and men.

—*Norman K. Denzin*
Champaign, Illinois

1

INTRODUCTION
Studying Alcoholism

Hell is our natural home. We have lost everything. We live in fear of living. Alcohol was our only friend. We found ourselves in alcohol and then it turned against us and tried to kill us. No other friend would do that to you. But we kept on drinking because we had to [Female alcoholic, 58 years old, sobriety date unknown].

In this study I examine a basic question: How do ordinary men and women live and experience the alcoholic self active alcoholism produces? I understand alcoholism to be a self-destructive form of activity in which the drinker compulsively drinks beyond the point where he or she can stop drinking for any extended period of time, even if he or she wants to. I adopt the point of view of those self-defined alcoholics who bring their lived experiences to the tables and meeting rooms of Alcoholics Anonymous. I assume that each alcoholic is a universal singular, epitomizing in his or her lifetime the experiences of all alcoholics (see Sartre, 1981: vi).

Alcoholism has, since 1955, been designated as a form of physical, as well as mental, illness by the American Medical Association. An inquiry into alcoholism is also a study in mental illness, but into a form of mental illness to which alcoholics give special meaning. The practicing alcoholic may be said to live an emotionally divided self (James, 1961; Denzin, 1984a). This, then, is a phenomenological study in biography and society, for it joins the private problems of alcoholics with the public discourse and the public experience that surrounds alcoholism's presence in American society (Bertaux, 1981; Gusfield, 1981; Mills, 1959; Beauchamp, 1980; Madsen, 1974).

Alcohol is the most abused chemical substance in the world (Royce, 1981). According to a recent psychiatric, epidemiological survey, 13.6% of Americans at some time in their lives have suffered from alcohol abuse and alcohol dependence (*New York Times*, 1983). In the United States some 9 million people are estimated to be alcoholics and a recent Gallup poll estimates that one-third of Americans have a drinking problem. The "mental illness" associated with alcohol abuse is thought to rank second to depression as the most prevalent mental disorder in American society. The human and economic costs of alcoholism are incalculable, and are barely reflected in the statistical facts that record alcoholic-related suicides, broken marriages and families, loss of work productivity, ruined lives, personal degradation, and the loss of self, income, sanity, and physical health (Cockerham, 1981: 169). Alcoholism, alcohol, and alcoholics touch the lives of one out of seven Americans at some point in their lifetimes.

ALCOHOL USE IN THE UNITED STATES

It is estimated that 7 out of 10 Americans drink, at least occasionally (Royce, 1981: 3). In a survey of the incidence of problem drinking in the United States conducted in 1967, Cahalan found that 43% of the men and 21% of the women who drank had experienced serious problems directly related to the drinking of alcohol at some time in their lives (Johnson, 1973: 183; Cahalan, 1970). Having, or having had, problems related to alcohol use is, then, if not a personal experience of the individual who drinks, at least a problem he or she is aware that others have had.

A social text has been written that positions the problem or alcoholic drinker squarely within a matrix of medical, social, scientific, personal, economic, and ideological beliefs that performs two symbolic moves simultaneously (see Johnson, 1973). First, alcohol use is part of the experience of being a normal American, male or female, during the first two-thirds of the twentieth century. Second, alcohol abuse, although associated with selfhood, freedom, and the status symbolism of the new middle class (Johnson, 1973), must be dissociated from the self of the abuser. Alcoholism, being a disease or an illness, is not the responsibility of the drinker. Yet, the ethos of self-responsibility and self-control that permeates American culture makes alcoholism the personal responsibility of the drinker who abuses alcohol. This subtle interpretation of alcoholism as an illness, which has the self at its center, escapes general public understanding. Hence, although the popularization of the disease or medical conception of alcoholism has spread throughout American society, it remains an illness that is not like other illnesses or diseases (diabetes, cancer) the individual may incur. It is not a purely medical or biological problem. This understanding remains in place, despite the efforts by the American Medical Association, the National Council on Alcoholism, the World Health Organization, the National Institution on Alcoholism and Alcohol Abuse, and Alcoholics Anonymous to persuade the public otherwise (Beauchamp, 1980: 22-48; A.A. 1957: 235-251; see also Blane, 1968; Chafetez and Yoerg, 1977).

This vicious ambiguity that surrounds the American attitude toward the self and the disease called alcoholism is revealed in the Mulford and Miller survey of 1964 in which they asked a random sample of respondents to give their personal views of the alcoholic. Of the sample, 65% said the alcoholic was sick. There were 60% who said the alcoholic was weak willed, and 31% who said alcoholics were morally weak. Only 24% said the alcoholic was sick, without using any of the other labels (Johnson, 1973: 146; Mulford and Miller, 1964). Being weak willed and morally weak are two meanings directly associated with strength of self and with self-will or willpower. Vaillant's (1983: 1-11) most recent review of the meanings surrounding the disease concept of alcoholism confirm the Mulford and Miller (1964) and Mulford (1970) findings.

The American alcoholic, then, at least since the 1960s, has been perceived as being sick, as suffering from an illness or a disease, but lacking willpower and self-will. The disease or illness conception of alcoholism has not succeeded in removing the *stigma of self* from the conduct of the alcoholic who has alcoholism (see Beauchamp, 1980: 68; Kurtz, 1979: 199-230; Levine, 1978: 160).

The alcoholic typically has been contrasted with the normal social drinker (Beauchamp, 1980). The normal social drinker apparently possesses skills, powers, and immunities that allow him or her to drink within the range of normal conduct that our culture prescribes. That is, the normal social drinker does not have socially defined problems with alcohol. These problems do not exist because of attributes he or she possesses. These abilities are in the individual and in the terminology that culture and science use to describe his or her use of alcohol. Locating the ability to control or not to control alcohol in the individual shifts attention away from the culture, the social groups, and the historical social structures the person inherits from society. By positioning the normal social drinker midway between the problem, alcoholic drinker and the person who abstains, American society has driven its obsession with self-control into the mind of every man and woman who comes in contact with alcohol. That is, control is a personal phenomenon that can be manipulated by willpower and the methods of modern behavioral science. The mythical social drinker who drinks normally thus epitomizes America's relationship with alcohol, alcoholism, and the alcoholic.

SITUATING THIS STUDY

The "alcoholism" that the alcoholic confronts on a daily basis is experienced as a relationship with the world. Consequently, it must be studied interactionally and interpretively as a structure of experience that is produced and reproduced, over and over again, in the lived experiences of the "alcoholic" man or woman.

As a study in lived experience, this investigation necessarily becomes an examination of temporality, emotionality, and interaction. That is, the alcoholic's being in the world is temporal. Alcohol alters his or her inner stream of emotional, temporal experiences. The alcoholic's interactional experiences with others are woven through an alcoholically altered inner stream of consciousness. The alcoholic confronts "reality" from the vantage point of the social world of alcohol, which, like the world of emotionality, is a separate province of reality (Denzin, 1984a: 95). Although embedded in the everyday life world, the world of alcohol stands distinct from that world. Yet when in the world that alcohol gives him or her, the drinker takes that world everywhere. The alcoholic cannot just walk away from it, as one might walk away from the work or family worlds one also occupies. Like the world of emotion, the world of alcohol shatters the taken-for-granted assumptions of the everyday world, rendering its assumptions and presuppositions meaningless and irrelevant.

Alcoholism and alcohol cut through every structure of the subject's life, leaving nothing in his or her world untouched. Consequently, a study of the self of the recovering or practicing alcoholic becomes an inquiry into the meaning of existence as existence is lived by the man or woman who places alcohol between himself or herself and the world of others. This investigation is an extended essay on the understanding of what I term "alcoholic existence." By disclosing the meanings of existence as seen from the point of view of the recovering alcoholic, I hope to shed light on what it means to live at this moment in the twentieth century. The active alcoholic is a person who, for some extended period of his or her life, approaches the world through an altered state of consciousness.

Alcoholic subjects find themselves, as Marx might say, inserted into a mode of existence and into a moment in history over which they have no control. Alcoholics find that history is going on behind their backs. Alcoholics drink in an attempt to control their relationship to these events that are occurring in front of and behind them. They find that they are the victims of their own actions and that their lives have lost meaning for them. They experience divided selves and hate themselves and everyone who surrounds them. As they alter their consciousness in order to change their beings and presences in the world, they find that the world destructively acts back on them.

"Normal" Time and Emotion

The alcoholic lives a *dis-ease* of time and emotion that is experienced as an uneasiness with self. This uneasiness is dealt with through alcoholic drinking. Alcohol obliterates or neutralizes the alcoholic's fear of time and self. Fearful of time, the alcoholic dwells in the negative emotions of the past. Such self-feelings undercut and undermine the alcoholic's ability to confront the present and the future in a straightforward manner.

In contrast to alcoholic time and emotion stands "normal" time and feeling. "Normal" temporality and "normal" emotionality conceptualize these processes in a reflective, purposive fashion. This allows the person to incorporate self-feelings and temporal experiences into ongoing action in a nondisruptive, non-self-destructive way. Normal emotionality does not dwell in the negativity of the past. It is not fearful of the present and the future. Normal emotionality does not undercut the self-structures of the person. Alcoholic emotionality does. Alcoholic temporality turns away from the present and leads to the production of negative emotional experiences, which further locate the alcoholic in the addictive cycle of drinking alcoholism turns upon.

An understanding of the alcoholic requires an interpretation of "normal" time and emotion, for the alcoholic attempts to achieve a state of "normalness" through the drinking act. Afraid of not being normal, the alcoholic drinks alcoholically so as to cover up this fear. The alcoholic hopes that the next drink will allow him or her to experience time and self-feeling in the way that normals do.

THE SIX THESES OF ALCOHOLISM

Six theses, or interpretive positions, structure my understanding of alcoholism (see Chapter 5 for an extended discussion of each). The first is the "Thesis of the Temporality of Self." This thesis assumes that the alcoholic lives his or her experiences in the world primarily through the altered temporal consciousness that alcohol produces. This means that the alcoholic is always out of temporal synchronization with fellow interactants. Thought and emotional processes are dulled or sped up as a result of the alcohol consumed. Alcoholism is a disease of time.

The second thesis concerns the relational structures of the alcoholic's self. It assumes that the alcoholic lives within alcohol-centered social relationships that have been distorted and twisted by the effects of alcohol on the alcoholic's self. In contrast to more normal social relationships in which affection and love may bond two individuals, in the alcohol-centered relationship, alcohol becomes the object that joins interactants in a combative, competitive, negative, hostile relationship. The emotionality of self is the third thesis. As indicated above, alcoholism is a dis-ease of emotionality and self-feeling. The alcoholic experiences negative, painful emotions on a daily basis. Alcohol blunts the ability to feel emotionality. Feelings are always filtered through the altered temporal consciousness alcohol creates.

The fourth thesis is the "Thesis of Bad Faith." I suggest that alcoholics and their significant others attempt to escape alcoholism by denying its existence. Structures of denial, self-deception, lying, and bad faith thus lie at the heart of the alcoholic's alcoholism (see Sartre, 1956, on bad faith).

The fifth thesis is the "Thesis of Self-Control." This thesis, following from the fourth, asserts that alcoholics believe they are in control of themselves and the world that surrounds them. As Bateson (1972a: 312) has argued, the alcoholic's self-pride leads him or her to risk taking a drink, even when knowing that self-control will be lost. Pride in self ties the alcoholic into a competitive relationship with alcohol. The alcoholic drinks in order to prove self-control.

The sixth thesis is the "Thesis of Self-Surrender." This interpretation argues that the alcoholic's recovery begins when he or she surrenders to false self-pride, breaks through the systems of bad faith, and comes to accept his or her alcoholism. Until such surrender, recovery cannot begin. In this volume I take the alcoholic up to and through surrender. In the next volume in this series, I examine the recovery process that follows from surrender.

The Alcoholic Self

A basic premise organizes the Six Theses. Every alcoholic I observed drank to escape an inner emptiness of self. This emptiness, often traced to early family experiences of death, parental loss, sexual abuse, drug abuse, or alcoholism, was manifested in terms of a fundamental instability of self. In this regard the alcoholic grotesquely displays the inner narcissicism and tendency toward madness that Lacan (1977), Lasch (1983, 1985), and Kohut (1984) have located at the core of human existence. The self-other experiences, the self-ideals, and the ideal selves that the alcoholic pursues are largely imaginary and out of touch with the world of the real. Alcohol sustains these imaginary ideals. The alcoholic lives in the realm of the imaginary and this may be a troubled world of sexual and emotional relations that reflect the alcoholic's unstable inner self. As a result of living in the realm of the imaginary, the alcoholic is unable to take the attitude of the other, to use Mead's (1934) phrase. He or she is unable to enter into and find a place in a society of preexisting selves. His or her imaginary life will not permit this. Intense preoccupations with self shut the alcoholic off from others. Because alcohol's psychological and physiological effects cannot be shared emotionally, the alcoholic's self is cut off from the world of normal interaction with others (see Tiebout, 1954).

These six theses, and the basic premise that organizes them, are drawn from three sources. They are based on my reading of the scientific literature on alcoholism. They are contained, in different form, in Alcoholics Anonymous's theory of alcoholism (see Chapter 3). Most important, they are grounded in my empirical materials.

EMPIRICAL MATERIALS

I examine the stories of self that active and recovering alcoholics bring to Alcoholics Anonymous, a worldwide organization of recovering alcoholics whose estimated membership in 1985 was over 1 million in over 58,000 groups in 110 countries. My materials are drawn from a five-year period of study, primarily in a medium-sized community of 150,000 in the eastern part of the United States. I have observed the workings of A.A. in over 2,000 open and closed meetings. I have gathered observations from substance abuse treatment centers and detoxification programs. I have had discussions and interviews with active and recovering alcoholics and their family members who belong to Al-Anon and Alateen. I also have had conversations with treatment personnel, physicians, psychiatrists, social workers, hospital emergency room nurses, and alcoholism counselors who make it their business to work with alcoholics. I have firsthand experience with alcoholism in my own family.

In addition to these sources, I have examined the literature of Alcoholics Anonymous including *The Big Book,* or *Alcoholics Anonymous* (1976). Other sources include *Twelve Steps and Twelve Traditions* (1953), *As Bill Sees It* (1967), *Came to Believe* (1973), *Living Sober* (1975), *Dr. Bob and the Good Oldtimers: A Biography, with Recollections of Early A.A. in the Midwest* (1980), *"Pass It On": The Story of Bill Wilson and How the A.A. Message Reached the World* (1984), *Lois Remembers* (1977), *The Grapevine* (the international monthly journal of Alcoholics Anonymous), *Twenty-Four Hours a Day* (Hazelton, 1975; this book is not authorized by A.A.), and numerous materials printed and distributed by the World Services Office of A.A.

The community or social world of alcoholics I observed numbered over 200 regular members who maintained near or continuous sobriety (as determined by self-report) by attending one or more meetings a week. Within this number there were 5 distinct groupings of recovering alcoholics. There was a core number of members (15) who had been sober over 10 years—one for 22 years—and the remainder averaging 14 years. These members were the "old-timers" in the A.A. community. There was a second group, with 50 members, who had been sober 5 to 10 years. The third group, numbering 40, had been sober from 2 to 5 years. The fifth group of 80 members had been sober less than a year, 45 for 6 months or more, 30 for 6 months or less. The most "slips" (returns to drinking) occurred within this group.

Within this broad fivefold structure there were other segments or smaller groupings. There were two women's groups, one gay and lesbian group, one young people's group, and seven Narcotics Anonymous groups that drew largely from the younger A.A. pool. I observed over 700 individuals who came and went or visited A.A. meetings during this period of time and defined themselves as alcoholics in meetings. A large proportion of this pool of individuals were patients in the two treatment centers in the community.

Traditionally, "two or more alcoholics meeting together for purposes of sobriety may consider themselves an A.A. group, provided that, as a group they are self-supporting and have no outside affiliation" (A.A., 1985: ii). Because two persons constitute a group for A.A.'s purposes, and therefore can have a meeting, and because the A.A. community I studied regularly saw the participation of "old-timers" in meetings, it would not be uncommon at any meeting to have members whose sobriety spanned the time frame of less than a day to over 15 years.

However, chronological age and sobriety date (days, months, years of continuous sobriety) often are widely divergent within A.A. Interactional age (Denzin, 1977: 162) or A.A. experience may bear little relationship to the individual's real age, sobriety date, A.A. age, or birthday. Thus in the community of recovering alcoholics I studied there were 2 individuals under the age of 25 with 4 years of sobriety, and 2 members under the age of 18 with 2 years sobriety each. There were numerous members over 45 who had less than 6 months of sobriety. Similarly, at least 5 members had over 10 years A.A. experience, but not one of them had succeeded in gaining over 9 months of sobriety. Slips, discontinuities in sobriety, and age at the time of the first serious encounter with A.A. disrupt and distort the relationship among these 3 age or temporal structures.

These temporal discrepancies potentially are present in every encounter that occurs between A.A. members. The gaps and distortions that arise among these 3 temporal structures (chronological age, length of continuous sobriety, and interactional experience with A.A.) support and underwrite the A.A. position that it is a 24-hour, one-day-at-a-time program that its members practice. The often-heard statement at A.A. meetings, "Whoever got up earliest this morning has the most sobriety at this meeting," is a pivotal point of departure for every recovering alcoholic—just as it is for every A.A. member who slips and comes back.

I observed fewer open meetings than closed meetings. An *open meeting* is open to any individual who has an interest in alcoholism. He or she need not be an alcoholic to attend. A *closed A.A. meeting* is attended only by individuals who have a desire to stop drinking and who may call themselves alcoholics, as the only requirement for A.A. membership is a desire to stop drinking. Persons who attend closed A.A. meetings typically identify themselves as alcoholic during the meeting when their turn to speak comes: "My name is Bill and I'm an alcoholic."

In the community I studied the number of meetings had increased to at least 4 closed A.A. meetings every day. In total there were 2 open meetings, 37 closed meetings, and 5 Al-Anon (meetings for spouses, friends, or relatives of alcoholics) meetings weekly. There were two alcohol treatment centers in the community, and six others within a fifty-mile radius of the city. There was a social club for alcoholics and the members of their families. There was no intergroup organization that connected the groups, as there typically is in communities over 150,000. The organization, or network, that existed between groups was coordinated by a small group of individuals who had an average of 14 years of continuous sobriety. A 24-hour answering service was maintained by the groups, however. The oldest meeting in the community dated from 1960.

My methods, described elsewhere (Denzin, 1978, 1982, 1984a), combine life histories with ethnographic, thick description, and phenomenological interpretation. For want of a better word this may be termed an *ethnography* of the alcoholic experience.

But it is also a case study of the lives of those men and women who were drinking and recovering during my fieldwork. I weave life stories and stories of self throughout my analysis, presenting alcoholics to the reader as they present themselves to fellow alcoholics. I also combine, in a variety of triangulated forms, a multiplicity of materials and methods including interviewing, observation, participation, archival analysis, textual criticism, semiotics, and the study of fictional and autobiographical accounts of alcoholism as given by such persons as John Berryman (1973) and Malcolm Lowry (1947).

At a deeper level, this inquiry is, in Foucault's (1970, 1977, 1980, 1982) senses, an archaeological and genealogical analysis of the micro power structures and discourses of knowledge that have congealed and coalesced to produce the alcoholic subject. This is a study of power, temporality, and the human subject. It is a study, too, of the forces that have produced the alcoholic subject within recent American history.

My intention is not to offer a new theory of alcoholics. Rather, I desire to remain as close as possible to the actual experience of alcoholism itself. I shall, in the main, employ terms that are derived from the lived experiences of alcoholics as they come to learn the language and the meanings of Alcoholics Anonymous. My analysis is interpretive, and will become causal only when the word *"cause"* is used by the alcoholic subject as he describes events that caused him to act in one way and not in another.

In the next chapter I offer a critical reading of the existing theories of alcoholism and alcoholics. I will indicate which of these theories should be set aside, if only temporarily, in favor of a social phenomenological interpretation of the alcoholic self.

A basic problem with my empirical materials must be noted. With few exceptions I did not observe alcoholics drinking. Nor did I observe any more than a few in their home or work settings. My materials are taken from the self-stories alcoholics tell around the tables of A.A.

There is a retrospective bias in these accounts. They do not report directly lived experience. Yet the experience that is reported upon, even though it has occurred in the immediate or distant past, becomes, in the moment of telling, an account of the self in the present. All I have, then, are the stories alcoholics tell and the observations I have of these alcoholics as they move from one meeting to another. From these stories I have extracted the picture of the alcoholic self that is offered in the following chapters.

This work should be evaluated by the following criteria. Do the interpretations of the alcoholic self illuminate and reveal alcoholism as a lived experience? Second, are the interpretations based on thickly contextualized materials that are historically and temporally grounded? Third, do the interpretations engulf and incorporate prior understandings of alcoholism and the alcoholic self? Fourth, do the interpretations cohere into a meaningful totality that produces understanding, however provisional and incomplete? If these criteria are met, I shall be satisfied.

Part I

DIFFERING VIEWS OF ALCOHOLISM

2

SCIENCE AND ALCOHOLISM

Consider the following account given by a 53-year-old printer at his second A.A. meeting after a 6-month absence. He has been attempting to stop drinking on his own for 2 years.

I can't get off the damned stuff by myself. When dad died he made me promise that I'd quit. I promised him, but I can't. I just can't seem to get to where I was when Dad died. The old man drank a quart of Old Fitzgerald everyday for 30 years, then he quit cold when the doctor told him to. My sister's an alcoholic, she can't quit either. The boss says Frank you've got to quit. I try, but you know I get those shakes in the morning on the way to work. I stop and get a half-pint of Peppermint Schnapps, so they can't smell it on my breath, and I drink it and then I quiet down, start to smile, and feel good. It starts to wear off about the middle of the morning. That's why I keep the cold beer in the ice chest in the trunk of the car. I go out for a smoke and sneak a beer. That gets me through to noon. Then I take lunch at Buddies and have a couple shots of Schnapps, with the beer that everybody else has. I can make it through the afternoon. Then I stop after work and really hit it. I get so shook up about not being able to stop that I seem to drink more. I keep drinkin till I pass out every night. The wife understands, and when I mark the days off on the calendar when I ain't had a drink she's so proud of me. I just think I ought to be able to do this thing by myself. The old man did. But I can't. I guess I'll just have to keep coming back to you people. My body's starting to show the effects now. The Doc says the liver can't take too much more of this. I don't know, when I take that drink these problems all go away. But they're there when the drink wears off.

This drinker displays the three criteria of alcoholism that are employed in this investigation. He calls himself an alcoholic. He cannot abstain from drinking for any sustained period of time and once he starts drinking he cannot stop. He qualifies as an alcoholic subject, the topic of this chapter. He is, in short, a gamma alcoholic, an example of the predominating species of alcoholism in the United States. He is the type of alcoholic most likely to come to Alcoholics Anonymous (Jellinek, 1960: 33).

My intentions are to review critically the classic and contemporary theories of alcoholism, to lay bare the underlying assumptions that structure current scientific understandings of this phenomemon as it currently presents itself to American society. A single thesis organizes my discussion. The scientific literature on alcoholism has, with the exception of the works of Jellinek, Madsen, and Bateson, produced an image of the alcoholic subject that is disconnected from the lived experiences of persons who live alcoholism on a daily basis.

I will treat the following topics: (1) the picture of the alcoholic subject as given in the anthropological, sociological, psychological, and psychiatric literature; (2) scientific theories of alcoholism, including genetic, learning theory, sociocultural, and interactionist formulations; and (3) an evaluation of these theories from a social phenomenological point of view. In discussing the scientific theories of alcoholism, I will give special attention to radical behaviorism. I will examine in detail the concepts of "craving" and "loss of control." I also will apply Lindesmith's (1968, 1974, 1975, 1977) theories of opiate addiction to the "addiction" experiences of the alcoholic.

THE ALCOHOLIC SUBJECT

The alcoholic subject, the subject of the classical and recent scientific literature on alcoholism, comes in several varieties: Skid Row (Wiseman, 1970; Spradley, 1970), chronic (Straus, 1974), alpha, beta, delta, gamma, epsilon (Jellinek, 1960); asymptomatic drinker, alcohol abuser, alcohol dependent (Vaillant, 1983); blue collar or college educated (Vaillant, 1983); primary-secondary (Madsen, 1974; Fox, 1957); American Indian (MacAndrew and Edgerton, 1969); black (Watts and Wright, 1983); female (Gomberg, 1976); gay and lesbian (Schuckit and Duby, 1983), a winner of the Nobel Prize for literature (Vaillant, 1983; Duhman, 1984); upper class or middle class, old and young (Royce, 1981); rural and urban, Finnish and Swedish (Room, 1983). There are, in short, no typical alcoholic subjects, only individuals who have been identified as alcoholic or as having problems with alcohol.

Nor is there an agreed-upon alcoholic or prealcoholic personality type (Solomon, 1983; Barnes, 1983), although some (Menninger, 1938; Knight, 1937) have spoken of an alcoholic personality. This conception persists in the literature, as does the search for such a type (Williams, 1976: 243-250). Catanzaro (1967: 38-40) suggests that the following characteristics, in various combinations, may "have formed the seed bed in which alcoholism grew": (1) high levels of anxiety in interpersonal relations; (2) emotional immaturity; (3) ambivalance toward authority; (4) low tolerance of frustration; (5) low self-esteem; (6) feelings of isolation; (7) perfectionism; (8) guilt; (9) compulsiveness; (10) angry overdependency; (11) sex-role confusion; and (12) an inability to express angry feelings adequately (see Madsen, 1974; MacAndrew and Edgerton, 1969, for criticisms of such formulations). Narcissism (Tiebout, 1954; Zwerling and Rosenbaum, 1959) also has been associated with the alcoholic personality (see Roebuck and Kessler, 1972: 96), as have defiance, grandiosity, and resentment (Tiebout, 1949).

To speak of an alcoholic personality type is to appeal to an objectively definable alcoholic or prealcoholic human nature that underlies and structures the problem drinker's actions in the world. Such an appeal presumes an essential structure to alcoholic human nature that precedes alcoholic existence. The explanatory recourse to a fixed, innate, or semi-impermeable personality structure that precedes alcoholic experience, or apparently calls out alcoholic conduct, is wholly incorrect and inappropriate. The fact that a "normal" personality type has never been identified also undercuts the attempt to locate an alcoholic or prealcoholic personality type.

However, the literature remains preoccupied with *who* this subject is, *when* he or she became an alcoholic, *why* this occurred, and whether or not he or she can be taught or *resocialized* so as to no longer be a problem drinker. Accordingly, this literature can be interpreted as offering a series of answers or hypotheses to causal questions concerning the etiology and natural history of alcoholism, although few natural history investigations have been undertaken, the majority being cross-sectional, sample surveys (Vaillant, 1983). The alcoholic subject is both the *effect* of causal agents that play upon him or her as alcohol is and is not consumed, as well as the *cause* of the effects that are experienced as a result of these factors, including continuing to drink. A circular model of causation that revolves around the alcoholic subject thus organizes this scientific literature.

The Alcoholic Experience

The individual whom science identifies as being alcoholic typically is assumed to have passed through the *prealcoholic* and *prodomal* phases of alcoholism. He or she is in either the *crucial* or *chronic* phase of the illness (Jellinek, 1962: 359-366). This alcoholic subject will have moved from socially motivated drinking to being a drinker who experiences "rewarding relief in the drinking situation" (Jellinek, 1962: 359). He or she soon "becomes aware of the contingency between relief and drinking" (Jellinek, 1962: 361). In this early, prealcoholic stage of drinking the subject will move between occasional and constant relief drinking. In the *prodomal* phases of drinking the subject will experience the onset of "blackouts." His or her drinking behaviors will indicate that beer, wine, and spirits have ceased to be beverages— they have become drugs the drinker needs. In this phase the drinker will begin to drink surreptitiously, will gulp drinks, feel guilt about doing so, and display a general preoccupation with alcohol. Alcohol consumption will be heavy, although overt intoxication is infrequent. This phase may last from 6 months to 4 or 5 years. It ends with the onset of "loss of control, which is the critical symptom of alcohol addiction" (Jellinek, 1962: 363).

Loss of control, Jellinek argues, means that any drinking of alcohol starts a chain reaction that "is felt by the drinker as a physical demand for alcohol." Once a drink is taken the "gamma" alcoholic may drink until intoxication, or until he or she is too sick to ingest any more alcohol. Loss of control develops gradually, and does not occur every time the subject drinks (Jellinek, 1960: 145).

After recovery from intoxication "it is not the loss of control— that is, the physical demand, apparent or real—which leads to a new bout after several days or weeks. The renewal of drinking is set off by the original psychological conflicts or by a simple social situation which involves drinking" (Jellinek, 1962: 363). Once the alcoholic drinks again he or she displays an inability to control the quantity drunk. It is still possible to control whether or not he or she will drink on any given occasion. The problem drinker will be drawn back to drinking when tensions arise, for a drink has become the remedy for reducing tension and anxiety. An alcoholic drinks to prove that he is the "master of his will" (Jellinek, 1962: 363). The drinker does not know that he or she has undergone a process that no longer makes it possible for him or her to control the amount of alcohol he or she drinks.

With the periodic loss of control emerge complex rationalizations the drinker gives him- or herself for drinking. The drinker locates explanations that "prove" that control has not been lost. Grandiose behaviors followed by periods of abstinence, a marked loss of self-esteem, signs of aggressive behavior, and changes in drinking patterns appear in this, the crucial phase of alcoholism. At this point, the subject's life has become totally "alcohol centered."

> The "physical demand" involved in the loss of control results in continual rather than continuous drinking. Particularly the "matutinal drink"...shows the continual pattern. The first drink at rising, let us say at 7 a.m., is followed by another drink at 10 or 11 a.m., and another drink around 1 p.m., while the more intensive drinking hardly starts before 5 p.m. [Jellinek, 1962: 365].

The *chronic phase* sees alcohol dominating the subject's daily round of activity. He or she suffers a loss of tolerance for alcohol. "Half of the previously required amount of alcohol may be sufficient to bring about a stuporous state" (Jellinek, 1962: 366). Trapped within a drinking cycle, in which the craving for a drink appears at regular four-hour intervals, the alcoholic finds that guilt and remorse have become reasons to continue drinking. The addict drinks to relieve the stresses created by excessive drinking. He or she craves the expected effect of relief from the withdrawal effects being felt (Jellinek, 1960: 146).

Although these reactions to excessive drinking give the appearance of an "alcoholic personality," they are but secondary behaviors superimposed over "a large variety of personality types which have a few traits in common, in particular a low capacity for coping with tensions" (Jellinek, 1962: 367).

The alcoholic subject (in the crucial and chronic phases of alcoholism) displays the following characteristics: polydrug use, experiences with hospitals and emergency rooms for alcohol-related illnesses (comas, gastritis, hepatic disease, peripheral neuropathy, nutritional deficiencies, cirrhosis, internal bleeding, convulsive disorders, alcohol psychoses, hallucinosis, acute withdrawal reactions, rationalization, resentments, sexual impotency, loss of efficiency at work, geographic moves, changes in friends and family, changes in drinking places, emotional and physical violence, traffic accidents, and feelings of guilt about drinking (Jellinek, 1960, 1962; Vaillant, 1983: 25-31; Keller and McCormick, 1968: 14; Guze et al., 1963). This individual will live from inside an alcoholic body. The vital organs of the body will be affected by alcohol intake. Vitamin B and C deficiencies, fractures and other bone injuries, heavy and frequent bruising, dermatitis, a weakening of the body muscles, subdural hematoma, hypothermia or loss of body heat, and adrenal failure are all common.

Alcohol routinely alters the drinker's consciousness of self and relations with others. It is a drug that quickly establishes its presence in the world, the body, and the consciousness of the heavy drinker. Psychological and physiological dependency upon it therefore is not surprising, for it produces all the classic symptoms of addiction: changes in tolerance, cellular adaptation or tissue change, and withdrawal. Chemically it is a sedative, a hypnotic, a tranquilizer, a narcotic, a depressant, and, sometimes, a hallucinogenic, as well as an anesthetic. It is like most barbituates in these respects, except that it is both a stimulant and a depressant, is socially acceptable as a respectable addiction to millions, and is selective in its addictive effects, leading 1 in 7 drinkers (some estimates say 1 in 12) to become addicted to it (Royce, 1981: 7-8).

Alcoholic Interactions

Layered, or woven, through the above-mentioned physiological effects of alcohol upon the body and consciousness of the alcoholic will be the interactional effects of alcoholism upon his or her comportment. The interactional style of the alcoholic carries over into all of his or her dealings with others. This will include the alcoholic's mode of self-presentation, the manner in which he or she manages emotion, stress, frustration, dealings with others, making jokes, accomplishing daily routines, following rituals and commands, taking turns in conversation, deferring to others, listening; how he or she sleeps, eats, drinks, drives an automobile, makes love, shows affection to his or her children, pays bills, keeps appointments, plays golf, and reads the newspaper. Alcoholism's effects are thus integral parts of the alcoholic's self-presence in the world of others.

The public symptoms or signs of alcoholism are twofold: physiological, in terms of effects on the body, and interactional, in terms of interactional style, mode and manner of speaking, and so on (see Goffman, 1967: 137-148, on the mental symptoms of mental illness and the public order). The alcoholic's situational improprieties and forms of public misconduct lead others to define him or her as a threat to the normal interactional orders of home, work, and public places more generally understood. His or her misconduct is taken as a symptom of an underlying disorder that may or may not be defined as alcoholic, psychotic, insane, violent, or just plain unacceptable. (On the mental illness labels that are applied to alcoholics, see Solomon, 1983: 670-712.)

SCIENTIFIC THEORIES OF ALCOHOLISM

Scientific theories cluster into three broad groupings, depending upon the predisposing factors to alcoholism that are emphasized. These groupings are (1) biological-genetic-medical, (2) psychological-psychoanalytic, and (3) anthropological-sociological (Kissen, 1977: 1; Biegel and Ghertner, 1977; Vaillant, 1983: 2-11). I will take up each of these groupings in turn.

Genetic Theories of Alcoholism

Goodwin (1976, 1979), Goodwin and Guze (1974: 37-52), Madsen (1974: 44-64), McClearn (1983), and Grove and Cadoret (1983) have summarized the basic findings on the genetic antecedents to alcoholism. Goodwin (1979) suggests several innate variations in the response to alcohol that could predispose a subject to abuse or avoid the use of alcohol. These factors include (1) adverse reactions to alcohol, including the "flushing" response observed in Japanese subjects, which could lead to an intolerance to alcohol; (2) innate factors that allow large quantities of alcohol to be ingested; and (3) innate differences in the way alcohol affects the brain, leading to more euphoria for some subjects than for others. After a thorough review of family, twin, adoption, genetic marker, and animal studies, Goodwin and Guze (1974: 49) conclude, "While a genetic factor cannot be ruled out, conceivably it can be ruled in."

Recent work by Schuckit and Duby (1983) also has shown a possible familial factor in the metabolism of alcohol. Nonalcoholic "male relatives of alcoholics were found to produce higher levels of blood acetaldehyde to a standard oral dose of alcohol when compared to an age- and sex-matched control group" (Grove and Cadoret, 1983: 51). A biological predisposition to alcoholism or to alcohol abuse may, then, be inherited, just as learning how to drink, how to abuse alcohol, when, and for what reasons surely is grounded in part in one's family experiences (Goodwin, 1976: 48-49). Certainly conceptions of excessive alcohol use and abuse are learned in the family context, as well as in the broader fields of social experience that encompass the subject (Goodwin, 1976: 48; Jessor et al., 1968; McCord, McCord, and Mendelson 1960; Vaillant, 1983).

These observations suggest that although there is no genetic or hereditary theory of alcoholism per se, the weight of the evidence warrants sensitivity to genetic, biological, and biochemical factors, as well as to factors learned and transmitted in the family context (but see MacAndrew and Edgerton, 1969: 83-90). Recent arguments suggest an interactional and dialectical relationship between hereditary and environmental factors (Lewontin et al., 1984) in the genesis of alcoholism.

The *integration hypothesis* of Ullman (1958: 48-54) would suggest that a family, work, religious, or ethnic group will have lower rates of alcohol problems when it has clear rules surrounding how alcohol is to be used. When members of the culture are exposed to alcohol at an early age and are given appropriate adult models who drink in moderation socially and who discourage intoxication, then rates of problem drinking or alcoholism will be low. The Italians and the American Jewish community have been identified as two cultures that have integrated alcohol use successfully into their group structure (Bales, 1946; Beauchamp, 1980: 43), but not the Irish (Stivers, 1976), American black (Kane, 1981; Watts and Wright, 1983), or Hispanic communities (Kane, 1981). The American teenage culture has not integrated alcohol use successfully either (Mandell and Ginzburg, 1976: 167-204).

The integration hypothesis would mediate the genetic predisposition argument concerning the etiology of alcoholism, but it will not explain how certain members of "alcohol-integrated" cultures come to be defined as alcoholic. Clearly, however, genetic predispositions are mediated by cultural, or group, effects, for "experiences in groups produce alcoholics" (Rubington, 1977: 382).

BEHAVIORAL SCIENCE
THEORIES OF ALCOHOLISM

Being "an alcoholic is a symbolic interaction process" (Mulford, 1969: 122). Drinking alcohol is a social act that has inner, covert and outer, overt phases that merge in the stream of experience of the drinker. Attached to the world through a circuit of selfness, the drinker's inner and outer worlds of experience are mediated and interpreted through interior self-conversations and self-indications. The self mediates the drinking act. The physical act of grasping a drink and drinking it is mediated and preceded by inner, covert actions, making it difficult, if not often impossible, to delineate firmly the line between inner and outer experiences; that is, between thinking a drink and taking a drink. The self of the drinker is always ahead of her in experiences yet to be taken, or just behind her in actions that are still being completed and felt.

The major behavioral science theories of alcoholism are causal. They seek to locate anterior and inner psychological states that precede the actual taking of a drink. They seek, too, to locate in the drinker's social, psychological, and cultural environment factors or forces that would condition or shape the psychological predisposition to drink (Madsen, 1974: 103-109). Three psychological-psychoanalytic theories—the simple *tension-reduction model* of alcoholism of Horton (1943) and Bacon et al. (1965), which has been elaborated and incorporated into the "learning theory" of alcoholism; the *power theory* of McClelland and associates (1972); and the *dependency theory* of McCord et al. (1960), Blane (1968), Knight (1937), Lisansky (1960), and White (1956)—compete with one another. Three anthropological-sociological theories—the "time-out" theory of MacAndrew and Edgerton (1969), Bateson's (1972a) "Cybernetics of self theory of alcoholics," and Madsen's (1974) "Anxious American Model"—locate the sources of problem drinking in cultural ambiguities in American society. (See also Jessor et al.'s, 1968, multivariate theory.)

I will take up each of these theoretical formulations in turn, understanding that no one of them accounts for the full range of drinking patterns observed in alcoholics.

Tension-Reduction Theory

The *tension-reduction*, or *anxiety-reduction*, model assumes that drinking is a learned means of reducing conditioned anxiety that is present in the psychological and social environments of the drinker (Conger, 1951, 1956; Horton, 1943; Ludwig, 1983). An initial dependency on alcohol is assumed to become established in predisposed individuals who learn to use alcohol to achieve states of euphoria and to reduce feelings of anxiety or tension. Because alcohol is its own reinforcer, producing reduction in unpleasant cognitive and emotional states, its continued use persists even in the face of negative stimuli and social reactions (Mello, 1983: 136). An "addiction-memory" sustains its continued consumption (Mello, 1972: 221). Alcoholism is thus regarded as learned behavior (Mello, 1983; Vogel-Sprott, 1972: 504) and should be understandable in terms of learning or reinforcement theory (Mello, 1983).

Ludwig (1983) has extended the "opponent-process" theory of motivation of Solomon (1983) to the question "Why do alcoholics drink?" His is perhaps the most elaborate tension-reduction learning theory model. He assumes that early alcohol use yields positive affective, or euphoric, states that are greater than the mild dysphoria associated with withdrawal from the drug. Because withdrawal represents an opponent of euphoria, the best way to remove this effect is to use the substance that produces the positive effect. This strengthens the opponent process of withdrawal, which requires an increased consumption of alcohol. Over time, individuals drink more to feel normal. The secondary conditioning of neutral stimuli within drinking situations brings the start of drinking behavior more and more under the control of conditioned stimuli. These conditioned stimuli elicit a subclinical "withdrawal syndrome which...is associated with craving...that directs the alcoholic to an effective source of relief from dysphoria" (Ludwig, 1983: 210). In those conducive drinking settings where craving is likely to occur, the first couple of drinks heighten craving and consumption of alcohol. A chain-conditioning process "in the absence of psychological, physical, or situational determinants, ensures that alcoholics will continue to drink until they reach their hypothetical pharmacological ceilings" (Ludwig, 1983: 211). Loss of control is thus located in this chain-conditioning sequence, which produces a relative inability to regulate or control alcohol intake. After the end of a drinking bout a relapse to drinking may occur through the ability of these conditioned stimuli to elicit the subclinical withdrawal syndrome and the related automatic craving experience (Ludwig, 1983: 211). A vicious circle of addictive behavior (Kissen, 1977: 5) is set in motion, and the behavior continues to produce the negative effects that are not sought, yet in order to remove the negative effects the act that produced the effects must be engaged in. Withdrawal becomes a conditioned stimulus for the conditioned response of drinking. Craving, withdrawal, and loss of control, familiar symptomatic behaviors of the alcoholic, are thus located in the addictive cycle wherein alcohol becomes both the stimulus and the response to the very conditions its use is intended to remove or alleviate.

A causal circularity is embedded in the tension-reduction, behavioral learning theory model. This point, which will be taken up next, has not impeded the implementation of variants on the tension-reduction social learning model in treatment centers. The assumption since Davies's (1962) article, "Normal Drinking in Recovered Alcoholics," has been that at least certain types of alcoholics could be resocialized to drink normally again (see Davies, 1960; Pattison, 1966; Pattison et al., 1968, 1977; but see Pendery et al., 1982). A resurgence in behavioral learning, tension-reduction, and social learning theories has appeared with the recent advent of increased federal funding for alcoholism research (see Madsen, 1974). It is to these theories that I now turn.

Learning Theories of Alcoholism

The most recent, influential, and controversial versions of the learning theory of alcoholism are given in Mello (1972, 1983) and Sobell and Sobell (1978). Building upon Skinner's operant theory of learning, the behavioral theory of alcoholism and alcoholics is not a theory of alcoholism. Rather, it represents an attempt to apply operant methods of conditioning to either determine the alcoholic's preferred pattern of drinking (Mello, 1972: 224) or attempts to modify the alcoholic's "alcoholic" drinking style, so as to produce a normal pattern of social drinking (Sobell and Sobell, 1978: 33).

Drinking, as with Ludwig's (1983) formulations, is hypothesized as being learned, acquired, and maintained "as a function of its consequences...the consumption of alcohol is preceded by certain events (antecedents), internal and/or external, followed by various short- and long-term consequences" (Sobell and Sobell, 1978: 33). Drinking behavior is defined as a discriminated operant response. The atheoretical structure of the Mello and Sobell and Sobell formulations makes no determination of the nature of the motivation, the intentionality, the self-conceptions, or the relations with others that might involve the alcoholic in the drinking act. In short, these models do not consider alcoholic drinking from a symbolic interactionist or interpretive point of view. Consistent with Skinnerian behaviorism (Skinner, 1953), these models make no assumption about hypothetical constructs that might intervene between events and behavior in alcoholic drinking (Mello, 1983: 137).

The basic concepts in these behavioral formulations are (1) the complex of discriminating stimuli that are present for any person at any time; (2) behavioral options (operants), which include appropriate and inappropriate drinking responses in an experimentally controlled environment; (3) reinforcement, which is any event that maintains behavior or increases the probability of the recurrence of that behavior; and (4) punishment, which is any event that decreases the rate of emission of a behavior. The behavioral effects of stimulus events and reinforcement and punishment schedules thus increase or decrease the likelihood of any unit of behavior being emitted, that is, drinking or drinking inappropriately. This behavioral model focuses on the consequences of behavior. There is no analysis of the inherent properties of the stimulus or reinforcing event; their properties are determined behaviorally. The Mello and Sobell studies offer, then, behavioral analyses of the reinforcing *effects* of alcohol (Mello) and adversive conditioning sessions on drinking behavior (Sobell and Sobell).

The Mello studies involved four reinforcement schedules: fixed interval, extinction of one minute, differential reinforcement of zero response and random sequencing, or multiple-chain scheduling of reinforcement. The Sobell and Sobell Individualized Behavior Therapy (IBT) sessions occurred in a simulated bar setting in a hospital. A variable-ratio electric shock avoidance schedule was employed when inappropriate drinking behaviors (as defined by the subject's treatment goal) were emitted. Videotapes showing the drinker intoxicated also were employed by the Sobells. Mello's studies involved the uses of individual operant conditioning booths and a modified driving machine. In both situations the "alcoholic" could work to earn money to buy alcohol that was dispensed automatically by the machine. The subjects in the Mello studies were, "for the most part, homeless men with a history of repeated incarceration for public drunkenness" (Mello, 1972: 224). The subjects in the Sobell study were gamma alcoholics who had "voluntarily admitted themselves to Patton State Hospital for treatment of alcoholism" (Sobell and Sobell, 1978: 82).

The conclusions from the studies reported by Mello (1972, 1983) and Sobell and Sobell (1978) may be summarized as follows. Sobell and Sobell reported success for their experiment. They concluded that they had succeeded in "shaping" the behaviors of the gamma subjects in their study so that they could practice controlled social drinking upon discharge from treatment. Their experimental group was reported to have been functioning significantly better throughout a two-year follow-up than were subjects in a control group who had been treated with the traditional methods of abstinence. An additional third year of follow-up by Caddy et al. confirmed Sobell and Sobell's conclusions (Pendery et al., 1982: 170). The effect of the Sobell study was to put before the American public and the scientific community of alcoholism researchers the proposals that gamma alcoholics could be returned, through IBT, to normal social drinking. This conclusion contradicts the earlier position of Jellinek (1962) and Alcoholics Anonymous (1976).

The Mello studies and others summarized by her (1983: 254, 259-260) lead to the conclusions that (1) subjects did not display loss of control in free drinking programs; (2) subjects never consumed all of the alcohol supply that was in front of them; (3) subjects could initiate periods of abstinence and could control the amount they drank; (4) the amount subjects drank could be manipulated by a work reinforcement schedule; (5) abstinence could be bought; (6) alcoholics will taper off and control their drinking; (7) some alcoholics can drink socially; (8) alcoholics do not display craving and loss of control, as these two phenomena have been conceptualized historically in the literature; and (9) alcoholics will continue to drink, even after alcohol produces negative, dysphoric effects for them.

Observations

Midway through her first experiment with alcoholics in the individual operant conditioning booths, Mello (1972: 228) observed that "it became apparent that neither subject's performance was coming under stimulus control as would be expected in the usual performance on a multiple chain schedule from a sophisticated pigeon." If Mello's subjects did not perform like sophisticated pigeons, they did display control over their drinking conduct in ways that permitted the above-listed conclusions to be drawn.

The Sobell subjects did not have the same experiences as those in the Mello experiments. The Pendery et al. (1982) follow-up of 18 of the 20 subjects in the controlled drinking experiment revealed that (1) of the first 16 admitted into the study, 13 were rehospitalized for alcoholism treatment approximately one year after discharge (this was contrary to the Sobell statements that their controlled subjects were functioning well in each of the follow-up periods for year 1 and year 2); (2) of the subjects studied in Caddy et al.'s (1978) third-year follow-up, 6 performed well 100% of the days, but Pendery et al. found that 4 of the 6 had engaged in excessive drinking during the third year (1 of the 2 who was rated as doing well had been hospitalized three times since discharge from the Sobell experiment for alcoholism); (3) the long-term drinking histories of the 20 subjects throughout a ten-year period (until the end of 1981) revealed that the one drinker who had been controlling his drinking after the end of the first year was still doing so, 8 controlled drinking subjects were still drinking excessively and regularly, and 6 were abstaining at the end of the follow-up, but only after multiple hospitalizations for alcoholism. "Four of the controlled drinking subjects eventually died alcohol-related deaths" (Pendery et al., 1982: 174). One was found floating face up in a lake, another died of a massive myocardial infarction (alcohol induced), another of respiratory failure, and another committed suicide, jumping from a pier into the bay.

These findings led Pendery et al. (1982: 174) to conclude that there is no evidence "that *gamma* alcoholics (in the Sobell study) had acquired the ability to engage in controlled drinking safely after being treated in the experimental program" (italics in original). These findings are an indictment of the behaviorial therapy employed by Sobell and Sobell, and it is an indictment of the learning theory that underlies their model. I shall take up a critique of this model in a moment, but first it is necessary to reflect on Mello's conclusions that her experiments (and those of others) demolish the twofold belief in the literature concerning the alcoholic's loss of control over drinking once the first drink is taken and the related belief of "the fatalistic craving" of alcohol (Mello, 1972: 282). Because these two phenomena are so closely interrelated, I shall treat them together in my discussion.

Craving and Loss of Control

Mello (1972: 259) states:

> The disease concept of alcoholism has long been encumbered by the notions of "need" and "craving" which are frequently advanced to account for addictive drinking. Craving has been defined as a loss of control over drinking and it implies that "every time the subject starts drinking, he is compelled to continue until he reaches a state of severe intoxication (Mardones, 1963: p. 146). The circularity inherent in this reasoning is evident. The lack of experimental data about drinking patterns has led to an implicit reification of concepts like "need" and "craving" which are defined by the behavior that they are invoked to explain. . . .

> No empirical support has been provided for the notion of "craving" by direct observation of alcoholics subjects in a situation where they can choose to drink alcohol in any volume at any time by working at a simple task. Although most subjects have consistently consumed enough alcohol on the first day of the experiment to raise their blood alcohol above 150 mg/100 ml, subsequent drinking patterns have been highly variable.

Mello (1972: 259-260) then concludes that no subject allowed to program his or her drinking freely has shown "loss of control" or a tendency to drink to oblivion. She suggests that these findings (1) argue against the validity of the general construct "craving" and (2) may lead to "more rational therapeutic approaches to problem drinking which acknowledge individual differences in potential capacity for controlled drinking." She does indicate, however, that these findings do not explain the problem of "readdiction," or the return to drinking by alcoholic as compared to "problem drinkers" (Mello, 1972: 261).

It must be noted that her criticisms of the craving and loss of control concepts fail to take account of Jellinek's (1960: 42-43, 139-146, 153-154) careful analysis of these phenomena as they occur in the latter stages of alcoholism, in particular Jellinek's point that loss of control does not occur 100% of the time (Jellinek, 1960: 145), and craving typically is set off "only in the presence of withdrawal symptoms" and these are late developments in gamma and delta alcoholism (Jellinek, 1960: 43).

Mello's arguments lend support to the IBT program of the Sobells, yet her inability to account for the phenomenon of "readdiction," or the return to noncontrolled alcoholic drinking, undermines her basic thesis that alcoholics can be taught to control their drinking. Indeed, the problem of readdiction restates the issue of "craving" and "loss of control." Readdiction pinpoints the failure of experimental studies of controlled alcoholic drinking. Mello (1972: 261) states the problem ironically: "The fact that the alcoholic is vulnerable to readdiction upon reexposure to the agent [alcohol] is one constraint on social drinking."

Mello (1972: 261) fails to establish her point that the concept of craving is a "logically and empirically inadequate explanatory concept to account for addictive drinking." That is, alcoholics who return to drinking reexperience the "craving for a drink" phenomenon, and once taking the first drink they set in motion an addictive cycle of drinking that is not unlike the cycle they broke when they became abstinent (or dry) for a period of time.

It is necessary to examine Mello's argument and her experimental findings in detail. I will begin with the Multiple Chain Schedule of Reinforcement experiment, in which alcoholics were given free access to alcohol on a 24-hour basis. Mello argues that her alcoholics drank enough alcohol on the first day to raise their blood alcohol level to a stable level, after which time they consumed an estimated 12 to 18 ounces of alcohol per day (half bottle). On the basis of this finding she argues that alcoholics can control their drinking and not drink to complete intoxication each time they take a drink.

A second experiment saw 13 of 18 subjects drinking 32 ounces of alcohol within a 24-hour period (Mello, 1972: 239). Prior to the cessation of this experiment, when alcohol would be withdrawn from the alcoholics, 5 of 23 subjects increased their intake, 9 decreased their intake slightly, and 6 "increased their blood alcohol levels in the 24-hour period immediately prior to cessation of drinking" (Mello, 1972: 241).

Three points may be taken from these findings. First, Mello's alcoholics were consuming large amounts of alcohol on a regular basis. Second, once they reached a stable level of blood alcohol, they stabilized their drinking at a high plateau, so as to avoid withdrawal symptoms. Third, in anticipation of withdrawal, rather than lowering their intake, they increased it, revealing anticipated craving upon cessation. Loss of control, or drinking to excess, thus occurs when the alcoholic believes his or her supply is about to be ended. *When he has a stable, regular drinking supply, the alcoholic in fact stabilizes his drinking at a high, alcoholic, addictive level.* Mello misunderstands the phenomenology of alcoholic drinking behavior and the craving process as it is experienced and anticipated by alcoholics. Her studies thus fail to offer a test of the craving and loss of control hypotheses.

Lindesmith on Addiction and Craving

Alfred Lindesmith (1947, 1968, 1975; Lindesmith et al., 1975, 1977) has examined the addiction process with narcotic users in great detail. His work illuminates the phenomenon of alcoholic craving and loss of control. By drawing upon it I am not suggesting that alcohol addiction is exactly like narcotic addiction. There are, however, important parallels. He suggests that withdrawal effects appear 4 hours (approximately) after the addict takes the last injection. (See Jellinek's remarks, above, on the alcoholic's 4-hour drinking cycle in the critical phase of addiction.) If no further drugs are taken withdrawal symptoms increase in intensity for about 72 hours and the most noticeable effects of the drug disappear after 2 weeks. An injection of the drug during withdrawal causes the withdrawal effects to disappear within minutes. This reaction is biological.

With full addiction (as evidenced with Mello's subjects) regular drug use produces a tolerance for the drug, or a drug balance in the body. The main effect of the drug is to maintain this balance, to prevent withdrawal symptoms, and to cause the addict to feel normal. The user may experience a "kick" when he or she shoots up, but during the several hours between injections it is difficult to determine if the person is under the effects of the drug or not.

According to Lindesmith et al. (1975: 227), the initial experience with heroin often is perceived as unpleasant. Alcoholics report similar statements when they discuss the first time they ever drank. They give accounts of vomiting, painful hangovers, and headaches the next day. Even when the first experience is pleasurable, the attitude it produces is not the same attitude that is expressed after addiction. This means that the "falling in love" with heroin or alcohol that pleasure theorists espouse cannot be considered a causal factor because causes must precede effects, rather than follow them.

In the initial period of drug use radical changes occur that reverse the drug's effects for the user. The original depressing effects of the drug vanish and are replaced by stimulating ones. However, euphoria or the positive effects of beginning drug use soon vanish. They are replaced by the negative effects of relieving the withdrawal distress and achieving normality. Tolerance builds up for the drug, for more and more of it is needed in order to relieve the distress effects of withdrawal.

Craving for the drug is located in the experience of taking the drug for the relief of withdrawal symptoms. "It is the repetition of the experience of using drugs to alleviate withdrawal distress (when the latter is recognized and properly identified) that appears to lead rapidly to the changed orientation toward the drug and to the other behavior that constitutes addiction" (Lindesmith et al., 1975: 226). Addicts, Lindesmith et al. (1975: 226) argue, do not get hooked on the pleasures of the drug (for example, as with opium), but on the experiences "of relief that occur immediately after a shot in a matter of five or ten minutes." Addiction is established in the experiences that occur immediately after each injection, and not in the way the user feels during the remaining time between shots.

The beginning drug user, like the gamma alcoholic in the critical phase, takes a shot every 4 hours. Addiction is established in this injection experience. It occurs approximately 10 minutes after each shot and not by how the user feels the other 230 minutes in each 4-hour interval. Those who think of drugs use in terms of being high, as being a euphoric or solely pleasurable experience, focus on the 230 minutes and not on the 10 minutes that follow the injection. They think of addiction as an ecstatic pleasure that extends throughout the intervals between shots, to be renewed by the next shot. But addicts report that they feel normal between injections, and they are the final authority on this, as alcoholics are authorities on alcohol use (Lindesmith et al., 1977: 518).

The addict (and the alcoholic) situation may be illustrated as shown in Figure 2.1. The rhythm of regular "fixes," injections, or drinks of the drug moves into the center of the subject's life, as he or she becomes addicted, "falls in love" with, or learns to crave the drug (Lindesmith et al., 1975: 228). All other activities are drawn progressively into the orbit of the drug rhythm, organized around it, and subordinated to it. The drug has taken control of the user's life.

Normal subjects report that they are unable to understand how anyone could become addicted to heroin or alcohol (see Lindesmith, 1975: 151; Beecher, 1959: 334). The same attitude characterizes the beginning drinker or drug user, who has no intention of becoming an addict or alcoholic when he or she first uses or takes a drink. However, as Lindesmith (1975: 151) notes in regard to the heroin addict, this self-confidence begins to fade when the user has his or her first experience with withdrawal, which is likely to be met with surprise and perhaps fear. The taking of a drink or the injection of a shot to

Addict's Experience with Heroin

(or alcohol)

The Heroin Rhythm

(or alcohol rhythm)

Figure 2.1: The Addict and the Alcoholic Situation.

remove the withdrawal effects quickly establishes in the user's or
drinker's mind the connection between the drug and the feeling of
withdrawal, however.

The addict, or alcoholic, soon moves to an injection, or drinking,
schedule that locates drug intake at the center of his or her life. To
return to Figure 2.1, the heroin or alcohol rhythm becomes the temporal structure that organizes every other activity (and perhaps thought)
in the user's life.

It must be noted, however, that the addiction to alcohol that the
alcoholic experiences takes several years to establish, although addiction to heroin and other narcotics can be established relatively quickly.
Furthermore, the fact that alcohol consumption is regarded as a normal social practice in our culture makes for an entirely different set
of attitudes toward the drug at the outset. Once addiction to alcohol
has been established (Jellinck's prodomal, critical and crucial phases of
alcoholism) the processes that Lindesmith describes for the narcotic
addict appear to fit the alcoholic experience (see Jellinek, 1960:
115-121).

The Pleasure Theory

Those investigators who explain addiction in terms of the pleasure
theory (McAuliffe and Gordon, 1974; Ludwig, 1983; Mello, 1983)
presume that the drug must produce intense pleasure to be as power-
fully addicting as it is. Even the opponent-process theory of Ludwig

(1983; see discussion above) must argue that the pleasurable effects of alcohol overcome the negative, dysphoric effects of withdrawal, hangovers, alcohol-related illness, high financial costs, self-degradation, the threat of arrest, DUIs, loss of family, and so on. Such theorists persist, however, in attempting to explain addiction in terms of the "high" that is experienced when the drug is taken.

There are two problems with this explanation. The first has been suggested. This is the absence of pleasure, as reported by alcoholics and addicts, in the time that intervenes between injections or drinks. Except in the few moments that follow the drug injection, the addict is, according to Lindesmith et al. (1975: 228), "one of the most miserable, unhappy types in our society." A similar description can be given to the alcoholic in the critical and chronic phases of alcoholism. The second problem with the euphoria theory lies in its tautological structure. The high that is the supposed key to addiction is part of the phenomenon of addiction. In this case the condition that is said to explain addiction is "simply part of it" (Lindesmith et al., 1975: 227). To equate the high with the cause of addiction is equivalent to saying that the cause of a person's illness is the high fever he or she is experiencing.

The alcoholic's or addict's statement that he likes the high that alcohol or heroin gives him is simply proclaiming that he is addicted to the drug (Jellinek, 1960: 64). These statements do not explain how he acquired this attitude or definition in relationship to the drug in question.

Euphoria, following Lindesmith's (1975: 149) metaphor, may be thought of as the bait that lures the user into a trap. The pleasure theorists seem to view addiction not as a trap, but as the rational pursuit of pleasure (Lindesmith, 1975: 149). Lindesmith suggests that they are so preoccupied with the euphoric bait on the addiction hook that they fail to see the hook—the painful and unpleasant effects of addiction. The key to addiction lies not in euphoria, but in the experience of taking the drug to relieve withdrawal symptoms.

Craving and Relapse

Addicts who relapse (Lindesmith, 1975: 147) do not do so out of a desire to avoid withdrawal effects, for they have passed through this stage when they stopped using. Nor do addicts return to drug use out of a desire animated by the pleasure principle, for, as Lindesmith has shown, the pleasures that are felt in the addiction arise only after the addiction has been established. The pleasure theory again confuses effects with causes. The crucial etiological question in the case of craving for drugs (or alcohol) and readdiction is to explain how the craving is contracted, learned, and brought into existence. Craving arises in conjunction with the use of the drug after physical dependence has been established (Lindesmith, 1975: 150). It is at this point that the compulsive and irrational aspects of the addict's behavior come into existence. A preoccupation with the supply, the fear of not having a fix when it is needed, and the hiding of the supply occur at this point in the addictive cycle. At the same time the ecstatic praise that the addict extols upon the drug appear in this phase, for this euphoric pleasure has become a motive for the continuation of drug use. Alcoholics, in a parallel fashion, will extol and speak eloquently of the effects of the first drink of the day, or of the drink that removes the shakes and the trembling feelings that they are experiencing.

The Two Forms of Craving

Mello (1972) fails to distinguished between the two forms of craving suggested by Jellinek (1960: 141), Isbell (1955), Ludwig (1983: 201), and Lindesmith (1975: 147). *Physiological* (or nonsymbolic) craving is located in the withdrawal effects felt as the drug leaves the subject's body. *Psychological, symbolic,* or *phenomenological* craving arises when the subject feels a compelling need, or desire, to drink or use, irrespective of (and often in the absence of) any withdrawal symptom. In phenomenological craving the subject's consciousness centers on the drug and on the effects she imagines will be produced were she to drink or use. As she imagines herself drinking or using she may produce shadow physiological effects that simulate the "real" effects of the drug in the body.

The following two statements from alcoholics who returned to drinking after lengthy periods of abstinence speak to phenomenological craving. The first speaker had been sober for four and a half years.

> I could imagine the taste of that stuff in my throat. I could feel my mind clear of the fear I felt. I imagined those feelings for two months. Finally, one Saturday morning I went to Walgreens and bought a half-pint. I told myself I'd drink half of it and throw the rest away. I took one drink, drank the half-pint, drank it, bought another, drank it, then bought a fifth, drank part of it, went to work drunk, walked through the front door, out the back, drove cross town, hid my car, checked into a motel and kept this up for three days. Then I went back to work, drinking a fifth every day. This lasted two months, until I ended up on the mental ward again, right back where I was four and a half years

ago, drunk, insane and out of my mind. I came back to A.A. after that. I accepted the fact that I was an alcoholic [field conversation, July 5, 1981, recovering male alcoholic, 75 years old, retired, 10 years sober].

The next speaker had been sober three months, having gone through a treatment center three months earlier:

It was a Sunday afternoon, mid-July. Everybody was gone. I'd been cleaning out my garage. I think I was angry at something. Suddenly the thought came over me that a drink would taste good. A straight shot of gin, warm and sweet. I knew my wife had thrown a bottle of wine behind the wood pile last spring. Least I thought she had. All I could think about was that bottle. I moved every stick of wood in that pile and the bottle wasn't there. Then I checked the neighbor's garden cause she'd thrown a bottle in there. No bottle. I gave up. I didn't drink that day, but the next Friday I went out and bought a bottle of that new 110 proof Irish whiskey and drank three shots. Put it back, got another, said I'd save it for a week, next day I finished it. I was off, then, on a four and one-half month binge that had me drinking every-day. I finally came back to you people in late November and accepted that I was an alcoholic. [field conversation, August 4, 1982, male alcoholic, 54 years old, academic, 4 years sober].

These two alcoholics began their relapses when they experienced phenomenological cravings for alcohol. Physiological craving was not present in terms of withdrawal symptoms, although each imagined the taste and effects of alcohol. Once each subject went back to drinking a loss of control was experienced. Hence their relapse sequence was as follows: (1) phenomenological craving, (2) imagined physiological craving, (3) actual drinking, and (4) loss of control, followed by attempts to control drinking, but drinking at an alcoholic level throughout the relapse.

Relapse occurs because the user has failed to replace the heroin or alcohol rhythmic center of his or her life with an alternative structure of experiences that do not involve drug ingestion. He or she remains psychologically addicted to the phenomenological, interactional, social, and cultural experiences (that is, lifestyle) that addiction brings.

Alcoholic Craving and Readdiction

Lindesmith suggests, then, that relapse or readdiction occurs because the user previously has been changed by the drug-using experience. The user has acquired new conceptions and attitudes as well as new knowledge of his or her body and its capabilities and the effects of the drug on the body. This is not an experience that can be altered easily or let loose of. The user's changed conceptions of self (produced by the drug) remain after he or she has stopped using or drinking. Similarly, an alcoholic drinker who controls his or her drinking will still drink to obtain the effects of total obliteration that complete intoxication has produced in the past. In short, Lindesmith's arguments suggest that alcoholics are addicted to and crave the experience that alcohol produces, independent of alcohol's addictive effects on their bodies. Further, his position suggests that "craving" is neither constant nor always present. It is only physiologically present when the effects of withdrawal are felt. It is felt at the moment when the drug is taken to relieve withdrawal symptoms. Loss of control will not occur if the alcoholic has stabilized his or her blood alcohol level at a level at which withdrawal symptoms are no longer felt. This is the state that Mello's subjects quickly tried to obtain and then maintained throughout her experiments.

Loss of control occurs—that is, the alcoholic drinks to oblivion— when the subject desires to maintain the high that previously was experienced in the early stages of drinking, but finds that the high can no longer be obtained or sustained. Having drunk past the point where the high would be felt, the subject continues drinking, not because of a loss of control, but in an attempt to prove that he can control his drinking and experience the feelings he once felt (see Bateson, 1972a, and the discussion below).

Reflections on Mello

These remarks suggest that the concepts "craving" and "loss of control" are necessary constructs in the explanation of alcoholic drinking. They reference opposite sides of the addictive process. When alcoholics are in control of their drinking, their behavior is being controlled by the alcohol in their bodies. No longer feeling withdrawal symptoms, they have drunk themselves into a steady-state where they feel normal. This is the state they desire, not euphoria; although they may define feeling normal in euphoric terms. They will drink and experience the negative effects of the drug so as to achieve this normal state. Hence the phenomenology of their drinking turns on the cognitive and emotional definitions of self they attach to the drinking experience and to the effects alcohol brings to their lived bodies. They are addicted to the experience of being normal, but they can be normal only by drinking alcoholically. Mello's studies fail to capture this pivotal feature of the alcoholic's drinking.

A similar set of reflections can be directed to the Sobell studies. They apparently succeeded in controlling at a socially acceptable level the drinking behaviors of their alcoholic subjects while in treatment. In fact, they succeeded in bringing their subjects' blood alcohol levels up to normal, so that withdrawal symptoms were not felt while in treatment. However, their subjects were addicted to the experience of addiction, and to the experience of controlling for themselves their drinking patterns. Once they left treatment they attempted to take control over their own drinking. They quickly returned to a level of readdictive drinking that required more than a few ounces of alcohol a day to relieve the withdrawal symptoms that were felt. This interpretation is supported by the fact that 13 of the first 16 subjects in the experiment were readmitted for alcoholism treatment within a year of discharge.

The Self and Addiction

A theory of addiction (and relapse) cannot explain addiction or relapse solely in terms of the effects that the drug in question produces for the user. Not only are such explanations tautological, and hence untestable, but they fail to locate the key factor in addiction, which is the user's symbolic and interactional relationship with the drug. The self of the user lies at the core of the addiction process. This self, in its many forms, structures and defines the user's relationship to heroin or alcohol. As Jellinek (1962) and Bateson (1972a) argue, self-pride and denial lie at the core of the alcoholic's relationship to alcohol, drinking, and alcoholism. Alcoholics believe that they can control their use of the drug. They also deny that they have problems when they drink. Self-pride and denial thus lock them in the drinking cycle that constitutes addictive, alcoholic drinking. Addiction can be explained only by going outside the presumed causal effects of the drug in question. Three "causal" agents thus lie at the core of alcohol and drug addiction: the self of the user, his or her physiological and lived body, and the drug in question. I turn now to a critique of the radical behavioral learning theory that underlies the research discussed above.

BEHAVIORISM, LEARNING
THEORY, AND ALCOHOLISM

The empirical evidence from the Pendery et al. follow-up of the Sobell experiment and the results reported by Mello effectively refute

the key features of behavioral learning theory as it has been applied
to the drinking practices of alcoholics. That is, gamma alcoholics, as
conditioned by Sobell and Sobell, were not able to sustain a socially
controlled, nonalcoholic drinking program. Mello's subjects continued
to drink at alcoholic levels throughout her experiments. Her data thus
support, rather than refute, the centrality of "craving" and "loss of
control" as key elements in the gamma alcoholic's drinking patterns.
Both of these bodies of research lend support to Lindesmith's argument that addiction occurs when the alcoholic learns to drink so as
to remove the negative effect of withdrawal symptoms.

These studies effectively undercut the ability of learning theory to
account for or control alcoholic drinking. This is so because, consistent with Skinner (1953), these researchers refuse to deal with the
cognitive, emotional, interactional, and self-reflective foundations of
alcoholic drinking. Their arguments are premised, first, on Thorndike's
(1913) Law of Effect (a behavior is maintained by it consequences,
"a reward or reinforcement strengthens either the response it follows, or the connection between that response and a stimulus"; Zurriff,
1985: 188). Second, they assume the simple principles of classical and
operant conditioning (an unconditioned stimulus can be replaced by
a conditioned stimulus that will elicit the same response previously
associated with the unconditioned stimulus). Alcoholics refuse to con-
form to Thorndike's Law of Effect. They will not submit to Skinner's
theory of operant conditioning and they will not model their behaviors
in terms of simple Pavlovian theories of aversive stimuli. The alcoholic's denial system, self-concept, and concept of "pride in drinking"
lead him or her to drink over and over again, even in the face of
disaster and failure. Contrary to Thorndike or Skinner, the alcoholic
denies the Law of Effect as it supposedly applies to his or her behavior.
(see Tiebout, 1949, 1953, 1954, for a discussion of the "ego" factor
in alcoholism).

Problems with Behaviorism

As a theory and a method in the field of alcoholism research, radical
behaviorism (1) is anti-introspective; (2) is against the use of mentalistic
constructs such as meaning, motive, intention, or self; (3) makes no
presumption about causal factors that lie outside the immediate
behavioral field of the alcoholic; (4) rejects cognitive or emotional interpretations of alcoholic learning; (5) attempts to remove a theory of
the alcoholic subject from the phenomenon of alcoholism; (6) rejects
first-person accounts by alcoholics as being of any use in the under-

standing of alcoholism; and (7) aims, following Watson (1913) and Skinner (1953), to be a purely objective, experimental branch of natural science.

These seven features of behaviorism make it particularly unsuited for the interpretation and understanding of alcoholism. This is so for the following reasons. First, the very factors that behaviorism excludes (meaning, intentionality, self, language, first-person accounts) stand at the center of alcoholism, for the alcoholic actively produces and defines her alcoholism as she becomes progressively addicted to alcohol. Second, behaviorism ignores the lived-body of the alcoholic, as that body and its withdrawal symptoms are defined and given meaning by the alcoholic. Third, behaviorism's search for causal factors ignores the fact that physical causality (as given in stimuli and reinforcement schedules) do not operate at the level of lived experience for the alcoholic. (See Merleau-Ponty, 1967; Sartre, 1956: 477). Fourth, because the alcoholic's self-system stands at the center of her alcoholism, any theory that attempts to explain alcoholism by ignoring the self is doomed to failure.

Fifth, a learning theory's concept of learning is unable to deal with the complex forms of learning that involve self-mediating processes (Bateson, 1972b) that are based on language and verbal interaction (Chomsky, 1959). Sixth, learning theory appears to be unable to reverse the negative, self-destructive behaviors that stand at the core of alcoholism. Seventh, behaviorists have been unable to locate a functional law that would connect some property of drinking with some property of a reinforcement schedule that would produce invariant control over drinking behavior.

Eighth, the temporal structure of behaviorism teleologically confounds effect with cause. Reinforcement schedules are presumed antecedent causes which supposedly affect rates of drinking behavior, when in fact drinking (the effect) becomes the cause for following or not following the reinforcement schedule. Because the subject mediates and defines stimuli and reinforcement schedules, any system that stands outside the subject's definitional system is flawed from the beginning. There are, that is, no stimuli, responses, or reinforcement schedules that stand independent of the subject's definitional field of experience. The start-stop, static model of conduct that behaviorists assume is unable to account for the creative, novel drinking behavior of the alcoholic.

Ninth, the reverse anthropomorphism of behaviorism (Kuhn and Hickman, 1956: 18-20), as applied to alcoholics, only recognizes those characteristics of man that have been found in nonhumans. By Mello's own admission, her early experiments failed to produce alcoholic subjects who would respond like "sophisticated pigeons." Such a failure would be otherwise benign in its effects, were it not for the fact that behaviorism, as employed in the Sobell studies, was used as a tool that destroyed human lives. It is necessary to call a moratorium on radical behaviorism as it currently is utilized in the field of alcoholism research. (See Redd et al., 1979: 8-10, for a critical reading of radical behaviorism as applied to the complex forms of behavior that alcoholism represents.)

PSYCHOANALYTIC THEORIES

The following two theories develop psychoanalytic themes of sexuality and childhood experiences as central components of alcoholism in adulthood. They are variations on personality theories of alcoholism, for they seek to locate the motivation for alcoholism in the personality makeup of the drinker.

Power Theory

McClelland et al.'s (1972) *power theory of drinking* refutes the tension, or anxiety reduction, theory that argues that men drink primarily to reduce their anxiety. They suggest that in cultures in which high amounts of anxiety are contained in folk tales, less drinking, rather than more, occurs. They also suggest that at the individual level small amounts of alcohol have no or little effect on anxious thoughts. Some experimental studies (Nathan et al., 1970; Cappell and Herman, 1972: 59) have indicated that anxiety increases during drinking.

McClelland's power theory argues that men who have accentuated needs for personal, not social, power drink excessively. Such men have power fantasies while drinking that express aggressiveness, thrill-seeking, and antisocial activities. Doubts about sexual potency and feelings of weakness are suppressed. A desire for personal dominance over others, a desire to gain power, glory, and influence is expressed in the fantasies of heavy drinkers when they drink. These fantasies reflect a world that is a competitive arena for males who must establish their dominance over one another. Personalized power fantasies increase as the level of alcohol consumption increases. Drinking is viewed as a means for the male to feel stronger. Men with exaggerated needs for personalized power receive direct gratification from these powerful fantasies that alcohol fuels. They want power but feel weak. They drink in order to feel powerful.

This formulation, which has not been well developed for women who are heavy drinkers or alcohol abusers (Williams, 1976: 278), does not offer a convincing argument for those males who have the need for personal power but do not become heavy drinkers (McClelland, 1972: 335). Nor does it account for those heavy drinkers who do not have power fantasies. It is not at all clear how McClelland's theory would deal with MacAndrew's and Edgerton's (1969) and Lemert's (1958, 1964, 1967) argument that the behaviors and thoughts that are felt when under the influence of alcohol are patterned and learned culturally. It is not the effects of alcohol that fuels the power fantasies or the aggressive actions of the drinker, but the culture. That is, power fantasies are part of being male in patriarchal cultures. McClelland's findings are therefore the artifacts of those cultures that are alcohol ambivalent, permissive, and overly permissive (Pittman, 1967: 6-12). Abstinent cultures (Islam, Hindu, ascetic Protestant) should, and do, present problematic materials for McClelland's theory (see McClelland et al., 1972: 249-250). Similarly, the type of drinker described by Spradley (1970: 252-262), the one who has no desire for personal power but drinks to excess, appears troublesome for the power theory.

Dependency Theory

McClelland goes to great lengths to refute dependency theory, which contends that heightened masculinity is a reaction formation against underlying dependency needs felt by the male (Williams: 1976, 254-256). Psychoanalytic in orientation, this theory assumes that the prealcoholic has a permanently unfulfilled desire or need for dependency, but is ashamed of this need. The prealcoholic male desires maternal care and attention, yet wants to be free of this care. This produces a dependency conflict, the origins of which are to be found in childhood. A facade of self-reliant manhood is developed to mask this dependency need. Because drinking is a masculine activity it helps the alcoholic to maintain an image of independence and self-reliance. Drinking satisfies dependency needs by providing feelings of warmth, comfort, and omnipotence. Drinking recreates the maternal caring situation. Accordingly, the motivation for drinking lies in the desire to satisfy dependency needs—not to feel powerful. Concerns for power are surface representations shielding or hiding underlying dependency strivings. Dependency, not the search for power, is the main cause or feature of alcoholism.

Both the power and the dependency theories assume that alcoholics have an inadequate masculine identity. Each, in this sense, returns to a psychoanalytic theme regarding sexuality, anxiety, neuroses, and maladaptive adult behavior, all traceable to childhood family experiences. Power theory locates this lack in a need-conflict culture. Dependency locates it in the early childhood experiences of the drinker. Power theory assumes that alcoholics act in a powerful way because they are concerned with power, not with underlying dependency needs. Both theories, then, take the same action patterns as a point of departure—heavy drinking, and masculine aggressiveness—but reach different conclusions concerning the cause or motivational reasons for alcoholism. It is probably the case that alcoholic males seek not only power, but also desire warm relationships with their mothers or with other women; just as women probably seek power and warm relationships with their mothers, their fathers, and with other males and females. The same criticisms that were applied to the power theory can be applied to the dependency theory.

ANTHROPOLOGICAL THEORIES OF ALCOHOLISM

I will now review the three major anthropological theories of alcoholism.

Time-Out Theory

MacAndrew and Edgerton's (1969) *"time-out" theory* of drunken comportment is both a critique of the alcoholism literature that seeks to locate invariant personal psychological effects in alcohol consumption and a cultural-anthropological argument for the thesis that all societies create time-out periods when their members are not held accountable for their actions. Alcohol is ingested during those time periods. Hence, drunken comportment is culturally patterned behavior and has very little to do with the psychological needs of the drinker, or the biochemical effects of alcohol on and in the drinker's body.

They marshall considerable evidence to support the following points: (1) There are societies in which drunken comportment does not display the "disinhibited" effects commonly ascribed to alcohol; (2) There are societies in which drunken comportment has undergone historical transformation; (3) There are societies in which drunken comportment varies from one situation to another (MacAndrew and Edgerton, 1969: 61). They argue that drunken comportment is learned behavior. The presence of alcohol in the body does not necessarily produce disinhibition. Over the course of socialization people learn from their societies how to be drunk and how to comport themselves when they have consumed alcohol. Because all societies appear to have "time-out" periods and because many, if not most, societies prescribe and permit the use of alcohol, drunken comportment will vary from one society to another, as will, presumably, the effects of alcohol consumption on the drinker's personal and social worlds.

Strictly speaking, MacAndrew and Edgerton's thesis is not a theory of alcoholism. It is, however, a powerful anecdote to much of the prevailing literature that argues for the near universal effects of alcohol upon human consciousness (McClelland et al., 1972: 2). Still, continued, prolonged use of alcohol has negative effects upon the human body and these effects apparently transcend cultural definition and interpretation. The MacAndrew and Edgerton argument can be read as closely supporting the position of Madsen (1974), who suggests that the American alcoholic lives in a culture that places a high value on the kinds of experiences that join alcohol consumption with adventure, thrill-seeking, and the quest for another "reality," other than the ordinary taken for granted world (Madsen, 1974: 107-108).

The Anxious American Thesis

Madsen's Thesis extends the cultural-anthropological position by locating American varieties of alcoholism within the shifting values of American society. Focusing primarily on two subspecies of gamma alcoholism, primary and secondary alcoholism (Fox, 1957), and consolidating the evidence on the genetic, hereditary, and learned components of heavy alcohol use and abuse, Madsen offers a multicausal model of alcoholism. He proposes that is there not only an ambivalence about alcohol use in American culture, but that the American ambivalence surrounding freedom and the escape from it places the person who is prone to become alcoholic in a position in which she is drawn to alcohol as a means of escaping the anxiety that surrounds her. Because alcohol has been given the cultural meanings of being both an anxiety reducer and the producer of euphoria, it is turned to in moments of high anxiety. The alcoholic mind is a product of the environmental stresses that reflect the generalized American anxiety regarding freedom, control, achievement, success, pleasure, adventure, love, nurturing, warmth, power, and caring. Conflicting values radiate throughout the society and these conflicts are lived and experienced in most prominent form in the lives of alcoholics who withdraw from society through alcohol in order to find a measure of comfort, security, and self-worth. Eschewing mono-causal motivational theories of why alcoholics drink, Madsen, drawing on his own observations with alcoholics in treatment centers and in Alcoholics Anonymous, suggests that alcoholics and heavy drinkers drink for such reasons as the following: death, oblivion, self cure, to escape from undefined pain, to fill a need, because they are addicted, for purposes of aggression, for fantasy purposes, because they are dependent on others, because they have no one to be dependent upon, because they cannot stop, because they do not want to stop, because they think they can drink normally, because they are happy, because they are depressed, because a loved one is ill or has died, because someone has offered them a drink, and so on. In short, heavy drinkers drink because they drink. Madsen's work has the value of being closely in touch with the lived experiences of alcoholic drinkers and recovering alcoholics. His inquiry attempts to position the understanding of alcoholism within American culture and American history in a way that other theories fail to do. He notes, with insight, that the alcoholic man or woman is a reflection of the society, the history, and the culture of which he or she is a member. Certain alcoholics perhaps take too far that American charge to "take time-out" from the everyday, mundane world of ordinary life. He or she, perhaps because of genetic and hereditary predispositions, as well as because of patterns of behavior learned in the family context, is drawn to alcohol in a way that other drinkers are not. And, he or she becomes a living victim of the value conflicts that endorse the use of alcohol as a means of escaping from conflict, ambiguity, loneliness, and alienation. Although Madsen does not draw upon the work of Gregory Bateson, he might well have, for Bateson's views on alcoholism anticipate and develop to a higher level Madsen's observations on the alcoholic's dilemma.

BATESON'S THEORY

Bateson's "Cybernetics of Self" theory of alcoholism (1972a) is the most advanced of any theory thus far offered in the field. It may be outlined in terms of the following arguments:

(1) The sober world and life of the alcoholic lead him or her to drink. In his or her drinking the alcoholic denies the insane premises of that world. Intoxication is a subjective corrective to the insane, sober world the alcoholic finds himself or herself in.

(2) "Pride" coupled with risk-taking lead the alcoholic to drink and attempt not to get drunk. The alcoholic's pride is mobilized behind the proposition "I can stay sober... [and] I can do something where success is improbable and failure would be disastrous." (Bateson, 1972a: 322)

(3) The alcoholic is involved in a relationship with alcohol and his or her significant others that is schmismogenic (given to self-destructive divisions and conflicts), competitive, symmetrical, and complementary. This network of social interactions leads the alcoholic to competitively drink in an attempt to prove self-control.

(4) Hence, even though the alcoholic knows he has lost control over alcohol and even though significant others call him alcoholic, he continues to drink in an attempt to prove self-control. Pride-in-self and risk-taking thus tie the alcoholic to a self-destructive drinking cycle that threatens to produce insanity and the loss of everything he values.

(5) Drinking represents a step out of sobriety and a symmetrical struggle with the bottle, in which the alcoholic has stopped drinking (in order to prove self-control), into a complimentary drinking relationship with alcohol. This move, Bateson hypothesizes, signals the alcoholic's desire for a complementary, sociable relation with himself or herself and with others.

(6) Each time the alcoholic drinks and fails to maintain control over her drinking, she produces an occasion to drink again, so as to prove to herself and to others that self-control has not been lost.

Observations

Bateson's theory attempts to analyze the alcoholic's inner phenomenological dialogues with self, yet structurally it locates the alcoholic in a materialistic society that is seen as promoting the use of alcohol as a means of dealing with emotionality, failure, success, and competition. Bateson's theory locates alcoholism, not in the alcoholic, but in his relationship to himself, to alcohol, and with others.

However, the major thesis that drinking represents a step from symmetrical struggle into a desire for complimentarity in social relations must remain problematic. The "step into complimentarity argument" does not deal well with those alcoholics I observed who sought to be alone when they drank. It is not a relation with others that is sought, so much as it is a desire to be at one with one's self, away from the gaze and the criticism of others.

Consider one of the passages from Lowry's *Under the Volcano* (1971, pp. 128-129) in which the Consul has been drinking alone, on the porch of his house. Finding a bottle of tequila hidden in his garden, he drinks from it. Careless of being observed, he finds that his neighbor has been watching him. He states: "He wanted...an opportunity to be brilliant . . . to be admired . . . to be loved." The loneliness, paranoia, and guilt of compulsive, alcoholic drinking are evident in Lowry's account. Hidden bottles, people looking over her shoulder, the desire for a quiet drink alone, the abrupt decision to be with others, the longing for love; these behaviors and thoughts are commonplace in the double-bind structures that trap the alcoholic drinker. Drawn to others yet fearful of them, drinking so as to overcome that fear; in these thoughts and others like them, the alcoholic displays the complexities, contradictions, and negations that characterize his total existence in the world—both with himself and with others.

These points are not developed sufficiently by Bateson (see Faulkner, 1981: 435-448, for a case that initially confirms, and then disconfirms, Bateson's thesis). That is, alcoholic drinking, which begins in the biography of the drinker as a symmetrical, competitive social act with others that permits moments of shared complimentarity or sociality, turns into an antisocial act that promotes separateness from others. As a social act it contains both structures of experience within itself. It permits the alcoholic in the later stages of his drinking career to escape from the maddening presence of others. The isolated alcoholic, bitter and alone, believes that if he drinks and does as others do he can for a moment become like and with them; even though as the alcoholic drinks he knows that he desires to be separate from them. The alcoholic is caught in the double bind of symmetrical and complementary structures of experience—desiring neither and wanting both at the same time. The symmetrical struggle is with the self, not with others. Because Bateson does not position firmly a double-bind relationship between symmetry and complimentarity, the dialectics of the alcoholic's inner and outer experiences with himself, alcohol, and others are not fully grasped.

AN INTERPRETATION OF SCIENTIFIC THEORIES OF ALCOHOLISM AND THE ALCOHOLIC

A complex and variegated view of alcoholism and the alcoholic is suggested in the theories just reviewed. A common theme or thread unites these views and this may be termed the *objective thesis* of alcoholism, alcohol, and the alcoholic. This thesis, which does not apply to Bateson, Jellinek, or Madsen, assumes that the mind and the body of the alcoholic may be studied objectively as a thing, independent of lived experience. Just as the objective, measurable effects of alcohol on the body may be studied, so too may the behaviors, the intentions, and the personality of the alcoholic. Such a view generates discussions of the symptoms that do or do not define who an alcoholic is. In each case alcoholism is not studied from within as lived experience. The objectivist thesis suffers from the following flaws or problematics.

First, objective science, behavioral, pharmacological, psychological, sociological, and epidemiological, orients itself to the phenomenon of alcoholism from a position that is at once controlling, rational, and normative. That is, these inquiries, taken as a totality, aim to control the uses and abuses of alcohol within human society. They do so from a rational, normative point of view that accepts drinking as normal and socially integrating, not understanding that alcoholics presume the antithesis of these standards. It is only in this view that the recent behavioral controversy within the alcoholism literature can be understood (Pendery et al., 1982).

Second, the objective point of view seldom admits within its scientific paradigm history the sexuality of the drinker (to any significant degree), the economic-political-social context wherein the experience of becoming an alcoholic appears, or the materialist world that structures and furnishes the technology that produces the alcohol in the first place (Denzin, 1977a, 1978). In short, the modern scientific view of alcohol, the alcoholic, and alcoholism is ahistorical, sexist, normative, and biopolitical in bias (compare to Foucault, 1982). It reflects the increasing thrust in American society to control the mind and the body of modern individuals by science and technological means.

Third, this literature, with the exceptions of Jellinek, Madsen, and Bateson, has not dealt with nor conceptualized alcohol as a means of dealing with the frightening demands of freedom and being in the world at this moment in the twentieth century. The attempt to investigate and interrogate scientifically the structures of alcohol-induced experience from the objectivist standpoint confronts and flies in the face of the alcoholic experience itself, which is an attempt to deny the control that the world of external, rational, scientific structures exerts over the daily existence of the alcoholic.

Fourth, because of the anterior focus of alcoholism research on forces that cause the alcoholic to drink or not drink, the temporality of the present and the future goes unnoted.

An essential part of the alcoholic's existence lies in the alcoholic's ability to change temporal consciousness. This allows the alcoholic to alter her relationship with herself and the surrounding world. These essential temporal features of alcoholism have escaped notice in the recent scientific literature. Failing to grasp the facticity of the alcoholic's situation, failing to understand that each situation for the alcoholic is different and unique, the literature has lost itself in the search for necessary and sufficient causes when such causes apparently do not operate in the alcoholic's life-world.

CONCLUSIONS

I have reviewed the dominating genetic, psychological, psychoanalytic, anthropological, sociological, and interactional theories of alcoholism. Each theory has been found wanting in one degree or another. Motivational, personality, and learning theories of alcoholism have been criticized. Recurring problems include how to account adequately for the dynamics of addiction, readdiction or relapse, craving, loss of control, the centrality of the self in the alcoholism process, and the actual lived experiences of the practicing alcoholic. A less than complete picture of the alcoholic subject has thus been produced by the theories of alcoholism that have been reviewed. Until the alcoholic self in located firmly in the center of the alcoholic experience, science will continue to remain out of touch with alcoholism.

I turn next to Alcoholics Anonymous and its theory of alcoholism and the alcoholic. This theory, contrary to scientific theories, has been written by alcoholics. It does, however, selectively rest upon the arguments of a small number of medical practitioners concerning the so-called "allergy and craving" theories of alcoholism. A.A.'s theory is a theory of the alcoholic self.

3

ALCOHOLICS ANONYMOUS
AND ALCOHOLISM

I turn in this chapter to Alcoholics Anonymous's theory of alcoholism and alcoholics. I will consider the following three topics: (1) Alcoholics Anonymous, science, and religion; (2) Alcoholics Anonymous's alcoholism; and (3) the alcoholic of Alcoholics Anonymous.

The alcoholic self who comes to A.A. finds an existing society of recovering alcoholic selves. In G. H. Mead's (1934) terms, Alcoholics Anonymous is an emergent society of preexisting alcoholic selves organized around the principles of recovery contained in the texts of A.A. Recovery involves learning how to take the attitude of the selves in this preexisting structure so that their attitudes can be applied to the individuals own experiences with alcoholism.

The problematic drinker will confront A.A.'s views at some point in his or her drinking career, usually as a result of a court order or the pressure of friends, family, employers, physician, psychiatrist, or psychologist, or because he or she has gone through a treatment center (Leach and Norris, 1977: 481). On rare occasions drinkers will come to A.A. claiming no outside influence or pressure. They will find a theory of alcoholism and an interpretive structure fitted to the experiences of problem drinkers that is likely to match their own. If they do not like what they find, they are told:

> Try to drink and stop abruptly. Try it more than once. It will not take long for you to decide, if you are honest with yourself about it...though

you may yet be a potential alcoholic. We think few to whom this book will appeal can stay dry for anything like a year [A.A., 1976, pp. 31-32, 34].

ALCOHOLICS ANONYMOUS, SCIENCE, AND RELIGION

Individuals who come to A.A. with problems with drinking bring a conception of alcohol, alcoholics, and alcoholism that has been differentially influenced by the "scientific-objective" theories just discussed. And, they will bring a personal "lay theory" of their problems that somehow must be fitted to the scientific and A.A. views of their problems.

If science in the traditional sense (Durkheim, 1973: 220-223) is understood to embody the principle that proposals for action in the world can only be made when rigorous, verifiable, causal knowledge has been obtained, then A.A. is scientific. It builds upon the following taken-for-granted assumption that is simple and causal: "If a man does not take the first drink he cannot get drunk." Yet A.A. does not inquire into the etiology, the causes, or the neurophysiology of alcoholism. It does not, as does science, ask causal questions, nor does it deal in absolutes or probabilities. As such, A.A. is an action-oriented, pragmatically structured set of experiences that combines elements of religion (James, 1904), depth and analytic psychiatry, medicine, existential philosophy, sociology, and social psychology (Bateson, 1972a: 331-335; Kurtz, 1979).

Alcoholics Anonymous presents itself to the problem drinker in simple, direct, ordinary language (see Maxwell, 1984; Rudy, 1986). In their meetings, A.A. members dissect, over and over again, the meanings of such ordinary words as power, control, resentment, emotion, sobriety, dry, fear, patience, anger, surrender, serenity, peace, love, and powerlessness. In the above senses, Alcoholics Anonymous is both scientific and not scientific. It is a blend of all of the above points of view into a workable lay theory of recovery from alcoholism. But unlike the personal theory of his or her problems the problem drinker develops (see Chapter 4), A.A.'s theory is grounded in a group perspective. It is a group, lay theory of alcoholism that finds authority in its spoken words and in the formal texts of A.A., including *Alcoholics Anonymous* and *The Twelve and Twelve*. The group and collective foundations of A.A. transcend the personal, lay theories of any given individual, drinking or not drinking.

Alcoholics Anonymous, however, is unlike science in the following critical respects. First, the essential structures of the A.A. traditions exist and are passed on through an oral tradition; that is, through the A.A. meetings. A.A. does not rely as exclusively upon the printed page for the transmission of its knowledge as science does. It is primarily an oral tradition.

Second, unlike science, which Durkheim asserted (1973: 220-223) can affirm nothing that it denies (that is, if it cannot be proven, it does not exist) and deny nothing that it affirms, A.A. affirms what it denies proof to, although denying what it rigorously affirms. That is, although arguing that a scientific proof for the existence of God can never be given, A.A. proposes a belief in a power greater than the individual (A.A., 1976: 48-49). It asks individuals to make a leap of faith and come to believe in a power greater than themselves. This Durkheimian power is collective. It is in the group and not in the group, or in the individual. It transcends the individual (Bateson, 1972a: 333). Yet it is defined individually. Although this power's existence cannot be directly nor even indirectly proven, its influence is involved daily in the group prayer collectively recited at the end of each meeting.

Similarly, doubting, but not denying that recovery from alcoholism can occur if the 12 steps are not taken, A.A. strongly urges each individual to follow its suggested steps to recovery. Hence A.A. affirms what it says cannot be proven, although denying, or at least rigorously doubting, the possibility of what it affirms. As a consequence, third, unlike science, which can establish nothing that is not based directly or indirectly on these two principles, A.A. moves forward, without records, regularly kept statistics, or information on whether or not its methods and assumptions do in fact work. (See Leach and Norris, 1977: 470-507, for a review of the first three A.A. sobriety surveys.) It directs its members, instead, to read the 44 life stories of recovery given in the *Big Book,* and A.A. regularly reports the recovery experiences of its members in its international monthly journal, *The Grapevine.*

Fourth, much of modern behavioral science (Bateson, 1972a: 336) builds upon the Cartesian dualism that posits an objective world that can be studied, interpreted, and controlled by the methods of modern inquiry. Alcoholics Anonymous denies this dualism. It denies also an objective view of the world, locating the alcoholic subject, instead, in a world that is intersubjective, noncausal, spiritual, collective, and distinctly oriental, as opposed to western and occidental.

Fifth, because of its traditional notions of alcoholism as a disease (see below), because it does not keep records on its members, and because it conducts its primary work within "closed" meetings, A.A. is regarded by many as being antiscientific and not amenable to scientific inquiry (Maisto and McCollum, 1980: 18-19). That is, A.A. is regarded as having closed its doors to science (Sagarin, 1969). This belief is challenged by A.A.'s Eighth Tradition, which welcomes the findings of science as they contribute to a better understanding of alcoholism. The antiscientific belief persists in the scientific literature on A.A., this despite the fact that *The Grapevine* regularly reports research findings on alcoholism.

Sixth, A.A.'s emphasis on a power greater than the individual places a wedge between this belief system and the rationality of modern science that in most forms is atheistic if not agnostic. A.A.'s religious spirituality and its pragmatic program of action, which in Weber's terms (1946: 153) is a practical ethic to action, speaks to man's ills in ways that no modern behavioral science can. Alcoholics Anonymous's elective affinities (Weber, 1946) with the pragmatic (James, 1955; Dewey, 1922; Mead, 1964), existential themes of religion, psychology, and psychiatry make it a practical, secular, scientific, and spiritual ethic. It blends, then, science, religion, and common sense in ethical and practical ways that no one of these points of view alone can do. And, because its simple focus is on alcoholism and the drinking act, it is not drawn off into unrelated areas of scientific, religious, political, and cultural concerns in which its local knowledge (Geertz, 1983) on alcoholism would prove to be unworkable or divisive.

Seventh, because A.A. accepts the disease conception of alcoholism, it is at least on the side of those alcoholism researchers (Jellinek, 1960; Keller, 1978) who regard it as a disease. Yet within the alcoholism literature the controversy over whether or not alcoholism is or is not a disease, and, if so, is it a unitary disease (Maisto and McCollam, 1980: 20-25), rages on. A.A.'s incontrovertible position on this matter also can be seen as placing it outside the realm of modern behavioral science as that science studies alcoholism (Sobell et al., 1980).

Eighth, and closely related to point seven, is A.A.'s position, taken from the physician William Silkworth, that abstinence from alcohol is mandatory if recovery is to be achieved (A.A., 1976: xxviii). Many behavioral researchers call for alternatives to abstinence, arguing that abstinence may, for some drinkers, be dysfunctional to social and psychological functioning (Sobell and Sobell, 1978: 29; Maisto and McCollam, 1980: 19). Such researchers call for individualized behavior therapy programs fitted to the drinking patterns of each individual, assuming that nonproblem drinking may be an alternative for many "alcoholic" drinkers. These programs are designed to bypass the "severe social stigma of being an alcoholic on this continent" (Sobell and Sobell, 1978: 28). They attempt to resocialize the problem drinker into nonproblem, controlled drinking patterns.

The abstinence versus controlled drinking controversy aligns A.A. with the nondrinking position, suggesting that its stance is detrimental to the recovery of certain types of drinkers. It is argued also that A.A.'s position produces or contributes to the large population of "hidden ex-alcoholics" (Sobell and Sobell, 1978: 28; Beauchamp, 1980: 49-66). A.A.'s humanistic desire to offer a path to recovery for the "alcoholic" drinker is thus countered by the behavioral scientist's desire to control the effects of alcohol on the problem drinker.

In the above senses Alcoholics Anonymous constitutes a structure of beliefs and assumptions that stand to the side of modern behavioral science as it approaches the alcoholism problem in the modern post-industrial society. The essential ethical and philosophical stance of A.A., which is anti-Cartesian and antiscientific control, places it fundamentally at odds with much of modern science as well. As Bateson (1972a: 33) forcefully argues:

> If we continue to operate in terms of a Cartesian dualism of mind versus matter, we shall probably also continue to see the world in terms of God versus man; elite versus people; chosen race versus others; nation versus nation; and man versus environment. It is doubtful whether a species having *both* an advanced technology *and* this strange way of looking at its world can endure.

A.A., Bateson contends, offers a way out of this dilemma, and it is a dilemma when it is first confronted by the problem drinker who has been taught by science and religion to be in control of himself or herself and drinking.

ALCOHOLICS ANONYMOUS'S ALCOHOLISM

A.A. defines the alcoholic as a sick person, suffering from an obsession, a fatal malady, a progressive illness that is physical, mental, spiritual, emotional, and self-destructive (A.A., 1976: xiii, 18, 30, 92; A.A., 1953: 22-23, 32-33, 107). The illness that alcoholics have is alcoholism. This illness is placed in remission only through death or abstinence from alcohol. It is treated by A.A. and A.A. meetings. The illness, alcoholism, and the sick person—the alcoholic—are thereby located within an interpretive circle that for A.A. remains forever closed and forward moving. It is nearly impossible, in this respect, to separate A.A.'s conception of the alcoholic from its conception of alcoholism. The two are intimately interwoven in what for A.A. is a life or death matter. "To drink is to die" (A.A., 1976: 66). This is A.A.'s reasoning and this is the circle in which it places its members.

A.A. believes, and quotes the physician William Silkworth, that "real alcoholics" have an allergy to alcohol. Silkworth states:

> We believe, and so suggested a few years ago, that the action of alcohol on these chronic alcoholics is a manifestation of an allergy; that the phenomenon of craving is limited to this class and never occurs in the average temperate drinker. These allergic types can never safely use alcohol in any form at all ... this phenomenon, as we have suggested, may be the manifestation of an allergy which differentiates these people, and sets them apart as a distinct entity.... The only relief we have to suggest is entire abstinence [A.A., 1976: xxxiv-xxvi].

Bill Wilson, the cofounder of A.A., described Silkworth's position in a letter to the psychoanalyst C. G. Jung in June of 1961:

> It was his theory [Silkworth's] that alcoholism had two components— an obsession that compelled the sufferer to drink against his will and interest, and some sort of metabolism difficulty which he then called an allergy. The alcoholic's compulsion guaranteed that the alcoholic's drinking would go on, and the "allergy" made sure that the sufferer would finally deteriorate, go insane, or die [A.A., 1963].

Elsewhere in his letter to Jung, Wilson speaks of reading William James's *Varieties of Religious Experience* while being hospitalized for his last bout with active alcoholism. He discusses his realization that the conversion experiences James analyzed involved ego collapse. Jung, in reply to Wilson, suggested that the alcoholic craves a spiritual wholeness that is contradicted by drinking: *"spiritus conta spiritum"* (Leach and Norris, 1977: 455, italics in original).

Several salient factors must be extracted from the above quotations and statements from Silkworth, Wilson, and Jung. The first is the allergy theory of alcoholism. As Jellinek (1960) noted, the conception of alcoholism as an allergy had been set forth as early as 1896. It did not originate with Silkworth. Second, although the notion has been discredited scientifically (Leach and Norris, 1977: 454), it continues to be used by A.A. members. As Jellinek (1960: 87) notes, the figurative use of the term "alcoholism as an allergy is as good as or better than anything else for their purposes, as long as they do not wish to foist it upon students of alcoholism." Third, Silkworth's formulations isolate a particular class or type of drinker who suffers from this allergy. Fourth, he locates the phenomenon of craving at the core of the allergy. Fifth, he advocates abstinence and the experiencing of an entire psychic change in the life of the drinker.

Wilson's letter to Carl Jung takes the allergy formulation to its most severe extreme: death, insanity, or institutionalization. Sixth, he positions the drinker's self centrally in the process of alcoholism, noting that the drinker often drinks against his or her own will and interest. Seventh, he builds upon Silkworth's position that an entire psychic change is required, noting that he was prepared for a conversion experience. Connecting this experience to William James's *Varieties of Religious Experience* has permanently located James, along with Jung, in the annals of A.A. (A.A., 1976: 26, 28, 569-570). Wilson notes the importance of the appearance of his friend Edwin T. at that moment in his life when he was most desperate and ready for a conversion experience. In Edwin T. he found another person with whom he could communicate. Eighth, Wilson notes that the ego or self of the alcoholic must be shattered. Silkworth's presentation of the allergy formulation thus entered Wilson's life at or during a time period when he was most ready to receive it.

Ninth, Carl Jung's remarks to Wilson elaborate the pivotal point that the conversion that occurs must be spiritual. It reveals a thirst or desire for wholeness. The alcoholic experiences, as James had remarked in *Varieties of Religious Experience* (1961: 150), a divided self (Denzin, 1984a). That self cannot be united or joined, James and Jung argued, without a conversion experience. More important, Jung argued that alcohol stands in the way of the spiritual experience.

This position is developed in A.A. as an individual, yet collective, version of spirituality is discovered. (See A.A., 1973.) Indeed, A.A.'s *Twelve Steps* are described as "a group of principles, spiritual in nature, which if practiced as a way of life, can expel the obsession to drink and enable the sufferer to become happily and usefully whole" (A.A., 1953: 15).

The disease or illness that alcoholics in A.A. believe they have is, then, spiritual, mental, and physical. Before the mental and spiritual sides of the illness can be treated, however, the alcoholic often must receive physical treatment, the object of which is "to thoroughly clear the mind and the body of the effects of alcohol" (A.A., 1976: 143). As noted earlier the alcoholic will, in all likelihood, suffer from vitamin deficiencies and any number of alcohol-related disorders including cirrhosis, diabetes, internal bleeding, pancreatitis, and jaundice.

THE ALCOHOLIC OF ALCOHOLICS ANONYMOUS

A.A. distinguishes four types of alcoholics or problem drinkers. These four types of heavy drinkers are all regarded by A.A. as candidates for their program. They correspond in varying degrees to Jellinek's alpha, beta, gamma, and delta alcoholics (Jellinek, 1960: 38-39). However, Jellinek argues, as indicated in Chapter 2, the gamma alcoholic is probably the type most likely to come to A.A. (Jellinek, 1960: 38). A.A.'s four types of drinkers have passed through the prealcoholic and prodomal phases of alcoholism and are in or near the crucial or chronic phases of the illness as described by Jellinek.

A.A.'s Typology of Alcoholics

The primary alcoholic that Alcoholics Anonymous directs its program to is the individual who has "lost the power of choice in drink" (A.A., 1976: 24). This is the drinker who is unable to not take the first drink, this in spite of the suffering and humiliation he or she may have suffered "even a week or a month ago" when he or she last drank (A.A., 1976: 24). Called the *real alcoholic,* this individual is described as follows:

> But what about the real alcoholic? He may start off as a moderate drinker; he may or may not become a continuous hard drinker; but at some stage of his drinking career he begins to lose all control of his liquor consumption, once he starts to drink.

> Here is the fellow who has been puzzling you, especially in his lack of control. He does absurd, incredible, tragic things while drinking.

A.A. (1976: 21-22) gives the following additional characteristics to the "real" alcoholic. He or she (1) is almost always insanely drunk; (2) becomes antisocial; (3) gets drunk at the wrong time; (4) is dishonest about alcohol; (5) goes on drinking sprees; (6) goes to bed intoxicated, yet reaches for a drink the first thing in the morning; (7) hides alcohol; (8) uses medications for sleeping purposes, mixing these with alcohol; and (9) visits physicians, hospitals, and sanitariums because of alcohol-related problems.

A.A. (A.A.: 110) compares the "real alcoholic"—the drinker who has been placed in one institution after another, who has been violent, and insane while drinking, who drinks on the way home from the hospital, and who has had delirium tremens—with three other types of heavy drinkers. The *first type* drinks heavily, sometimes continually. He spends a great deal of money on alcohol, and the mental and physical effects of alcohol may be showing, but he does not see them.

This type of alcoholic may be an embarrassment to his family and friends when he drinks too much, which is often. He may be certain that it is possible to control his intake of alcohol, and is insulted if told he is an alcoholic. A.A. states that "this world is full of people like him. Some will moderate or stop altogether, and some will not. Of those who keep on, a good number will become true alcoholics after awhile" (A.A., 1976: 109).

The *second type* of heavy drinker has the following characteristics: (1) he shows a lack of control over his drinking; (2) he gets violent when he drinks; (3) he tries to stop, or go on the wagon, and fails; (4) he has started to lose friends and his work suffers; (5) he drinks in the morning to control nervousness; (6) he is remorseful after a heavy drinking spree; and (7) he thinks drinking moderately is possible. Of this drinker A.A. states: "We think this person is in danger. These are the earmarks of a real alcoholic. Perhaps he can still tend to business fairly well. He has by no means ruined everything. As we say among ourselves, *He wants to stop*" (A.A., 1976: 109, italics in original).

The *third type* of drinker has gone further than the second type. Friends are lost and homes nearly destroyed. This individual cannot work, or hold a job, and has begun to make the rounds of emergency rooms, hospitals, detoxification centers, and treatment centers. This type admits he or she cannot drink like other people. He or she does not know why and may want to stop, but cannot (A.A., 1976: 110).

Having isolated the "real" alcoholic and compared his or her career to the trajectory of other types of heavy drinkers, A.A. further characterizes this alcoholic as a person who has led a double life. Like a stage actor, she attempts to maintain a certain reputation of being in control of her drinking and career. Yet she is haunted by the guilt that was produced by the last drinking spree, and is fearful that others may have seen her when she was drunk. She attempts to push these memories to the side, believing that the next time she drinks such an event will not occur again. The real alcoholic is "under constant fear and tension—that makes for more drinking" (A.A., 1976: 73).

This drinker will have attempted any of the following methods to control her drinking: (1) drinking only beer, (2) limiting the number of drinks, (3) marking the bottle and not drinking below that line, (4) never drinking alone, (5) never drinking in the morning, (6) keeping alcohol out of the house, (7) going on the "wagon" or "taking the pledge," (8) never drinking during business hours, (9) drinking only at social gatherings and parties, (10) switching from bourbon to vodka because it is odorless, (11) drinking only natural wines, (12) agreeing to resign from work if she ever gets drunk on the job again, (13) taking a trip, (14) not taking a trip and always staying at home, (15) engaging in a rigorous exercise program and joining a health club, (16) seeing a psychiatrist, (17) reading inspirational religious books, (18) accepting voluntary commitment to treatment centers, (19) taking antabuse, (20) joining a church, (21) taking the geographical cure by moving from one city or part of the country to another, and (22) changing wives, husbands, or lovers (A.A., 1976: 31). This list could be extended indefinitely, for the alcoholic who has yet to come to A.A. will have tried any or all of these methods and others as well in an effort to control her drinking.

However, these methods are doomed to failure for, according to A.A., "no real alcoholic *ever* recovers control" over alcohol (A.A., 1976: 30). The actual or potential alcoholic "with hardly an exception, will be *absolutely unable to stop drinking on the basis of self-knowledge*" (A.A., 1976: 39, italics in original).

The double life the "real" alcoholic leads will have left no area of his or her life untouched. Work, sexuality, family, relations with friends, personal health, the desire for wealth, power, material possessions and finances, lifetime goals and ambitions; these pivotal points and others of the same magnitude will have been touched, altered, and perhaps destroyed by the alcoholic's illness and by his or her behavior patterns (A.A., 1953: 42-43). Not only is alcoholism a family illness, but it is an illness, A.A. argues, that cuts to the core of the self of every individual who is involved with the alcoholic, whether wife, child, close friend, father, mother, or employer (A.A., 1976: 104-150). A.A.'s alcoholism and A.A.'s alcoholic are relational phenomena.

THE ALCOHOLIC SELF

The excessive, addictive use of alcohol by the alcoholic is traced by A.A. to the self of the drinker. A.A. states, "self, manifested in various ways, was what had defeated us" (1976: 64), and, alcohol or "liquor was but a symptom" of the illness the alcoholic manifested while drinking (1976: 64). The causes and conditions of that illness are located, as just indicated, in self and in the emotions of self—chiefly resentment, guilt, anger, and fear. These emotions are rooted in the alcoholic's past, the wreckage of which he or she is told to "clear away" and to "Give freely of what you find and join us.... We realize we know only a little... The answers will come, if your own house is in order.... God... will show you how to create the fellowship you crave" (A.A., 1976: 164).

Thus A.A.'s alcoholism is transformed into an emotional illness, into an illness of self, emotionality, and being in the world. The alcoholic is an emotionally ill individual. The alcoholic's illness is rooted in the emotions she attaches to herself and to the past she has constructed while drinking. A.A. believes that while drinking she was insane, defining sanity as "soundness of mind." A.A. states that "some will be willing to term themselves 'problem drinkers,' but many cannot endure the suggestion that they are in fact mentally ill" (A.A., 1953: 33). Continuing this line of interpretation, A.A. argues that "no alcoholic, soberly analyzing his destructive behavior, whether the destruction fell on the dining-room furniture, or his own moral fiber, can claim soundness of mind for himself" (A.A.'s 1953: 33).

A double structure thereby is embedded in A.A. conception of alcoholism and the alcoholic. Connected to self, emotionality, unsound thinking, a past that cannot be let loose of, and the excessive, addictive, craving, allergenic use of alcohol, alcoholism becomes a disease, or illness of living in the world. Alcohol becomes but a symptom of A.A.'s illness. A.A.'s double structure, then, addresses how not to take the first drink, so as to keep the symptom of the illness out of the alcoholic's mind and body. But second, it addresses the emotional and mental illness, or complex of "unsound thinking structures," that have been built up around the alcoholic's self and relationship to the world of others. At the second level, A.A. becomes a structure of group interactions whose primary purpose is to help each alcoholic stay sober today so as to be able to maintain emotional balance and emotional sobriety, one day at a time (A.A., 1953: 88, 90). Recognizing that "all people, including ourselves, are to some extent emotionally ill, as well as frequently wrong" (A.A., 1953: 92), A.A. offers, through its steps and its daily meetings, a structure of tools and a supportive group environment in which the problematics of living sober may be dealt with (A.A., 1976: 554). A.A. thereby locates the recovering alcoholic in a materialistic, social, and historical world that is filled with other individuals who are also emotionally ill, if not alcoholic. In this move A.A. informs the recovering alcoholic that he is no less ill than those with whom he routinely interacts. Because the alcoholic has a set of tools and a group structure at his disposal he is, in fact, better able to deal with that world than are those who have not yet found A.A.

ALCOHOLIC STIGMA AND UNDERSTANDING

Accordingly, the stigma that A.A. might attach to itself, to its members, to alcoholism, and to being alcoholic, is reduced, if not removed, by joining symbolically the recovering alcoholic with a structure of experience that is transcendent and in harmony with the "fellowship of the spirit" that A.A. has located in a power greater than the individual (A.A., 1976: 164). That power which is in the group, in the texts of A.A., and in a God as understood and defined by each member, thus becomes the core of the "fellowship of the spirit" that A.A. says restores the alcoholic to sanity and removes the compulsion to drink.

A.A. (1975: 70) suggests that the alcoholic, when comfortable in the new identity of "recovering alcoholic," share this information with others. To do so, it is argued, increases self-respect and serves to "chip away at the cruel old stigma unfairly placed by ignorant people on victims of our malady." Such statements also "help to replace old stereotyped notions of an 'alcoholic' with more accurate perceptions" (A.A., 1975: 70).

A.A. surrounds any prospective member with an aura of understanding, sympathy, and compassion that he or she may have not found elsewhere. The problem drinker who is a "real" alcoholic will know if she is in the right place when she attends her first A.A. meeting, or so A.A. contends. The new member will find others who truly understand her, perhaps for the first time. Dr. Bob, the cofounder of A.A., described his meeting with Bill Wilson as follows:

> Of far more importance was the fact that he was the first living human with whom I had ever talked, who knew what he was talking about in regard to alcoholism from actual experience. In other words he talked my language [A.A., 1976: 180, italics in original].

A.A. assumes and rests upon a theory of understanding that presumes that understanding derives from shared, common experiences, even when the experiences that are understood have not been experienced together (see Denzin, 1984a: 145). That is, A.A. provides a common field of shared, interactional experience that problem drinkers immediately are able to enter into. They find themselves in the company of others who have been where they have been. They find themselves, perhaps for the first time, experiencing an interaction with others that is grounded on true or authentic emotional understanding (Denzin, 1984a: 145). What they have sought and did not find in alcohol they find in front of them in the faces and the voices of persons who call themselves alcoholics. But these others are not drinking today. They have been practicing alcoholics who have sat in the same chairs when they came to their first A.A. meeting. They find a field of common experience in which emotional understanding is embedded and they will return (See Denzin, 1984a: 145).

A theory of emotional understanding and of emotionality thus underlies the inner workings of A.A. and A.A.'s theory of alcoholism and the alcoholic. This theory, which will be articulated in following volumes, sets A.A.'s view of alcoholism and the alcoholic drastically apart from the behavioral, medical, and psychological theories of alcoholism discussed in Chapter 2.

CONCLUSIONS

A.A's theory of alcoholism and alcoholics may be summarized as follows:

(1) Alcoholism is a threefold illness involving emotional illness, physical deterioration, and physical addiction, and a moral or spiritual emptiness on the part of the person.
(2) Alcoholics have an obsessive craving for alcohol that produces an allergic reaction in their bodies.
(3) Alcoholics have lost the ability to control their drinking, or to stop drinking by themselves.
(4) Self-pride, self-delusion, and denial are central to the alcoholic's alcoholism, for the self and its emotions lie underneath the public symptoms of alcoholism.
(5) Alcoholism is a family or relational illness.
(6) Recovery from alcoholism requires abstinence. No alcoholic can ever return to controlled, social drinking.
(7) Recovery requires an admission of powerlessness over alcohol and a willingness to admit a power greater than the person into one's life.
(8) A destruction of the "alcoholic ego" (surrender) is required if recovery is to occur.
(9) Surrender will eventually be accomplished by a conversion to a "spiritual" way of life.

Science has challenged A.A.'s core ideas, including the allergy theory of alcoholism, the disease conception of alcoholism, and the craving and loss of control hypotheses (Jellinek, 1960; Beauchamp, 1980; Mello, 1972, 1980; Sobell and Sobell, 1978). It may even be argued that A.A. unscientifically reifies the concept of alcoholism, making it a causal force in the life of the drinker, when the term references only an unagreed upon set of understandings concerning problem drinking. Yet A.A.'s practical theory and method for recovery remain unchallenged as one of the most effective or major treatment modalities for alcoholism (Kissin, 1977: 41).

Central to A.A.'s effectiveness is the emotional theory of understanding that underlies the working of the A.A. group. Coupled with this theory of understanding is A.A.'s basic point that the self of the drinker lies at the center of his or her problem. Most alcoholics eventually understand this argument. Bateson's theory of alcoholism, as discussed in Chapter 2, also builds from this position, as does my own. I turn in the next chapter to the lay theory of alcoholism and problem drinking that problem drinkers develop.

4

ALCOHOLICS AND ALCOHOLISM

When I was an undergraduate I took a course on alcoholism. That was back in the early '60's. It was just about the time Jellinek's book on the disease concept came out. My instructor, who is a leader in the field, spent the entire course (as I remember it) rejecting Jellinek. When I began having problems drinking I could never bring myself to believe that I had a disease. I knew the scientific meaning of disease and A.A.'s wasn't scientific. I thought I could control it myself [field conversation, November 20, 1982, recovering male alcoholic, one year sobriety, college professor].

In this chapter I examine the folk, or lay, theory of alcoholism. This theory is organized around the meanings the heavy, or problem, drinker gives to the terms alcoholic, alcoholism, and alcohol. (See Thune, 1977; Wallace, 1982.) This will be the third theory of alcoholism the problem drinker confronts (scientific theories and A.A.'s formulations being the other two). The lay theory of alcoholism will be the primary interpretive framework the alcoholic employs, for it allows him or her to continue drinking. In fact he or she may construct (as the drinker above did) a position against these other theoretical structures.

I will take up two main topics: the structural constraints on the lay theory of alcoholism and the essential structures of this theory. These structures will be analyzed in terms of the alcoholic's theories of (1) self, time, and causality; (2) denial and rationalization; (3) successful drinking; and (4) alcoholism.

STRUCTURAL CONSTRAINTS ON
THE LAY THEORY OF ALCOHOLISM

I define a lay theory as an interpretive account of human behavior developed by the person on the street (Schutz and Luckman, 1973). This theory may draw upon common sense, scientific knowledge, personal prejudice, or the collective wisdom of a social group. It may be a "well informed theory, or a theory riddled with inaccuracies and scientifically out-dated understandings. It will be fitted to the biography and life experiences of its user. It will be a theory that weaves the self and the history of the subject into a coherent tale, or story, that may be sad or happy" (Goffman, 1961a). *A lay theory is a theory of self.* It is theory that may or may not be shared or accepted by others. The alcoholic's lay theory of alcoholism seldom is acceptable to the significant others that make up his or her world.

Previous chapters have sketched in detail the scientific, cultural, historical, and social structures that shape the conceptions of alcohol, alcoholism, and alcoholics that the lay drinker in American society is likely to confront. Because alcohol consumption is woven so deeply through every fabric of society, the drinker, if he has problems with alcohol, finds it difficult, if not impossible, to avoid alcohol's presence in his life. He lives in a culture that drinks.

It is against this background of alcohol's necessary, pervasive, yet problematic presence in his or her world that the problem drinker develops a lay theory of drinking, alcohol, and alcoholism. This theory also will draw upon images of the alcoholic or problem drinker as given in the popular culture, including its national magazines, its films, its novels, its popular music, and its television. However, those social and cultural facts will be modified to fit the facticity of each drinker's drinking experience. Lay theories will draw upon, synthesize, ignore, transform, and rewrite the cultural, religious, scientific, medical, and personal facts and images in the possession of the drinker at the time she comes to the realization that she has problems with alcohol. This stock of knowledge (see Schutz and Luckmann, 1973) will be utilized in such a way as to deny the stigma that might be associated with being a problem drinker. Self-responsibility for drinking-related problems will be denied. The self-pride of the problem drinker will be drawn upon so as to place symbolically the blame for the problems she has experienced on others. The inability of others to understand the drinker and her drinking patterns will be interpreted within a resentful, interpretive framework. That is, these others (employers, family, friends) do not understand why the drinker has to drink the way she does. At root, the problem drinker will believe that it is a moral and legal right to drink. Further, the drinker will believe that she can control, through self-will, her drinking. This complex of beliefs may have been sustained for years. They are part of the core structures of the self of the drinker. They also are woven through the basic elements of the drinker's culture and society.

THE LAY THEORY OF ALCOHOLISM, ALCOHOL, AND ALCOHOLICS

This theory has a threefold structure. First, it locates the drinker centrally within the drinking act, offering temporal and interactional accounts, disclaimers, and explanations of why he drinks as he does when he does (Scott and Lyman, 1968; Hewitt and Hall, 1973; Hall and Hewitt, 1973; Hewitt and Stokes, 1975; Sykes and Matza, 1959; Dewey, 1922, Mills, 1940; Schutz and Luckmann, 1973: 208-233; Sartre, 1956: 446-447; MacAndrew and Edgerton, 1969; Rudy, 1985; Spradley, 1970). At this level, the theory locates the drinker in relation to other drinkers and to alcoholism, which is the most problematic form his drinking may take. It also attaches the drinker to a set of drinking practices that produce desired alterations in the inner and outer streams of emotional experience. Second, the lay theory focuses attention on alcohol as a meaningful social object that brings pleasure and comfort to the drinker. He or she will be attached to a favorite alcoholic beverage and to a favorite drink, perhaps scotch and water, "7 & 7," Jack Daniels, Old Busch, Blue, dry martinis, boilermakers, or gin and tonics. He will appropriate an image of himself in relationship to the drink that he drinks, perhaps deriving personal and social status from that brand and the places in which he drinks that favorite drink. Third, the lay theory will position the drinker in a world of interactional, emotional associates (Denzin, 1984a: 3, 92-93, 281). By so doing it allows the drinker to define his alcohol use against their interpretations of him as a problem or alcoholic drinker. This threefold structure of the lay theory turns, then, just as the scientific and A.A. theories discussed earlier do, on the meanings that will be given to the three terms: "alcoholic," "alcohol," and "alcoholism."

Lay Theory as Theory

These three elements of the lay theory are organized around the just outlined interpretive structures concerning (1) self, time, and causality, (2) denial and rationalization, (3) successful drinking, and

(4) alcoholism. The lay theory is more than a quasi-theory (see below) and more than a set of hypotheses the drinker holds about himself or herself, alcohol, drinking, and alcoholism. However, it contains conceptions of cause, effect, and hypotheses concerning alcohol's effects on the drinker's experiences. In this regard, it as a theory of self in relation to alcohol.

The lay theory is a theory, if theory is understood to refer to an interpretive structure that renders a sequence of experiences meaningful and understandable. It is a pragmatic theory of ordinary behavior, fitted to the particular biographical experiences of its user. It is woven through the life story the drinker tells about herself, for as life becomes problematic so too does her use of alcohol. Accordingly, her life story and theory of heavy drinking complement one another; although often it is not clear for the drinker whether the problems she has encountered in life are due to heavy drinking or whether problems occur because she is a heavy drinker. Before turning to the four major interpretive structures that organize the lay theory, it is necessary to examine briefly the place of cause, effect, and hypotheses in this theory.

Drinking hypotheses. The alcoholic's lay theory of heavy drinking (and alcoholism) contains a set of working hypotheses (Mead, 1899: 369-371) regarding the effects of alcohol upon his or her conduct. The alcoholic has learned that he or she cannot confront the world without alcohol. He or she knows when alcohol's effects are likely to be needed, when they are likely to wear off, and where to get the next drink, should it be needed. He or she has learned how to "manage" life while under the nearly continuous influence of alcohol. The alcoholic has learned where to get a drink early in the morning and late at night. He or she has learned how and where to drink while at work, at home, in the car, in public transit, and in other public places. He or she leads a secret life with alcohol, never far from its presence. Alcohol governs the alcoholic's life, thoughts, and actions in the world.

The alcoholic's theory of how and why he drinks is fitted to the practical, local knowledge he has of himself, his associates, and the taken for granted world he inhabits (Geertz, 1983: 73-94, 167-180; Garfinkel, 1967; MacAndrew and Garfinkel, 1962; Husserl, 1962). The following account, given by a 75-year-old recovering male alcoholic, sober for 15 years, reveals these features.

> I needed a drink every 30 minutes when I worked. I kept it under the counter at the store in a cleaning bottle. When I'd go into the back room to fill the bottle I'd take a drink of the stuff. My wife never knew why I had to keep the shelves of the store so clean and why it took so much

cleanser. I also hid the stuff in a spare tire in my car, half-pints inside the inner tube. I had it buried in the garden, and hidden behind canning shelves in the basement. I wore engineering boots to city council meetings so I could keep a half-pint inside them. I went to the bathroom a lot. I was drunk all the time and could have been arrested anytime in those 40 years for a DUI, but I never was [field conversation, August 10, 1984].

Denial and causation. The lay theory of alcoholism and heavy drinking is both a theory of denial and a phenomenological theory of cause and effect; that is, it is a theory of temporality and the drinker's place in the flow of inner subjective time (Schutz and Luckmann, 1973: 212). As a phenomenological theory of personal causation (Schutz, 1962: 22, 70-72; Schutz and Luckmann, 1973: 208-223) it incorporates "in order to" and "because" motives that account for why it is that drinkers drink the way they do when they do, and why they have the problems they do when they do. They drink in order to manage problems that arise and they drank yesterday because those problems were there and had to be dealt with then. In order to and because motives thus causally connect the future and past in the lived present of the drinker.

Quasi-Theory and Theories of Self

This theory is more than a quasi-theory (Hall and Hewitt, 1973; Hewitt and Hall, 1973) because it extends beyond "ad hoc explanations brought to problematic situations to give them order and hope" (Hewitt and Hall, 1973: 367-368). It is also more than just a set of accounts (Scott and Lyman, 1968) or disclaimers (Hewitt and Stokes, 1975) about the past or about future situations that are defined as problematic. This theory is backward and forward looking at the same time, yet most fundamentally it is grounded in the present; that is, in the now of the moment when the drinker must take another drink. It is not just a set of justifications for neutralizing the drinker's responsibility in a situation (Sykes and Matza, 1959) nor just a vocabulary of motives (Mills, 1940). Rather, it is a fully grounded interpretive system that positions the drinker against a world that would hold him accountable for his actions, today, tomorrow, or yesterday. Although certainly based on "common sense notions of human behavior and social arrangements" (Hewitt and Hall, 1973: 368) the lay theory of alcoholism incorporates all of the elements of accounts, disclaimers, techniques of neutralization, and quasi-theories of problematic situations into a workable theory of temporality and personal cause. Focused as it is around alcohol and drinking, it becomes a theory of self as drinker. As a theory of self it draws into its center every contingent life situation the drinker confronts and gives him a reason for drinking in that situation and not being the cause of what went wrong or became problematic.

In this respect it is like an elegant scientific theory of cause and effect that incorporates every deviant case that might challenge its causal efficacy. Because the self stands at the center of the theory, self as theorist is able, through the use of what Garfinkel (1967) has called *et cetera* and *ad hoc* clauses, to account for every misfortune it encounters. That is, there are no negative cases in the lay theorist's theory of his or her drinking conduct. There are, however, problematic events that cause the theorist to revise his or her theory of self in relation to those events. Consider the following, which evidences the drinker's ability to incorporate the problematic into his theory of himself as a drinker. The speaker is a 50-year-old architect, sober two years.

> I found myself in a motel with an empty whisky bottle, a copy of Elizabeth Bowen's short stories, broken glasses, and wearing the suit I had worn to a conference on the weekend. It was Wednesday morning. I couldn't figure out what I was doing there. Then I remembered a fight I'd had with my wife before I left for the conference. She said, "Don't drink!" And I said "What makes you think I will?" I was furious, that she could think that I couldn't control my drinking. Then I remembered I'd had a drink after my presentation which had gone well. Everyone was toasting me. It made sense to have a drink. Why not? I had two drinks and got mad at my wife for her thinking I couldn't control it. Then I bought drinks for everybody. I can't remember what happened after that, except leaving and taking a cab. I guess that's how I got in the motel. Once I'd figured it all out it made sense. I cleaned up, shaved, ordered a clean suit of clothes and went to the bar and had a drink with lunch. When I got home my wife was all smiles. I didn't tell her what had happened. She thought the conference was for the entire week [field conversation, July 2, 1983].

Self as drinker. The self as drinker theory structures the relationship of the drinker-theorist to temporality. This theory structures the understandings the alcoholic has about himself or herself, including such matters as sexuality, family, and work history. It speaks to deep, inner feelings concerning who the alcoholic wants to be, who he or she has been and who he or she is now. It also references "good-me," "not-me," and "bad-me" self-feelings, that is, desired self-feelings, feelings that produce dread, and feelings that produce anxiety (Sullivan, 1953: 72; Denzin, 1984a: 213).

The lay theory of the alcoholic is a theory of self, denial, and temporal causality. I shall take up each of these points in greater detail, beginning with the theory of temporality that is embedded in the lay theorist's theory of self as drinker.

THE LAY THEORY OF SELF AND TEMPORALITY

The above account of the architect who found himself in a motel room reveals the inner temporal ordering of causality as it is conceptualized by the heavy drinker. That is, the architect explains the present in terms of actions taken in the past. Those actions, in turn, justify his taking a drink once he determined why he had taken the drink that got him in the motel room in the first place. Be recalling the conversation with his wife he was able to understand why he bought the drinks for everyone after his presentation. He was still angry at her. That interpretation, in turn, justified the next drink he took. By not telling his wife of his troubles *he* was able to act "as if" he, in fact, had not taken a drink at the conference.

Temporal Consciousness

In part because alcohol alters the temporal structure of his or her consciousness, the heavy drinker is always located in a temporal world that is either sped up or spread out over that long duration Bergson (1974) called the present. Yet it is not the present that the drinker lives in; he or she lives in the past or the future, never completely in the now of the present. Alcohol spreads out the inner flow of time so that the past and the future can crowd out the present. The following excerpts from a letter Dashiell Hammett wrote Lillian Hellman in 1938, after 14 months of sobriety, reveal these temporal features of the drinker's consciousness, once alcohol has begun its work:

> Darling,
>   So after I phoned you I took a shot of scotch, the first I've had since when was it? and it didn't seem to do me any good, but I suppose it hardly ever does anybody any good except those who sell it to get enough money to buy detective stories or tickets to Elliott...
> and that damned barking bird is at work outside and if I don't look out I'll become a stream of consciousness writer and be discovered by Whit Burnett....I hope you can stop laughing long enough to read the rest of this letter; it gets
> better as it goes on.

```
     That's what I'd like to think,
       and like to have you
          think, but I know
           as well as you
            do that just
            about now
           what lit-
            tle im-
             agin-
              ati-
               on
                I
                 ,
                  v
                   e
                    g
                     o
                      t
                       i
                        s
                         u
                          s
                           e
                            d
                             u
                              p
                               a
                                n
                                 d
                                  s
                                   o
                                    .
                                     .
                              Love,
                      [Johnson, 1983: 150-151]
```

The physical text of Hammett's letter displays the effort to spread out
time, to draw out the writer's passage through time as long and as
dramatically as possible. More important, Hammett's thoughts are
located in the past, as these thoughts of his having used up his
imagination push the boundaries of the present further away from him.
He is in the past as he writes in the present and it is the past that he
laments. Yet the present in the form of the barking bird outside crowds
in. It is, however, a self of the past that Hammett is attempting to
recapture with his prose.

Temporal Causality

A confusion over temporal causality is produced, for while he or she is or was drinking the drinker loses track of time, thinking things occurred when they did not, or did not occur when they did. Berryman (1973: 17-18) offers an example:

> He heard himself looking down at the middle of the floor saying "sober for months" after Howarden, and he shuddered.
>
> It wasn't so.
>
> Not only was it not so but he had been forced to *learn* that it was not so, and now he had "forgotten" again. He was sincerely lost, relapsed back over ground gained long ago, months ago. He had given the same account of his first slip after Howarden when he came into Northeast in the spring, and happened to mention it to his wife that evening. "But Alan," she said, "that isn't so, dear. You had your first drink at the New Year's Eve party at the Browns."

Because the drinker is always present in his or her inner stream of thought, he or she is confused easily over temporal details, as Berryman was in his conversation with his wife concerning when he took his first drink after treatment. This becomes a source of confusion, producing resentment toward the other who traps the drinker in a temporal error. It produces contradictions for the self as well.

Temporal Existence

The heavy drinker lives an inauthentic temporal existence (Heidegger, 1962), for by locating herself either in the past or in the future she is unable to live in the now of the present. This inauthentic structuring of time alters the drinker's conception of causality and cause and effect. All events that occur in the world that surrounds her are filtered through a past or future temporal orientation. Hence they are given causal effects they cannot have in the actual world of the lived present. But because the drinker's temporality is teleological, the future does enter into the present and cause things to happen in the present. The following account reveals this teleological feature of the drinker's temporal thinking. The speaker is a 45-year-old male engineer, sober 2 years.

> I had stopped going to meetings and had started drinking off and on. I was going to Toronto to some meetings. I knew I was going to drink in Toronto so I bought a bottle of Jack Daniels to take with me so I would have a drink when I got there. My plane was delayed two hours so while I waited at home I decided to have a drink since I was going to have a drink in Toronto. This made sense since I was going to drink

in Toronto anyway. In an hour I had finished the bottle. I still had time before my plane so I went out and bought another bottle. To make a long story short, I drank that bottle too, missed my plane and lost $500 in my basement. I found the money a year later stuck in a book [field conversation, October 1, 1983].

If knowing you are going to have a drink in Toronto can cause you to drink four hours before you get to Toronto, then having someone tell you they will discuss a problem with you in a day or two when you are sober also can cause the drinker to drink now. Our references to Lowry's *Under the Volcano* present the Consul as outraged because Yvonne assumed he *would be sober* at a later time.

By absorbing externally produced events, perhaps the statements or actions of other individuals, into his inner stream of consciousness, the drinker places his own stamp of temporal causality upon them. They become his thoughts, actions, or statements and take on a temporal causality that is uniquely his. That is, the drinker fits them into the flow of other events with which he or she has to deal. Causally their meaning becomes temporal for they are inserted into the inner flow of other events with which the thinker must contend. Lowry (1947: 193, 196-197) offers a complicated example. The Consul has just received a postal card mailed to him by Yvonne a year earlier stating *"Darling, why did I leave? Why did you let me? Expect to arrive in U.S. tomorrow, California two days later. Hope to find a word from you there waiting. Love Y"* (1947: 193). Upon receiving the card, the Consul and Yvonne are invited to a friend's for drinks.

A letter written a year earlier, received today, carries meaning that it could not have had, had it been received a year ago. For if that had occurred, and if the Consul had written back, Yvonne would have learned that he had gone through with their divorce, and that he had not asked her to return. Yet she did return, and he loves her today. So today, if her letter had arrived that morning he would have told her that. But he could not tell her that without a drink and of course it was because he was drinking so heavily that she had left a year ago. All of the drinks that had transpired since she wrote the letter and he received it were thereby compressed into the present by the Consul, for, just as a year earlier, he needed a drink now. Similarly, his having gotten over her leaving and her return now made the year seem as if it had not passed. In fact last year's letter had been written yesterday; or so it seems the Consul was able to reason. The logic of this reasoning is dialectical, circular, and teleological. It inserts effect before cause, allows effects to produce causes, and causes to become effects. It is interactional, temporal, and based on the premise that for the drinker his or her thoughts are always able to transcend, if not nullify the passage of time. The drinker can make anything happen if he or she has the next drink, or so it seems. Power fantasies are realized when he or she drinks (McClelland et al., 1972).

Temporal Rhythm

The drinker's inner stream of experience assumes a temporal and melodic rhythm that is sustained by alcohol's effects upon his or her consciousness. Alcohol keeps the long spread of the present alive in the drinker's mind. The pitched high that alcohol gives is what the drinker seeks, over and over again; and he or she desires to maintain that state of mental experience at all costs. Once again Lowry offers an example:

> Oozing alcohol from every pore, the Consul stood at the open door of the Salón Ofélia. How sensible to have a mescal.... He was now fully awake, fully sober again, and well able to cope with anything tht might come his way [Lowry, 1947: 284].

But because alcohol's effects wear off, and because he or she dwells in a world of others, the drinker finds that other events intrude into his or her stream of consciousness, altering the temporal rhythm of his or her thoughts. The drinker is forced to accommodate these intrusive thoughts into his or her inner stream of experience.

Like an angry tryant, the drinker seizes these intrusive events and forces them into his or her inner world of thought. Snatching a request from the other who has forced his or her way into his stream of consciousness, the drinker dispenses with the other's presence as quickly as possible. Dealing with the other, thinking angrily about him or her, getting emotional, the drinker acts, impulsively, quickly, so as to be done with the other. Alex, a 41-year-old male, 2 years sober, recalls an exchange with his 3-year-old daughter on Christmas Eve:

> We'd given her this damned new bicycle which was red and came in a box. The wife had made me go out and buy it that afternoon. I got it home, tore the paper wrapping it, stuffed it under the Christmas tree and went to have a drink. The kid saw the package and wanted to open it. I said "No! Not now!" After supper she tore into it and said, "But Daddy, it's not put together! Won't you put it together for me?" I said, "Not now, I'm busy." The wife said, "Come on, honey, its Christmas." "O.K.," I said, "Christ, its my night, too." I grasped the damned thing, set my beer down, told the kid to get the wrench, got the wheels on the frame, turned it upside down so I could tighten the bolts, and fell

asleep under the damned thing. I woke up the next morning under the damned bike, feeling like a heel and mad as hell at the kid and the wife. We laugh about it today [field interview, April 2, 1983].

Acting quickly so as to move past the intrusion of an external event, the drinker places the event (in the above case a request) in his or her immediate past. But of course he or she has not acted toward these events, except in thought or impulsively through actions that leave the project unfinished. Hence, although the drinker thinks that an event has been dealt with because it was thought about, he or she has not. That the drinker fails tightens the circle of anger that attaches him or her to the other who has brought the request in the first place. Of course, in order to deal with this anger he or she must drink again.

The Temporal Self

The temporal self references those self-feelings that come at the alcoholic through the altered temporal consciousness alcohol produces. It is a self that floods the alcoholic's awareness, melodically and rhythmically, as a pulsating point of reference in his or her consciousness. It is the problematic that centers the drinker's consciousness. As alcohol's effects wear off, the drinker finds that she must return to herself for the self crowds its presence into her stream of consciousness. Lowry's Consul (1947: 223-289) exclaims the following:

That bloody nightmare he was forced to carry around with him everywhere upon his back, that went by the name of Geoffrey Firmin . . . deliver me from this dreadful tyranny of self. (I have sunk low. Let me sink lower still, that I may know the truth. Teach me to love again, to love life. . . . Let me truly suffer. Give me back my purity, the knowledge of my Mysteries, that I have betrayed.—Let me be truly lonely that I may honestly pray. . . . Destroy the world! he cried in his heart.)

Confronting himself in this state of mind, the Consul, like all heavy drinkers, drinks again, for what he seeks is the escape from self that alcohol gives him.

When forced to be responsible for actions that he has taken only in thought, the drinker rebels against those who attempt to hold him accountable for his actions. He withdraws, claiming misunderstandings on their part. The drinker is unable to bring into the outer world of experience the feelings, thoughts, and emotions he feels toward himself and toward them. Like Lowry's Consul he cannot speak the emotions he feels. He drinks again in order to deal with these emotional feelings that he can neither express nor feel when he is criticized by others.

The Real and the Imaginary

The alcoholic's world of temporal causality is, then, a fantasized, interior, "fictional" world of cause and effect. It is, though, a world that is real. The thoughts that are thought are felt, and felt as real feelings. These feelings and the thoughts about them lead him or her to drink. The line or the division between real and imaginary, the fantasized and the actual, is dissolved in the alcoholic's inner and outer streams of experience. Time, in all its inner and outer forms—past, present, future, when a thought was thought, a feeling felt, an action taken, or not taken—is all that connects the real and the imaginary in the alcoholic's world; time that is and self and alcohol.

Alcohol prohibits the expression of the inner self and the inner feelings that the alcoholic feels and thinks. Hence her inner world of being is cut off from the world of others. She is, as Lowry describes the Consul, truly lonely, even when in the presence of others. The alcoholic seeks to sink lower in order to find the ultimate meaning of herself to herself.

Alex, the alcoholic quoted previously, phrases this dilemma as follows:

I want to be alone, a loner. I want to live with ordinary people, but I don't want to be ordinary. But I can't live and communicate with ordinary people when I drink and when I don't drink I can't stand them either.

Summarizing the above comments on the lay theory of temporality, the following observations may be made:

(1) The inner temporal world of the heavy drinker is located within the long *dureé* of the present, yet the drinker dwells in the past or the future.
(2) The drinker drinks in order to keep the long spread of time alive in his or her consciousness.
(3) A confusion over temporal causality and the temporal ordering and flow of events is experienced continually; producing conflict, anger, and ressentiment toward others.
(4) The heavy drinker exists in inauthentic temporality.
(5) The heavy drinker imposes his or her own temporal ordering on the events and thoughts that intrude into his or her inner world of experience.
(6) His or her theory of causality is a theory of temporality that is both fictional and real. The logic of that theory of causality is dialectical, circular, and teleological.

(7) Sustained drinking maintains the structure of this inner world of dialectical temporality.

I turn now to the lay theory of denial.

THE LAY THEORY OF DENIAL

As a pragmatic interpretive structure that renders meaningful and understandable the subject's heavy drinking conduct, the lay theory of denial rests upon the conceptions of temporality and personal, phenomenological causes just outlined. More than a quasi-theory of problematic situations, it weaves the subject's theory of self as drinker into a total "worldview" that hinges on three pivotal processes: self, alcohol, and drinking.

The lay theory of denial is a theory of personal power, for the drinker feels she is in control of her world. She feels that alcohol and drinking are the keys to that control. The drinker derives power from alcohol and drinking. To take alcohol and drinking away would render her powerless. She understands power to be the control of self and other in the social situation and the lack of power to be the inability to control herself or others. Control of self and other involves interaction, the manipulation of knowledge, secrecy, and the control of information; most centrally information about how much she has had to drink. The drinker must deny, to herself and to others, the amounts she drinks, and how dependent she is on alcohol.

The power that alcohol gives to the drinker's imagination has been discussed elaborately by McClelland and associates (1972). A male alcoholic, age 29, at his second A.A. meeting, speaks of this power:

> I've been afraid to write my dissertation. I sit down with the materials, the paper and the typewriter and I have an anxiety attack. I get up, pour a glass of scotch, drink it and the fear goes away. I get courage and power to write. But I can't stop at one drink and I never get anything written [fieldnotes, June 10, 1984].

The alcoholic writer may become dependent on alcohol, finding, he or she believes, the power to create in alcohol. Athol Fugard, the South African novelist and playwrite, sober 17 months at the time of a *New York Times* interview (June 10, 1984: 19) states in regard to alcohol and writing that the alcoholic writer becomes dependent upon alcohol and upon the myth that creativity and writing come from alcohol. Such authors indulge in and endorse the romantic myth that alcohol produces creative works of art. Fugard cites the cases of Dylan Thomas, Brendan Behan, and himself to make his point.

The alcoholic's theory of power in alcohol is, Fugard suggests, a theory of self-deception. By claiming that alcohol fuels creativity, the drinker perpetuates the relationship constructed between himself or herself, alcohol, drinking, and the act of writing. The drinker reaches for power in the world through written words, yet is dependent on alcohol for that power. Hence, power is based, Fugard suggests, on a myth, a romantic notion that the power to think creatively can be given through alcohol. In this respect cause is confused for effect, the writer thinking that the cause of creativity is alcohol, when, in fact, alcohol is both the cause and the effect of the chain of thought when he or she drinks and attempts to write.

The alcoholic's power rests on an elaborate system of self-denial, knowledge manipulation, deception, duplicitous actions, secrecy, and evasion. The following statement from a female alcoholic, age 32, sober five months, underscores the centrality of secrecy in the drinker's world.

> I only drank alone, in the dark. Never in public, never with my husband, or with his family or mine. Nobody knew I drank until I came into A.A. and they said they were glad I was doing something because they thought something was odd. I got caught by my husband one morning. It was 3:00 a.m., I was alone in the living room in my chair, with my bottle of scotch, my cigarettes, the light out, the music on the stereo. He came home one day early from a fishing trip and caught me drunk in my chair. He'd never seen me like that. Then I had to tell him. It's hard for me to look at that chair today. I remember all the nights alone, when I got drunk in it, light out, being sad, angry, resentful. Full of feeling and afraid to show it [fieldnotes, April 30, 1984].

Drinking alone, in the dark, never in public, takes to the extreme the drinker's fear of being caught.

"Passing"

A system of explanation is constructed about his or her conduct that will stand the test of the everyday structures of the world the drinker inhabits. He or she must be able to "pass" as a normal human being who is not under the heavy influence of alcohol (Goffman, 1963b; Stone, 1976; Garfinkel, 1967). "Passing" as normal, he or she "disavows" any deviance he or she might produce (Davis, 1961). By so doing, or by attempting to do so, the drinker maintains a "secret deviance" (Becker, 1973). Knowing that he or she is a heavy drinker, but pretending not to be, he or she maintains his or her standing among normals, or so he or she thinks. All the while the drinker feels as though he or she is an "outsider" in a world he or she may hate, despise, resent, or regard as inferior (Becker, 1973).

Another female alcoholic, age 48, sober five years, phrased her attempts at passing in the following words:

> I always felt that only if I didn't open my mouth nobody could tell. I only drank wine, alone in my kitchen, never even in front of my husband. At parties I'd just hold my glass and smile. But then some fool would say something ignorant that I was an expert on and I'd feel that I had to hold forth. And I would, and then I'd make a fool out of myself and my husband would have to take me home. I could never keep my mouth shut [field interview, December 17, 1983].

A female alcoholic, age 33, sober one month since her last drink, who repeatedly attained 11 months of sobriety, but never onc full year, described her relationship to normals while she drank:

> Oh I was good at hiding it. I kept a constant buzz at work. I'd take a short drink before 8:00 in the morning. Kept a bottle in my desk at work, would pour vodka into my coffee cup. Nobody knew. They never knew me sober until I came into A.A. and then they wanted to know what had happened to me [fieldnotes, May 15, 1983].

The Other

The lay theory of denial hinges on self and on the relation the drinker has with others. As a system of denial it rationalizes continued drinking, neutralizes any responsibility the drinker might be held accountable for, and justifies any action that must be taken in order to obtain the next drink (Scott and Lyman, 1968). By denying self-responsibility for his actions, the drinker blames the other who holds him accountable and questions his drinking. In this respect the theory of denial becomes a theory of the other who holds the drinker accountable for his actions. The drinker altercastes (Weinstein and Deuteshberger, 1962) the other into the identity of a person who makes him drink. This subtle shift in causality is accomplished through those acts of the drinker that promote guilt and counter responsibility in the other's eyes. An alcoholic, age 65, sober 12 years, describes how he manipulated his wife into believing she caused his drinking:

> I had her believing she was crazy. She hid my bottles, poured them out. I was s'posed to do the hiding, not her. She got a bad case of the "nerves" and she went to a psychiatrist. He told her my drinking was

her fault. She should leave me alone. That is, I needed it. But she wouldn't let up on me. Then she started to going to Al-Anon, over a year before I got in A.A., and she got off my case. I went down hill fast after that [field conversation, September 10, 1982].

A 45-year-old male alcoholic, sober two years, described his relationship to his wife as follows:

She bought the bourbon by the case. I told her I didn't like to go into liquor stores. They made me nervous. She thought that if she got it for me and made me happy, we wouldn't have fights. It didn't work though, cause I'd drink and then get mad at her for buying the wrong brand, or whatever [fieldnotes, July 11, 1983].

By manipulating the other into a position wherein she enables his drinking, the drinker absolves himself of responsibility for his drinking conduct.

If the drinker lacks a significant emotional other, or if she rejects those that she has, responsibility for her drinking is shifted to an "imaginary" other, often the other side of her divided self. A male alcoholic, age 42, in A.A. for 12 years, with 10 months of continuous sobriety stated this situation as follows:

When I drink another side of me takes over. The drinking side. Before I drink my sober self tells me not to drink, and I don't. If I want to drink all I have to do is take a drink and then the alcohol and my other self talk to me and tell me to have another drink. Too many times I've done this. My drinking self can't stand what the sober self accomplishes and it wants to tear it down. With one drink I can start a chain of events that will destroy everything I've accomplished while being sober [fieldnotes, June 11, 1982].

This is called talking yourself into a drink. If the lines between the subject's sober and drinking self are not drawn firmly, then an emotional ambivalence will characterize the inner dialogues that precede a drink. All of the reasons for not drinking will be set aside in favor of the one reason the drinking self gives the subject for taking a drink. Calling alcohol a friend, the drinking self will talk the sober self into picking up that drink. And once the first drink has been taken the drinker will not be able to stop with one drink. The drinker sets in motion a sequence of events that will make him or her accountable once again for the state of consciousness and actions taken. Drinking himself or herself drunk, or into sobriety, the alcoholic will turn against the drinking self and hate or despise that self for having taken the first drink. The alcoholic will disclaim responsibility for drinking, blaming it on a side of himself or herself that he or she does not understand. In H.S. Sullivan's terms (1953: 161-162), he may relegate the drinking side of his self to the "not me" and the "bad me," arguing that a side of him that is not the "good me" lead him to drink. Guilt, remorse, and self-anger may dominate the self-feelings the subject feels when he allows the "bad me" to talk himself into taking a drink. He will say that it was not the "real" self that drank. Further, if the subject took actions while he drank that he cannot remember, he will claim that it was the alcohol that was acting and talking.

An alcoholic male, an academic psychologist, age 47, speaking in a detoxification center one night before he was to start treatment stated:

> My wife would bring these conversations back to me in the morning. She'd report vile things I'd said, violent actions I threatened, crude sexual gestures, promises I'd made. I could remember none of it. I'd say she was making it all up just to get back at me. I hated her for it. Who does she think she is? I'd never never say things like that. I guess it's what they call a blackout. I just don't say things like that [fieldnotes, June 11, 1984].

Blaming Alcohol

The alcohol the subject requires is blamed for the actions that are taken when he or she drinks. The viciousness of this circle of drinking, taking actions that one cannot remember and denying responsibility for them, escapes the drinker's attention. His or her system of denial denies their occurrence. The drinker's self-pride is embedded so deeply in drinking and in the myth that his or her life is under control that he or she cannot see how alcohol destroys what it is intended to produce and sustain.

The drinker's self-pride is fused with the drinking act. Hence, in order to maintain her self-esteem she must continue to drink. Alcohol is conceptualized as a positive social object that brings beneficial effects to the drinker's self-pride and to his or her relationships with others. Indeed, the drinker feels that he or she cannot deal with others except through alcohol. The act of drinking secures a socially desirable self; a self that is valued and cherished—if not misunderstood—by others.

A female alcoholic, age 36, sober 8 years, explained why she drank the most expensive scotch:

> I was high-class. I wore the best clothes, went to the best hairdresser, had the best college education, came from high-status parents. My father was the head of a hospital. I had to drink the most expensive scotch in the world. And I did, a fifth a day for 5 years. Then it became a quart, and then I knew something was going wrong. Why did it take so much scotch to make me feel good [fieldnotes, October 7, 1983]?

A male alcoholic, sober four years, age 39, stated this relationship between self-pride and alcohol as follows:

> I'm a man, a strong man. Strong men drink boilermakers, shots of V.O., and glasses of Old Mill. That's what I did. When the old lady had me locked up over night in the city jail I couldn't believe it. She told the Chief of Police to leave me there the full limit [72 hours]. I hated her for it. How could she do that to me? I could control the stuff and she knew it. She was just trying to get back at me cause of the woman from Detroit [fieldnotes, November 13, 1986].

Self-Uniqueness

Beneath this position of pride in self is the drinker's belief that he or she is unique and hence must drink the way he or she does.

> Anybody with the problems I had would have drank the way I did. Two divorces, retarded kid, bankrupt, mother dying of cancer, I drank to blot it all out. Had to, no choice. At least the booze let me forget [fieldnotes, November 19, 1982, 58-year-old male alcoholic].

The alcoholic's belief in self-uniqueness involves the following assumptions. First, she takes seriously the assertion that every social situation is imminently personal and unique (Sartre, 1956; Garfinkel, 1967: 281-283). Second, she takes to the extreme the view that every human individual is unique, and hence unlike any other individual (Schutz and Luckmann, 1973). Third, she believes that her uniqueness is more unique than that of any other individual. Fourth, like the embezzler and white-collar criminal who believes that his or her problems are unshareable (Cressey, 1947; Benson, 1985), the alcoholic assumes that her problems can only be solved through individual means. She mobilizes self-pride and risk-taking behind this assertion. Fifth, the alcoholic resorts to actions that violate the trust others have placed in her. Her alcoholic drinking becomes a means of solving insurmountable, unshareable problems. Sixth, the alcoholic neutralizes the guilt she feels about her actions (including her drinking) by claiming that it hurts no one else. She may also make an appeal to higher authorities in justification of her drinking (see Sykes and Matza, 1959). Seventh, she feels that she is not guilty of any "true" violation of trust because she is doing only what she has to do in order to survive. Eighth, the unique lifestyle that she leads, the unique set of problems that she has inherited or that have been forced upon her, and the special problems that arise in the daily world of interaction, justify continued drinking at the alcoholic level. Recovering alcoholics call this "terminal uniqueness," and suggest that problems drinkers may die from this version of their illness.

The drinker's self is attached to the world through a circle of drinking conduct. That circle defines for him the essential meaning of who he is to himself. The drinker's essence lies in the drinking act. To stop drinking, or to contemplate stopping drinking, is unimaginable. Who would he be without alcohol? Alcohol fills a void, an emptiness that other people—including the alcoholic—cannot fill.

An alcoholic, who died from internal bleeding produced by varicose veins, spoke of why he drank:

> My counselor asked me, "Why don't you stop?" I said, "What else is there? It doesn't mean anything. Life, what is it anyway? Drink, take it all the way, push it, fight it, keep fighting it. Without booze there's nothing. It's all empty, dark. Who said it? Fitzgerald, 'the fear of early morning, alone, awake, terror of darkness.' That's why I drank, to beat the hell. When I die I want 'em to drink a bottle of whiskey and dance around the fire on my grave and say, 'He gave it HELL!'" [field conversation, August 29, 1980].

The drinker's theory of denial, to summarize, has the following features:

(1) It is a theory of power in use, for alcohol is regarded as the key source of personal power in the drinker's life.

(2) As a theory of self as drinker, the system of denial focuses on self, alcohol, and drinking.

(3) Dependence on alcohol is denied and hidden from others.

(4) Secret drinking is at the heart of the theory of denial employed by the heavy drinker.

(5) Control over alcohol is basic to the drinker's daily existence and he believes he can control alcohol and its effects upon him.

(6) The drinker's denial system blames others and the "not me" or the "bad me" components of the self for his drinking.

(7) Self-pride justifies the continuation of drinking, as does the belief that the drinker is unique and has unique problems that only alcohol can handle.

(8) The drinker's self is attached to the world through a circuit of drinking. He finds the core meaning of his existence in drinking and in alcohol.

(9) The alcoholic's system of denial is sustained by the belief that he will not fail the next time he drinks.

This last point, the belief that he will not fail the next time he drinks, is the core assumption that underwrites the alcoholics ongoing drinking project. The alcoholic's denial system sustains this belief, for it allows him to justify each time he drinks and encounters trouble. I turn now to an elaboration of this element of the subject's theory of drinking. At some point in his drinking career he did drink successfully and alcohol did do all these things for him. The alcoholic's denial system is based on a past "reality" that he believes to be true. He also believes that alcohol can work for him once again, as it did before.

THE LAY THEORY OF SUCCESSFUL DRINKING

At some point in her drinking career—perhaps for a time period that spans years, if not decades—the subject regarded herself as a successful drinker. By this she means drinking gave her the good feelings, the euphoria, the creativity, the release from pressures and anxiety, the comradery, the fellowship, the love, and the warmth of fellow humans that she sought and valued. As a successful drinker she had good times with alcohol and with others who drank with her. It was possible to control her intake of alcohol. She could control her behavior while drinking, and drink in a manner that was regarded as normal, if not unique. Even during periods of "out of control" drinking she did not suffer negative consequences that she could attribute to alcohol.

This picture of the past is held onto by every problem drinker. It is for the alcoholic a factually accurate picture. Because it is "factually" accurate, as it is remembered, it becomes the cornerstone of the system of denial the drinker constructs when her experiences with alcohol begin to go bad. That is, she believes that it is always possible to get back to the time when she drank successfully. Every negative experience is dispelled as accidental, as being caused by others. Her "bad faith" (Sartre, 1956: 70) flees the facticity of each problematic drinking situation, permitting the drinker to believe what she knows is not true. The alcoholic knows she is a problem drinker, but believes that she is not. Any problematic that might occur when she drinks is disarmed in advance. At the same time she clings to and seeks out the smallest pieces of experiential evidence that would prove that she is in fact drinking successfully.

Consider the following statements. The first is by a 52-year-old male alcoholic, an owner of a construction firm, sober 12 years:

> I remember how that gin would taste: warm, right out of the bottle I kept behind the seat in the pickup truck. I'd take a long swallow about 4:30 in the afternoon, before me and the boys would stop off at the bar for a few beers. It would be warm, bitter, sweet, hot, it tasted sharp

and clean. It would go all the way down to my toes and then come back up through my blood stream to my brain. I'd start to tingle, feel warm, then shiver and feel cold, then my head would clear. Those damned anxieties and fears would all go away. But it would come right back up and I'd vomit the gin. I'd have to do it twice more before it would stay down and then I'd start to be warm and feel good all over. I kept this up for three years. Everyday. The wife said I was crazy [field interview, May 13, 1982].

The negative experience of vomiting is disallowed in advance. It was a necessary step that had to be taken before the gin could bring the desired effects. The drinker goes on to report:

During this time in my life I made more money than I ever have, before or since. I had 25 men working for me. We built three banks. I drove a new Chrysler every year. We built a new home. I owned three condos and a vacation home down south. How could I be an alcoholic? I told myself it was the pressure, all those men working for me.

The problematic confronted by this drinker, the vomiting when he took the first drink, was discounted because of the above successes. These successes, however, were compounded by the following experiences:

It was after I started drinking in the morning, and getting sick when the wife could hear me, that she told me I had to do something. I told her to go to hell. We fought for weeks. I'd come home, grab a beer out of the fridge, after the gin earlier and the 6-pack I drank on the way home, go into take a bath and pass out. She knew something was wrong. Then I'd come to the supper table, yell at everybody, drive them all off, get 'em crying and all that, and then I'd either leave, or go into the bedroom with a bottle and shut the door. Finally it got so bad the wife told me to leave. I said good. I moved into the Moose, then I could drink whenever I wanted to and nobody would yell at me. That lasted a year, before I went to A.A. for help. I still didn't believe I was an alcoholic and at the old halfway house they kicked me out and told me to go drink some more. So I did, another year. Finally I gave up, went back, got help. Stayed there 6 months. Now I'm back with the wife and kids. I still remember how sweet that gin tasted [field interview, May 13, 1982].

This drinker's story of his history with problem and alcoholic drinking displays the features of the lay theory of successful drinking outlined above. Beer and gin were his favorite drinks. The taste and feel of the gin when it entered his consciousness were memories of drinking onto which he held. His financial successes during the period of the onset of his problem drinking nullified the problems he and his wife knew he was experiencing. Alcohol appeared to handle successfully the problems of anxiety he confronted in his work. His pride and self-will were attached to the drinking act. He was willing to give up his home and his family in order to continue his drinking. The problems he was experiencing while drinking were not of his making. His bad faith succeeded in convincing him that he was still a successful drinker. That is, even when the drinker has problems with drinking he still insists that he is a successful drinker.

The following statement is from a 48-year-old academic, sober 10 months. He had entered treatment 13 months earlier and drank 3 months after he was back at work. He drank off and on for 3 months. He states the following:

> I could never connect the problems I was having in my life and in my work with drinking. Somehow they were always disconnected. Drinking was just something I did. These problems just kept coming up. I would drink when I was down and I would drink when I was up. When I was up I felt strong and drank then too. I would remember all of my accomplishments and connect those to my drinking. Then I would drink more. Everything that I did that was good I always connected to my drinking; never the bad things, and there were more of those! I drank, too, out of fear of things that hadn't happened yet—a loss in my family, a sickness, whatever [field conversation, June 13, 1984].

This drinker separates problems from drinking. He regards himself as a successful drinker because his problems were never joined with his drinking. Connecting drinking to his successes and the good moments in his life, he sustains the image of himself as a successful drinker.

The following drinker, also an academic, is less sanguine. Sober seven days in A.A., after a four-month period of being dry and then slipping for two months before coming to A.A. for the first time. He states:

> Alcohol is supposed to make you happy. It cures depressions. Takes away anxiety, kills pain. Makes me laugh. Helps me sleep. But its killing me, slowly, slowly; its taking a long time, but its killing me. Why do I keep drinking this poison? It must be insanity, or irrationality. But I can't sleep. I put the headphones on from the stereo to blot out the dreams. And I dream and the dreams hurt. I get up and take a drink and kill the pain. But then I have to come off the sauce and I can't sleep then either. Its a circle and I can't seem to break out of it [field conversation, June 10, 1984].

The double-edged effects of alcohol, as a producer of both euphoria and depression, are well captured in these remarks. Drawn back to alcohol because of its killing, numbing, sometimes pleasurable effects, the drinker nonetheless feels that he is killing himself.

The same individual describes himself in greater detail, offering the following biographical information about himself and his family.

> My father was and is an alcoholic. He would close the family grocery at 6:00 and not come home until 1:30 a.m., after the tavern closed in the little Minnesota town we lived in. As a kid growing up I never saw him. Later when I was a teenager he bought a carnival. He wanted it to be a family business. Me and my four brothers worked it in the summers. It was embarrassing. He would yell at us in the kiddie rides, drunk. I left home to go to college and thought I'd escaped. I went off to become the successful drinker. I taught my friends how to drink. One night a friend asked me: 'How many drinks does it take before you become an alcoholic?' That was years ago. That line haunts me to this day. How many drinks does it take? [field conversation, June 19, 1984].

When does the drinker stop being a successful, heavy social drinker and become an alcoholic? This is the question that is being asked.

Another side to alcohol and drinking is given in the mass media, especially through its beer commercials. A male alcoholic, age 31, 2 years after treatment, during which time he had 2 slips, or returns to drinking, describes himself:

> Sometimes I don't know who I am. I watch the T.V. and see the commercials. I think I'm a product of Madison Avenue. When I think about drinking I hear, "Go For It!" "The Weekends are for Bud!" "Join the Pepsi Generation!" Who Am I? I pick up that stuff. It used to work for me. I started when I was 15, then I found grass and speed, then LSD and then coke. I've had an altered state of consciousness for so long I don't know who I am. Then I was unconscious for two years before treatment. I can't even find my own thoughts inside all the commercials and that shit! [field conversation, June 10, 1984].

This drinker nearly lost his job as a middle-level executive. He nearly lost his marriage. He was two thousand dollars in debt to drug dealers when he entered treatment, which he was forced into. Yet when he closes his eyes and thinks drinking, he sees and hears the commercials from Madison Avenue. These commecials, which do not depict the negative consequences of drinking, elaborate the inner fantasy life of the drinker because they picture only the positive effects and consequences of drinking.

This drinker knows that the picture of a successful drinker given in the mass media is not him, still he dreams of "Going For It!" The pictures in the commercials and the sounds in his mind evoke success. The heavy social drinker, the problematic drinker, and the alcoholic can all find pictures of themselves which normalize their drinking and make drinking an attractive, desirable social act. The mass media fuel that false image of self. Often the bad faith of the drinker can talk him or her into thinking he or she is like the drinker pictured in the commercials.

On other occasions the drinker will cling to a memory, or a picture of himself from the distant past, and attempts to drink himself into that picture. The speaker is 43-years-old, sober nearly 3 years.

> I had a bottle of Pouilly Fosse, 1962, in the Princess of China, a restaurant in Chinatown in San Francisco in 1968. It was a beautiful tasting wine. The meal was outstanding and the view across the bay, after dinner, with the sunset was gorgeous. That was a good night for me. Everything was the way it was supposed to be. For years I searched for that bottle of wine and looked for that taste, that moment, those feelings of that evening. I never found that bottle of wine and I never got back to that feeling. It used to make me sad as hell and I'd drink even more. Something had gone wrong and I didn't know what [field conversation, April 10, 1984].

This inability to get back into a state of consciousness that was once experienced haunts the problem drinker. His or her denial system, as outlined above, sustains this self-image image of as a successful drinker.

The essential elements of the lay theory of successful drinking are as follows:

(1) It is based on earlier historical moments in the drinker's past that are defined as having occurred.
(2) Unpleasant features of that history that might have been problematic, in which alcohol or drinking were involved, are neutralized and discounted through the drinker's bad faith.
(3) The drinker views herself in the present in terms of these past images of self.
(4) The successes the drinker achieved in the past, whether financial, family, work, or personal, are seen as being part of the picture she has of herself as a successful drinker. She connects drinking and successful drinking with successes in the other areas of her life.
(5) Even if the drinker comes from a family of unsuccessful drinkers, she regards herself as being a successful drinker, that is, not alcoholic.

(6) At some point in her career as a successful drinker, the drinker knows that she no longer drinks as her friends or drinking associates do.

(7) Beneath the image of herself that she holds onto and puts forth as being a successful drinker is the awareness that she probably is not what she claims to be. The drinker knows, in some part of her consciousness of self, that she is a problem drinker, if not an alcoholic.

It is this last awareness that produces the lay theory of alcoholism, or of heavy, problem drinking that the above pages have outlined. The lay theories of temporality, causality, denial, and normalized or successful drinking are all subsumed under what I have termed the lay theory of alcoholism, or of heavy, problem drinking.

THE LAY THEORY OF ALCOHOLISM

This theory, which is an interpretive structure that permits the drinker to go on drinking long after he and his emotional associates feel he should, revolves around the following 12 points. These points are deeply embedded in the personal history of the drinker.

(1) He may be a heavy drinker, but not an alcoholic.

(2) He deserves to drink and has to drink because he is unique and special. Even when he has to drink it is because he deserves it.

(3) There are problems in his life with which alcohol helps him deal. Without alcohol he could not deal with those problems and be a unique person.

(4) When drinking she escapes life's problems.

(5) When she has problems drinking it is due to matters over which she had no control. When she has problems it is the problems, not the alcohol, that create the problems.

(6) She is a social drinker who drinks heavily and doesn't drink any more than others do. Therefore she cannot be an alcoholic.

(7) Those people who say he has problems with drinking do not understand him.

(8) Therefore, if they make him angry, it is natural to drink more and to not interact with them.

(9) Life is still manageable and everything is under control, even if he does drink a little too much on occasion. After all he has never had a DUI.

(10) The reasons to quit are not strong enough, although quitting is possible if she wanted to.

(11) Therefore, no interference or help from others is necessary. All that is necessary is to be left alone so that she can drink and enjoy alcohol in solitude, or in the company of others who understand and who will allow her to take pleasure from the next drink.

(12) When drinking she becomes the kind of person she wants to be. Alcohol is her best friend.

CONCLUSIONS

The lay theory of alcoholism rests, as indicated above, on a threefold structure. First, it is a theory of causality that is both rational and logical, as well as being dialectical and contradictory. It is based on facticities, or lived factual experiences that are constructed and reconstructed in the drinker's mind. The drinker twists and constructs reality to fit his ongoing picture of himself as a drinker who needs alcohol. More important, he is a misunderstood drinker.

Second, the lay theory of alcoholism rests on a theory of denial that draws, third, on the drinker's theory of normalized, successful drinking. These three interpretive structures feed upon one another. They are woven or stitched into the picture of self the drinker desperately holds on to. Inscribed in his or her consciousness and in the divisions that separate the self is a deeply etched triadic picture that joins the self of the drinker with alcohol and the drinking act. His or her life is held together through and because of alcohol. To take alcohol away from him or her would be an act of destruction. It would be an act of such monumental consequences that the drinker dares not think of himself or herself as a nondrinker. To think that it is possible to exist without alcohol is unthinkable.

It is not surprising, therefore, that the drinker will go to any length to protect his supply, hide his drinking, rationalize his troubles, and exclude from his world those who say he has a drinking problem. Nor is it surprising for the drinker who has stopped for a period of time to be drawn back to drinking and to alcohol. After all, he has constructed an elaborate interpretive structure that allowed drinking long past the time when he should have stopped. In order for the drinker to start drinking again, all that is necessary is to resurrect a tiny part of that interpretive structure and he can tell himself once again that it is okay to drink because he can handle it now. Behavior modification treatment programs for problem as well as for alcoholic drinking are well suited to the alcoholic who does not wish to stop drinking. Such programs offer interpretive reasons for continuing a drinking career.

In this chapter I have developed in considerable detail the phenomenological and interpretive structures that underlie the problem drinker's theory of alcoholism. Analysis has revealed that for the problem drinker continued, heavy drinking is a necessity. The reasons for drinking are legion, the causes for drinking phenomenological and personal. The problem drinker constructs a personal theory of drinking behavior in the midst of a social, scientific, and political dialogue that surrounds alcoholism in American society today. This theory draws from this larger universe of discourse what is necessary for the drinker's survival. Knowing that alcoholics exist in the larger society and knowing that she may be one, the drinker goes to great lengths to avoid the label, as she continues to drink. In the next chapter I offer a summary of the foregoing in terms of "The Six Theses of Alcoholism." In Chapter 6, I show how this conceptual and interpretive structure that the problem drinker has built begins to collapse. I will show how the drinker must finally confront the fact that her self lies at the core of her relationship to the world. The self, caught in the webs of bad faith that she has woven, ultimately proves to be her undoing; that is, if she is to recover.

5

THE SIX THESES OF ALCOHOLISM

Thesis: "A position or that which is set down or advanced for argument." (Chambers 20th Century Dictionary, 1983: 1342)

I have now examined the three major theoretical approaches to alcoholism and alcoholics that a practicing problem drinker will confront. The theories of science, A.A., and the lay individual have been discussed in detail. In this chapter I return to the Six Theses of Alcoholism that were briefly sketched in Chapter 1. These theses are drawn from the above theories. They are based also on my empirical observations of individuals who have an "alcoholic self." The theses summarize the experiences of such individuals. They are derived from the presentations of self such persons make in the social worlds of alcoholism that center around A.A. meetings.

They are stated as theses. They are not hypotheses or testable propositions as such. They reflect points of interpretation in the structures of experience that constitute *the alcoholic circle,* including problematic or alcoholic drinking, denial, surrender, and the processes that underlie recovery.

The six theses of recovery (and alcoholism) are (1) the thesis of the temporality of self; (2) the thesis of the relational structures of self; (3) the thesis of the emotionality of self; (4) the thesis of bad faith; (5) the thesis of self-control; and (6) the thesis of self-surrender. I will discuss each thesis in order. But first I must examine briefly the basic premise that organizes the theses.

THE ALCOHOLIC SELF

The theses are organized around a single premise, contained in the term "alcoholic self." Divided against himself or herself, the alcoholic is trapped within an inner structure of negative emotional experiences that turns on extreme self-centeredness and self-narcissism. This narcissism, as Tiebout (1954) suggests, is grounded in three factors: (1) feelings of omnipotence, (2) an inability to accept high levels of frustration, and (3) a tendency to "do everything in a hurry" (Tiebout, 1954: 612). Freud's term, "His Majesty the Baby" (Tiebout, 1954: 612), has been applied to the alcoholic self who wants to rule the world in its own way. Although there is questionable utility in the three personality characteristics Tiebout ascribes to the alcoholic, his general point concerning self-centeredness and feelings of omnipotence seem useful and correct.

The narcissistic, alcoholic self uses alcohol as a "mirror" to the world. This mirror produces a distorted image of the alcoholic, for it fuels grandiose feelings of omnipotence. It also fuels an inwardness of thinking that leads the alcoholic to focus upon past failures. A resentment toward self and others is produced. This resentment is focused on gaps and failures in achievement. In particular, the alcoholic has internalized a conflicting set of inner, self-ideals. These ideals are derived, in part, from an original "mothering" or "fathering'" other and in part from his or her own version of those ideals as applied to himself or herself (Lacan, 1977: 2-5). The clash between these two structures of self (ideal-self derived from the mother and/or father, and self-ideal formulated by self) creates a fundamental instability of self for the alcoholic. He or she uses alcohol as a means of joining those two self-structures.

The alcoholic's unstable inner self runs to madness, fantastic self-ideals, imaginary fears, neurosis, isolation, and narcissism. It is held together through fragmented body self-images that incorporate self-dissatisfaction with a disdain, or dislike, for the physical body that houses the alcoholic's self. The alcoholic's self-other relations (Kohut, 1984) produce experiences that solidify this fundamental alienation from self. Because alcohol is his mirror to the world and the mirror to himself, the alcoholic dwells in the reflected self-images alcohol produces for him.

These inner structures of self come to life in the language, thought, and memories of the alcoholic self. Because alcohol modifies the cognitive and emotional thought processes of the subject, it is necessary to examine briefly the disorders of consciousness that are experienced by the alcoholic. These disorders are connected directly to the individual's relations with himself or herself, emotionality, time, and others. They also speak to the phenomenon of relapse, loss of control, craving, and denial.

Language, Thought, and Memory in the Alcoholic Self

Considerable evidence suggests that alcoholics in the prodomal, critical, and chronic phases of alcoholism suffer from, or display, the following language and thinking disorders: (1) short- and long-term memory loss; (2) a substantial dissociation of experience during drinking; (3) a clouding of consciousness, a disorientation of thinking, and an inability to understand language; (4) an inability to produce written or spoken language of a coherent form, evidenced in slow speech, poor articulation, improper sentence structure, an omission of small grammatical words and word endings; (5) a confusion over similar and dissimiliar terms, including the appropriate use of metaphor and metonymy, and a general inability to follow associative and syntactical rules or understandings; and (6) compensatory confabulation (Ryan and Butters, 1983: 487-520; Mello, 1972: 262-263; Wallace, 1984: 80; Keller and McCormick, 1968: 122-123; Urbina, 1984: 56; Oscar-Berman, 1984: 191; Jakobson, 1956: 90).

These disturbances, or irregularities, in thought and memory also describe the alcoholic in the first year of recovery. They are produced by the effects of alcohol and other drugs on the various hemispheres and regions of the brain, including the frontal system, and the right and left hemispheres (Ryan and Butters, 1983: 525-526). The continuity hypothesis, which suggests a continuum of impairment that extends from heavy drinkers to alcoholics with Krosakoff's disease has been proposed; that is, as the alcoholic progresses in his or her alcoholism the above effects become more and more pronounced (Ryan and Butters, 1983: 525-526).

Alcoholic Aphasia and Amnesia

These findings may be interpreted within the literature on alcoholic aphasia and amnesia. Alcoholics have been identified as suffering from Wernicke's disease (Keller and McCormick, 1968: 215). This is also termed *receptive aphasia* (Wallace, 1984: 80), and it is characterized by points two and three above (that is, dissociation of experience and a difficulty grasping and understanding language). Alcoholics also suffer a second form of aphasia termed *Brocca's aphasia* or *expressive aphasia* (Wallace, 1984: 80), which is displayed in points four, five, and six above.

Wernicke's disease often precedes Korsakoff's psychosis (or disease), which is also termed *amnestic-confabulatory psychosis* (Keller and McCormick, 168: 122) or *alcohol amnestic syndrome* (Urbina, 1984: 56). Although the "blackout" is the milder form of alcoholic amnesia, the Korsakoff syndrome evidences an inability to form new long-term memories (anterograde amnesia) and a loss of memory of past events that were once remembered (retrograde amnesia). The *organic amnestic syndrome* refers to short- and-long-term memory loss associated with organic pathology, often produced by substance abuse, including excessive alcohol use (Oscar-Merman, 1984: 191). This form of amnesia encompasses each of the six disorders outlined above. Victor (1965) argues that recovery from this syndrome "requires the formation of new memories and their integration with past experiences" (Keller and McCormick, 1968: 123). The alcoholic in the acute phase of the syndrome produces elaborate, often imaginary, conversations to cover for the fact that she has suffered a loss of memory. Problems memorizing new materials or following conversations are evidenced, as is a general inability to employ the "forward memory span" (Keller and McCormick, 1968: 122). In short, the alcoholic is able to think about and remember only the most recent of events. She has trouble incorporating new information into her memory and into conceptions of herself.

Figures from the Past

Suffering from these forms of aphasia and amnesia, the alcoholic appears to latch onto a few pieces of information about herself, to commitments she has made, and to significant others from the past. These figures from the past constitute a constant point of reference in the otherwise clouded alcoholic stream of consciousness. She knows, in short, her name, birthdate, social security number, address, spouse's name, place of employment, who her parents were, and where she is supposed to be next, although she may even forget or confuse these elementary pieces of information. She may not remember that she is an alcoholic and may drink again because of this. The alcoholic will also forget what happened the last time she drank, including the pain that was felt during withdrawal, and that she lost control over alcohol. She will experience the physical and phenomenological craving for alcohol within a temporal vacuum that does not associate drinking with past failures.

The threads that hold this discontinuous stream of thought together are emotional. Anger and resentment toward the past is held onto. A general fear of the future is experienced. A disorientation in the present is felt, as is a confused state of self-understanding concerning who the alcoholic is and why he is in the situation he now finds himself in.

The Circles of Alcoholic Thought

The alcoholic exists within a circular, conceptual, linguistic, and temporal space that confounds the effects of receptive and expressive aphasia with anterograde, retrograde, and alcoholic amnesia. The self is located in the center of this confusing linguistic circle. Bits and pieces of the past, the present, and future attach themselves to one another within this circle in ways that do not make sense. The alcoholic is like a half-completed jigsaw puzzle. Disconnected, unrecognizable pieces of the puzzle, like the fractured pieces of the self, lie all around in a disorganized pile. He or she doesn't know where to start, or how to start to put the pieces back together into some recognizable shape or form.

The alcoholically reflective self mediates these thought patterns. It attempts to make sense out of them, but finds that its every effort to be coherent, logical, rational, and orderly fails. Its thought and talk alternate between metaphor and metonymy. It races back and forth in time from distant experiences to events that occurred a moment ago. Holophrastic, repetitive speech displaces part for whole, confuses whole for part, and associates discontinuous thoughts with one another, as if they fit together in a rational, orderly thought sequence.

The ability to reason, to think coherently, logically, and with any kind of temporal order has vanished. The alcoholic's language continues to turn and twist metaphor and metonymy into patterns of speech that appear to reflect deep, inner, primary processes of self and consciousness. These primary speech patterns of self ordinarily are inhibited in common discourse. But they are the primary discursive structures of thought that order the alcoholic's self-dialogues. Partially released by alcohol, partially ingrained in his or her consciousness, they become familiar patterns of thought for the alcoholic. The twisted, poetic, metaphorical, metonymic patterns of speech thus serve to place him or her outside the realms of ordinary speech and interaction.

Consider the following account given by an intoxicated alcoholic:

I'm crazy, like a horse who wants to jump over a house. I'm out of the saddle, flying high over houses, I look down and see the person I

sleep with and work with lying in bed. I want to laugh at her and try
to explain all of this to her but I can't. I'm afraid to go downstairs and
talk to her. She's waiting for me. I want to get in the saddle and ride
again, I've got all this fear inside my head. If I could just slow down
it would be better.

But I can't slow down. I feel like my house doesn't belong to me
anymore. Nowhere is mine anymore. I want to get away and go riding
[field conversation, as reported September 20, 1985, 39-year-old alcoholic, lawyer].

This jumbled sequence of thought and speech moves from statements that equate house with horse, saddle with being in control,
omnipotence with looking down and seeing the woman he lives with
in bed, and craziness with being like a horse. His house becomes a
horse (metonymy). He is like a horse (metaphor). He mixes these tropes
in his speech, as he attempts to place himself within the stream of
consciousness he is experiencing.

Ten days later, in a treatment center for alcoholism, this speaker
raises the topic of relapse for discussion at an A.A. meeting. He states:

I've been thinking about relapse. I think I stood relapsed since I got
out of treatment last time. Maybe for four or five months. I was drinking
when I came in here. I don't remember getting a drink, and I don't
remember going out and starting to drink. All I remember is that I was
drunk and I couldn't stop. They told me the first time to watch for these
things but I didn't understand what they meant. How did it happen?
I want to know.

This statement could be interpreted within the framework of
"denial." That is, the drinker denies his alcoholism and wanted to
drink, so he did. It can also be interpreted within the discussion just
presented. That is, 10 days earlier this thinker was trapped within an
aphasic, amnesic structure of thinking that was alcoholically produced.
Drunk at that time, he could not remember taking a drink. Now, 10
days hence, as he is becoming sober, he cannot remember how he
started drinking after he left his first treatment center. Suffering from
a form of organic, amnestic syndrome, coupled with his earlier entrap-
ment in expressive and receptive aphasia, he is unable to remember
taking the first drink. Memory loss, coupled with denial, provide the
interpretation we are seeking for the situation he found himself in.

An interpretation of the Six Theses of Alcoholism, which now
follows, requires that the above discussion be kept in mind. The self,
language, and thought patterns of the alcoholic structure the opera-
tion of the processes the theses are meant to describe.

THE THESIS OF THE
TEMPORALITY OF SELF

The thesis of the temporality of self assumes that the alcoholic knows himself only through time and the temporal structures of experience that alcohol produces for him. As a temporal being, the alcoholic exists within authentic (inner) and inauthentic (chronological) outer time (Heidegger, 1962). The alcoholic knows himself as a being who moves through time. He knows that alcohol alters the flow of time in his inner stream of experience. By drinking, the alcoholic alters his relationship to himself, to time, and to the passage of time.

The self of the alcoholic contains in its inner core a conception of self as a drinker or a nondrinker. This master identity overrides all other conceptions the alcoholic has. The self, accordingly, is attached to the world through an interactional circuit that includes drinking or not drinking as pivotal activities that define and shape who she is to herself and to others. The self is made up of three inner structures the "good-me," the "not-me," and the "bad-me" (Sullivan, 1953: 161-162). The good me references positive feelings of self; the not me, self-feelings and actions that produce terror and horror for the drinker or the nondrinker. The bad-me refers to those self-feelings that produce anxiety and negative feelings of self. Across these three structures of self are two temporal conceptions of self: The self of the past and the self of the present. For the nondrinker the self of the past is the drinking-self of the past. The not-me and the bad-me are the central elements of this part of the past self. In the past he or she may have drunk so as to feel the "good-me" features of self. Now the not-me and the bad-me are the self ideals that drinking both brings into existence and neutralizes in terms of guilt or anxiety.

Within the temporal and interactional structures of the good-me, the not-me, and the bad-me, and the self of the past and the self of the present, is the fictional "I" of the subject (Lacan, 1968). This "I" is reflected only in the inner thoughts and feelings of the subject. It stands outside his immediate discourse with others. It is attached indirectly to his "real" interactional self through his thoughts and actions in the world. However, these actions do not, for him, reflect the deep inner meanings the alcoholic holds toward himself. These inner meanings are gathered together around the "I" of his inner self-conversations. The inner "I" of the subject is the moral self, the feeling self, the self that is the "real self" of the subject (Denzin, 1984a). For the drinking alcoholic, alcohol fuels this inner, fictional "I." Indeed, he believes that only alcohol can bring that conception of self before him.

These analytic and experiential structures of self give way in the flux of concrete experience to a consciousness of self that is always within reflective range of the subject. Haunted by who she is, could be, and has been, the active alcoholic lives within a temporal world that is circular and inward turning. Located within the circular confines of time, she is hemmed in by the past, the future, and the present. She knows herself through time. Who she is, has been, or will become ultimately hinges on actions she has taken and not taken, or will take.

A recovering alcoholic, sober 30 days, phrased this relationship between time and action in the following words:

> When I was drinking I always made momentous decisions and acted decisively—in my head. When it came time to act I always hesitated, waiting for the right moment to act. Then I would let alcohol make my decision for me and I wouldn't act. I was afraid to act and to move forward. Alcohol always gave me the excuse I needed [field conversation, 39-year-old male alcoholic, academic, July 9, 1984].

The thesis of the temporality of self rests, as the above discussion suggests, on three interrelated assumptions. First, alcoholism is a disease of time. Second, the alcoholic is a temporal being. Third, temporality defines an essential core structure of the alcoholic's self. I shall examine each of these assumptions in turn.

Alcoholism as a Dis-Ease of Time

Alcoholism is a disease, an uneasiness with time, temporality, and the alcoholic's being in time. It is a dis-ease of time. Malcolm Lowry (1947: 344) offers the following description of the Consul who is reading the letter Yvonne had mailed to him a year earlier:

> "Do you remember tomorrow?" he read. No, he thought; the words sunk like stones in his mind.—It was a fact that he was losing touch with his situation—. He was disassociated from himself . . . he was drunk, he was sober. . . . Do you remember tomorrow? It is our wedding anniversary.

The Consul is lost within time. He is ill at ease within time. He drinks to escape and control time. Alcohol, as noted in Chapter 4, speeds up and spreads out the passage of time. Within this spread-out horizon of time the alcoholic, as the Consul above, loses track of himself or herself. Fearful of time, fearful of the actions he or she must take in the world, the alcoholic confronts time with alcohol.

The Consul does not know if it is six in the evening or early morning. He is unable to remember tomorrow. Yet each of his states of inner experience—drunk, sober, hungover—collapses in upon him all at once. These inner experiences are temporal and alcoholically induced. The fact that they run together in his stream of consciousness evidences his loss over time and over his being within time. The alcoholic who drinks to make time stand still becomes a victim of the very inner consciousness he or she desires.

The Alcoholic as a Temporal Being

A recovering alcoholic, age 48, a carpenter, sober four years, described his relationship to time in the following words:

> When I drank I made time stop. I would look at the clock on my mantle, it would say 10:30 p.m., I'd drink a glass of whiskey and go flying inside my head. I'd be back years ago, or ahead, 10 years from now. I'd be happy, sad, angry, afraid, all at once. I'd stretch out my legs and reach for the glass and it would be empty. I'd get up to get another, look at the clock, it was 10:35 p.m. Here I was drunk, it was still early in the evening. I wouldn't be able to go asleep yet. The kids and the wife were still up, nothing was quiet like it was supposed to be and I was drunk! And it was only 10:35 [field conversation, December 7, 1982].

The alcoholic's dis-ease of time renders him or her a temporal isolate, an anomic temporal being. By attempting to escape time the alcoholic escapes himself or herself and is free to dream, but these dreams and this alcoholic time is not time with others. It is inner, private time that is unshareable and often unbearable. He or she is placed outside other people's time and thus becomes a different kind of temporal being. He or she is drawn to those others who share this disease of time.

The Consul inhabits lonely bars early in the morning. Other drinkers seek out the solace of their own company; still others seek crowded taverns during happy hours, which legitimately begin "drinking time" early in the afternoon. A recovering alcoholic, age 43, a chemist, sober two years, described his lunch patterns:

> I only had lunch at bars that served food. I of course drank my lunch. But "The Greek Bar and Grill" had a happy hour that started at 1:00. I could take a long lunch and legitimately start drinking early in the afternoon. The drinking crowd came in around 1:30, to beat the amateurs who came in around 3:30. We'd get the music rolling— "Margueritaville" by Jimmie Buffet—and the double gins and the day'd fly by. I'd hit the sun on the sidewalk about 4:30 and have the day under control. No problem with what to do about the day after that [field conversation, February 5, 1983].

Time and Self

The drink situation the alcoholic confronts (Lowry, 1947: 303) is whether or not to drink the drink that awaits. This decision is made as she attempts to hide from others the effects the drink she has just taken is having upon her. Locating the self of her inner consciousness in the experiences that alcohol brings, her self is a fiction. It is an imaginary "I," to borrow from Lacan (1968), Jakobson (1956), and Kristeva (1974), that has little if any connection to the "real" world of others. The "I" of alcoholic thought is fictional, narcissistic, heroic, dramatic, articulate, resentful, private, and angry. It is angry because it can never realize its inner "imagined" dimensions in "real" interactions with others. Its thoughts spill over beyond the boundaries of normal, orderly discourse. The words that surround this fictional "I" in the alcoholic's inner thought cannot find a form of acceptable display in the talk that would anchor this inner self in the public world of others. Her words are hollow, yet her inner thought is alive within a dialogue that is vivid, pictorial, dialectical, and unique. The unique structures of the self are known only to her.

The most literate alcoholic, then, is trapped within an inner world that knows no acceptable mode of external expression. Because time is ungraspable and because his thoughts exist only in time, in the fictional world his fictional "I" inhabits, the alcoholic experiences himself as a void in the world. He is nothingness (Sartre, 1956). Every action taken that would or could fill out the void of nothingness fails, or seems to fail. He can never succeed in bringing the "I" of his inner existence into the interactional world of others.

Normal Time Versus Alcoholic Time

It is necessary to compare alcoholic time with normal time. In suggesting that the alcoholic experiences a dis-ease or uncomfortableness with time, I imply a normative, or "normal," conception of time. Following Heidegger (1962), Schutz and Luckmann (1973), Mead (1934), and Parsons (1951), we may make the following points regarding "normal" time. First, everyday, purposive social action grounds the individual in the present, as the past and the future are taken as orienting perspectives for accomplishing goals in the near, or immediate, present. Second, "normal" time, unlike alcoholic time, is not oppressive, threatening, or anxiety producing. That is, the experiencing of "normal time" does not require the use of alcohol so as to overcome the fear of time. Third, alcoholic time is time that is lodged in the past or in the distant future. Normal time is lived in the present. Fourth, normal, healthy time is understood reflectively as being part of the person's ongoing presence in the world. Reflection on normal time and its passage does not produce flights back into the past, as alcoholic time does. Fifth, alcoholic time lodges the self and its emotions in the past. Normal time locates the self and its feelings in the present.

These differences between alcoholic and normal time suggest Heidegger's (1962) distinctions between authentic time and inauthentic time. Authentic time is lived in the present, without a fear of the past or the future. Inauthentic time is fearful of the past and the future. However, an easy application of Heidegger's distinctions to normal and alcoholic time cannot be made, for normal time also may be experienced inauthentically, as Heidegger so forcefully argued. To say that alcoholic time is defined by the use of alcohol so as to flee from time borders on the tautological. The operative distinction between these two modes of time lies at the phenomenological level. The alcoholic is simply uneasy in time. He is unable to deal with time on his hands. He cannot let go of the past and purposive actions that would commit him to a stance in the future are avoided. By drinking, time comes to a standstill.

The alcoholic is like the "workaholic" who deals with the fear of the future and the past by overinvolvement in task activities. The alcoholic uses alcohol, the workaholic work; both classes of individuals seek to avoid or escape time on their hands.

Modern societies have produced large groups of individuals who share certain features of the alcoholic's dis-ease of time. Scheler's (1961) man or woman of ressentiment is a victim of time and the negative emotions that trap them in the past of the future. The elderly who are fearful of death, women who experience traumas after childbirth and when their children leave home, racial and ethnic minorities who live in the oppressions of the past, students who are fearful of making life decisions, the recently divorced who face the future without spouses, and the unemployed worker who has no economic hold on the future all live a version of the alcoholic's dis-ease of time. These individuals are all candidates for alcoholism and drug addiction, for in these chemicals they will find a means of escaping time's fearful oppressiveness.

THE THESIS OF THE
RELATIONAL STRUCTURES OF SELF

The self of the alcoholic is embedded in the communicational and emotional structures that tie and connect him or her to others. The self is a relational phenomenon or, in H. S. Sullivan's words (1953), it is an interpersonal process. That is, the self is not in the subject. The self is in the relationships the alcoholic has with others. Alcoholism (and the process of recovery), accordingly, is a relationship to the world. It is not something located in the person, nor is it a disease or illness of the person. *The thesis of the relational structures of self asserts that the self of the alcoholic and his alcoholism can be understood only in terms of the relational structures he constructs, experiences, and gives meaning to. In short, he and his alcoholism are relational, interpersonal processes* (Bateson, 1972a: 324-325).

The alcoholic, like other subjects, conducts transactions with the world through the *relational circuit of selfness* (Sartre, 1956: 102-103; Denzin, 1984a: 60). The self does not inhabit his or her consciousness (Sartre, 1956: 103), rather it is lodged in the alcoholic's interactional relations with himself or herself and the others. Most pivotally, the self is located in alcohol and in the drinking situation.

The alcoholic's world of relational interaction consists of the following structures: (1) "real" and imagined, or fictional, others; (2) "real" and imagined "emotional" relations with these others; (3) the structures of self and self-feeling that are lodged in these relations with others; and (4) strategies and patterns of drinking and not drinking that exist alongside these relational connections that join the self with others. Each of these structures requires brief discussion.

"Real" and Imagined Others

The alcoholic's world is populated by others who are both real and imaginary. Malcolm Lowry's Consul carries on elaborate and detailed conversations with his half-brother Hugh, oftentimes confusing the "real" Hugh with the Hugh of his imagination. Similarly, the Consul finds himself engaging Yvonne, his separated and then divorced wife, in inner conversations that bear no relationship to the "real" Yvonne who appears at his doorsteps on the last day of his life.

John Berryman's (1973) Dr. Severance was an imaginary other, a fictional alter ego, with whom Berryman coversed as he charted his recovery process while in treatment. Bateson (1972a: 328) suggests that the alcoholic's others "are either totally imaginary or are gross distortions of persons on whom he is dependent and whom he may love." These others will be drawn from the alcoholic's immediate and distant family, world of work-related others, childhood, the mass media, friendships, and from the depths of his or her imagination. They are emotional associates (Denzin, 1984a: 281), or persons who are implicated in some fashion in his or her emotional worlds of experience. More specifically, however, they are "alcoholic" others, for they are entrenched in the alcoholic world he or she has constructed. They may be *enablers,* or persons who support his or her drinking, though passively and actively disapproving of it. They may be drinking associates who drink with the alcoholic and encourage him or her to drink. They may be authority figures, including a physician, member of the clergy, psychiatrist, employer, God, judge, the police, or parent.

The alcoholic's other may be a part of her, for through a disassociation of self, she may conceive of herself as being two persons: the alcoholic who drinks and the alcoholic who does not drink. The fictional "I" of the inner self may be the real other she speaks to and regards as most central to her life. In short, the line between "real" and imaginary may be virtually nonexistent in the inner self-conversations of the alcoholic. As she brings these imagined others into her inner world they assume a liveliness and presence that is felt to be real.

The alcoholic is the consequence of a chance occurrence, the meeting of a certain body and "psychosomatic reality" with a certain social environment, a certain mother, father, set of siblings or peers, a family structure, and a social world (Sartre, 1981: 48-51; Denzin, 1984a: 91). He or she emerges from a particular family unit. Those others who make up that world of family interaction indelibly impress on the alcoholic a biographical structure of experiences that will never be shaken or forgotten permanently.

The alcoholic is haunted by this childhood past, by its memories, its relationships, and its feelings. Absent mothers and fathers figure prominently in these memories. The alcoholic may drink in order to regain a sense of a past that was lost or never experienced in childhood.

The triadic relational structure of child-mother-father attaches the alcoholic to his or her family past. The adult alcoholic attempts to reestablish, through the drinking act and through the alcoholic consciousness that alcohol produces, a relationship to that triadic structure that is satisfactory. He or she lives out, in and through alcoholic consciousness, all of the anger, the resentment, the fear, the lust, the desire, the frustration, the anxiety, and the love that were or were not present in childhood and adolescence. The alcoholic may drink so as to kill his or her absent family other, or to recreate the other in his or her own eyes. In either case he or she drinks so as to live through this past what was in some sense unsatisfactory, painful, and perhaps morally horrifying. Many female alcoholics, for example, report sexual abuse experiences in their childhoods (Gomberg, 1977). They began drinking, in part, so as to blot out, or forget, these experiences.

Every recovering alcoholic I observed made reference, at some point in the recovery process, to these family others who continued to shape and influence their lives. The following account is typical:

> My father was an alcoholic. My mother was schizophrenic and a drug addict. It was painful growing up. I learned to drink to kill the pain. My mother's dead. I like my stepmother. She's good for my father. She's not my mother. I would like to see my mother today [field conversation, 38-year-old female alcoholic, accountant, in A.A. for 12 years, sober 11 months before a recent slip, June 9, 1984].

Malcolm Lowry's Consul describes (1947: 197-198) the pain of his relationship with his mother and his stepmother:

> The urgent desire to hurt...had commenced with his stepmother.... It was hard to forgive.... Harder still...to...say...I *hate you.*

Emotional Relations with the Alcoholic's Other

Bateson (1972a: 326) suggests that the relationship the alcoholic has with his or her real and fictional other is schismogenic and symmetrical. By the first term he means that the relationship is split, or divided, into competing and often self-destructive factions. Schisms have been generated. By his second term Bateson proposes that these schisms exist along an axis that both encourages and discourages more drinking on the part of the alcoholic. Rather than being complementary, as when one pattern of behavior (dominance) fits another pattern (submission), the symmetrical relation of the alcoholic and his or her other builds and escalates into more and more drinking. Though it is likely that his or her relationship to the other is both complementary and symmetrical, Bateson's point concerning the escalation of self-destructive patterns within the relationship is correct. These patterns, if allowed to persist, will destroy the *alcohol-centered relationship.*

That is, the interactional patterns within the relationship produce an alienation from the other. This fuels feelings of ressentiment (Scheler, 1961; Nietzsche, 1887), which undercut the emotional foundations of the relationship (Jackson, 1962; Steinglass and Robertson, 1983: 295-300). The alcoholic comes to hate those to whom he is closest, and is unable to either express the positive feelings of love and warmth that he feels, or feel the other's love and warmth for him. A desperate loneliness pervades all emotional relations with others.

A recovering female alcoholic, age 40, a nurse, sober four years, described her feelings toward her husband in the following words:

When I drank I lost all touch with love and my inner feelings for my husband (and my children). They tried so hard to get me to stop drinking that I only felt fear and anger toward them. I was afraid they would catch me drinking the wine in the kitchen and it would make me feel angry. I still don't know how to show my feelings toward them and its been over four years since I've had a drink! I'm still trying to get in touch with my emotions [field conversation, April 1, 1982].

The relationship the alcoholic has with the other escalates as he or she continues to drink. Often it escalates to the point of collapse. That is, the relationship is destroyed. More often the relationship stabilizes into an uneasy structure in which both parties relate to one another in hostile, antagonistic, and spurious interactional forms. The emotional fields of experience they share become hollow and empty, filled only by the anger and the remorse that alcohol produces. The emotionality that connects the alcoholic with his or her other is, to summarize, negative, spurious, and relationally destructive. The schisms that divide the relationship are increased each time a negative interaction and a negative emotional experience is produced.

Structures of Self-Feeling

Self-loathing, self-hatred, guilt, ressentiment, including envy, desire for spite, wrath, and anger (Denzin, 1984a: 285) characterize the self-feelings the alcoholic feels toward herself and toward the other who is nearest to her. Not only does she feel misunderstood by the other, but she feels anger and guilt over the fact that she is misunderstood. Moreover, the alcoholic's actions while drinking—which may have taken her into the self regions of the not-me and the bad-me—only serve to increase her self-loathing and guilt. As her alcoholic conduct leads her to violate her inner moral standards, anxiety and guilt increase. In short, half of this relationship with the other is built on negative emotionality. The alcoholic hates and loathes herself, therefore she hates and loathes the other.

This structure of interaction is self-generating, that is, it moves forward in terms of its own inner momentum. Each occasion of face-to-face interaction generates self-feelings that are, if not negative, ambiguous and ridden with anxiety. The feeling that the alcoholic will explode and turn on the other is ever present. Such feelings permeate the self-structures of the other, leading him or her to be always on edge and fearful of what might happen next. The expectations of negative interaction, in a self-fulfilling fashion, serve to increase the likelihood that such negativity will in fact be produced. In this sense the self-structures of the alcoholic and his or her other produce interactional structures that destroy the underlying premise of the relationship that brought them together, and now holds them together as hostages of one another. I turn now to the patterns of drinking that are built into the alcoholic's relationship with his or her other.

RELATIONAL PATTERNS OF DRINKING IN THE ALCOHOL-CENTERED RELATIONSHIP

At some point—probably early—in his relationship with the other, the alcoholic drank publicly and openly. Once his drinking becomes problematic, this pattern changes. He becomes a "hidden" alcoholic within the alcoholic-centered relationship he has established with his other (see Rubington, 1973).

The following concealment strategies were typical of the alcoholics I observed: (1) hiding alcohol in the laundry basket; (2) hiding half-pints in the corner of the bedroom closet; (3) pouring alcohol in empty laundry detergent containers; (4) hiding bottles of alcohol in desk drawers at work; (5) filling beer cans with vodka; (6) burying bottles of alcohol in the backyard and in snowbanks in the winter; (7) hiding glasses of alcohol behind books in bookcases; (8) filling oranges with gin; (9) carrying bottles of wine in shopping bags and large purses and drinking in the restroom; (10) drinking one or two large drinks before going to social gatherings; (11) drinking large amounts after the rest of the family had gone to bed; and (12) stopping for drinks before coming home for dinner.

The alcoholic's other may enter into this "hiding game" by pouring out her alcohol, throwing away bottles, asking her to mark the bottles or marking them herself, or fixing drinks for her. The other attempts to control the alcoholic's drinking through these actions and in so doing enables her. That is, an environment is promoted in which drinking becomes a competitive activity and a battle of wits. Each party focuses attention on the drinking act. The emotional content of the relationship is thereby reduced to the amount of alcohol the alcoholic drinks on a daily basis. In short, a chemical takes control of the interpersonal relationship.

THE THESIS OF THE EMOTIONALITY OF SELF

The thesis of the emotionality of self states that alcoholism, in addition to being a temporal dis-ease, is an emotional dis-ease, or a dis-ease of emotionality and self-feeling. The alcoholic is emotionally sick and inhabits a world of painful self-feelings and painful emotional experiences. His or her relations with others are emotionally distorted as well. That is, ressentiment, anger, fear, and the negative emotions outlined above permeate his or her emotional relations with others.

The alcoholic is uneasy in this emotionality, feeling pain and conflict in those emotional self-feelings that disclose his or her inner self to others. His or her inner self and inner feelings are masked through the manner of sociable comportment that alcohol gives. Yet basic to the alcoholic's relationship to the world are his or her self-feelings. These feelings, and the inner and the outer selves they are attached to, are negative, spurious, and fleeting. Their existence is dependent on the effects alcohol brings to the drinker's stream of experience. That is, the drinker feels himself or herself and his or her self-feelings first through alcohol and then through the reflected appraisals of others.

Accordingly, the interactive effects others have upon him or her are distorted by alcohol. The alcoholic's inner self is always at least slightly out of line with the self that is presented to and perceived by the other. Furthermore, his or her inner self-feelings are feelings that cannot be shared with the other, for they are alcoholically mediated emotions.

A recovering alcoholic, age 47, an academic, sober three years, reported the following conversation with his former wife:

> She said she never knew me except when I was drinking. She said she thought I never heard her when she said she loved me. She said I always seemed either too happy or completely depressed and all she ever wanted to do was make me happy. She couldn't understand who I was when I stopped drinking. I don't think I ever knew her either [field interview, July 10, 1983].

The self-feelings and emotionality of the drinking alcoholic have a three-fold structure: (1) a sense of emotionality in terms of an awareness that is filtered through the altered temporal consciousness that alcohol produces; (2) a sense of self feeling these feelings in terms of the emotional feeling that alcohol brings; and (3) a revealing of the inner, moral, deep, feeling alcoholic, drinking self through this experience (see Denzin, 1984a: 51; Heidegger, 1982: 137).

The Alcoholic Body

Because self-feelings are embodied states of consciousness (Denzin, 1985b) and because alcohol produces both minor and major alterations in his or her lived, physiological body, the alcoholic's sense of emotional experience is one in which bodily sensations play a major part. An undoubted authenticity is granted to emotional experiences simply because alcohol alters and affects the functioning of nearly every one of his or her vital organs. As the alcoholic drinks and feels the feelings he or she feels, and as he or she interprets those feelings, especially those that are emotionally significant, his or her central nervous system is processing this information within an alcoholically based biochemical environment. The drinking alcoholic's sense of self and emotionality is, then, quite literally alcoholic, for he or she experiences himself or herself only through the effects of alcohol.

His or her sense of self and emotionality is real in the illusively fictitious sense that alcohol makes effects real. The alcoholic is, after all, more than what alcohol does to him or her, but interactionally the other may not know this. Hence when he or she is defined as an alcoholic by the other the label is resented for the alcoholic knows that he or she is more than the label conveys. But because the drinker can only present himself or herself alcoholically, or through the structures of experience that alcohol produces for him or her, the other's assertions and labels are correct. This self-awareness serves to increase the ressentiment he or she feels toward the other.

The emotionality of self thesis, which suggests that alcoholism is an emotional dis-ease, points to the underlying emotional foundations of the everyday world the alcoholic must inhabit. That is, the taken for granted world that surrounds the alcoholic is one that is based on unproblematic emotionality (Denzin, 1984a). By making emotionality problematic through the drinking act, the alcoholic makes himself or herself a problematic member of the world of which he or she is a part. I turn now to the problem of bad faith and the alcoholic.

THE THESIS OF BAD FAITH

The Thesis of Bad Faith states that the alcoholic and his or her other attempt to escape the facticity of alcoholism by denying its existence. The alcoholic's theory of denial and his or her theory of normal, successful drinking supports the structures of bad faith that allow him or her to continue to drink. Blackouts and alcoholic amnesia produce a "learned" forgetfulness about the destructive effects his or her alcoholic drinking is producing.

The structures of bad faith that sustain the alcoholic's commitment to drinking are fourfold. They come before the drinker as *coefficients of adversity* (Sartre, 1956: 482), which are self-defined obstacles to action. In a self-fulfilling fashion the drinker prophesizes his or her own defeat in the face of these forces. He or she defines the situational forces as being insurmountable.

The four structures of bad faith are (1) the problematic of physiological addiction; (2) the problematic of social support and the strength of the enabling system to which the drinker belongs; (3) the obstacle of self, self-pride, self-defined fear, and the fear of failing; and (4) the problematic of time, typically phrased as follows: "How can I stop drinking for the rest of my life?"

These four problematics are the reasons the drinker gives to himself for not stopping drinking. He tells himself that the difficulties in stopping are more painful (as he imagines them) than are the current difficulties he encounters as a drinker. Accordingly, the alcoholic convinces himself that not only does he not need to stop drinking, but that he cannot stop drinking, even if he wanted to, which he does not. Therefore, there is no reason even to attempt to stop drinking because he cannot do so. In order to sustain this fourfold structure of bad faith he must bring, if only tacitly, the full force of his lay theory of drinking into place. The thesis of bad faith envelopes his theories of denial, of temporality, and of normal as well as problematic drinking. Each of these problematics requires a brief discussion.

The first structure of bad faith is embedded in the physiological structures of the drinker's body. She is addicted to alcohol. Her body needs alcohol on a regular basis, whether she wants a drink or not. As she interprets the signals and the feelings of her lived body, which produces trembling hands, headaches, morning vomiting, loss of appetite, and the craving for a drink, she drinks. The physiological and mental pain of not drinking is too great. She can never go long enough without a drink to overcome the pain of not drinking.

The second structure of bad faith is lodged in the social world of the alcoholic and in her circle of enablers. Her friends drink, so why can't she? The alcoholic sustains the myth that she is still a normal, social drinker. She succumbs to the social pressures of others who encourage her (or so the alcoholic believes) to drink.

The third structure of bad faith is located in the self of the drinker. He defines himself as a drinker. To not drink is to be without control over the fear that engulfs him every time he is in the presence of others. Closely connected to the third structure of bad faith is the fear of failing. Should the drinker make a commitment to stop drinking and not succeed, he would lose face in his own eyes and the eyes of his peers and family. Fearing that he cannot stop, not being sure that he wants to stop, the alcoholic brings the fear of failing in front of himself as a further justification for not stopping.

The fear of failing is embedded in the drinker's self-pride, and in his belief that he should be in control of himself (Bateson, 1972a: 312, 320). This belief, inscribed as it is in Western culture, leads the alcoholic to continue to pit his willpower and strength against alcohol. Indeed, by failing the alcoholic proves to himself that he cannot stop drinking. This becomes another reason for not stopping.

The fourth problematic is time. To think of herself as a person who will never take another drink again is impossible. The alcoholic confronts herself, then, with the insurmountable problematic of the universe of time that engulfs her lifetime. The drinker knows that she will never be able to stop drinking for the rest of her life, and that even if she can stop for a day, or a week, or a month, before she dies she will drink again. Knowing this, she conceives of stopping drinking as an impossibility. Hence, the alcoholic allows time to deter her from stopping.

These four obstacles, or problematics—the pain felt in the lived body, the social pressures of others, self-pride, fear, and the dilemma of time and temporality—are the self-defined adversaries that keep the alcoholic drinking long after he or she wants to stop. They are woven into his or her system of bad faith, always giving him or her a reason for not quitting today.

The following account, given by a drinker 35 years sober, a 68-year-old bartender, displays these four structures of bad faith that are at the heart of the drinker's self-system:

> I'd get up in the morning (it was after the War in Germany where I learned how to drink that good German wine), and puke in the throne, on my knees, my head in the bowl. I'd be shaking so that I'd have to tie a string around the first glass of beer at Shorties' Tavern around the corner. I'd pull the drink up to my mouth and get the first one down. Then I'd follow it with a double shot of Old Fitz. Then I'd go to the can and vomit, then come back and do the same thing all over. I'd keep the second round down and the shakes would start to stop. The boys from the Ford plant would cheer me on. "Have another one, Bill," they'd say. And I would. Then we'd be off to work. I'd be O.K. until 10:00 in the morning. We'd slip off for a couple of snorts and I'd make it till noon. Noon was eight beers and eight double shots. That would carry me until supper when we'd go back to Shorties and drink till closing time at 1:00 a.m. when I'd stumble home to start the whole thing over the next day. I wanted to sober up, but I could never get past the shakes. Everytime I thought about it I'd shake all over and get sick inside. How could I confront the boys and work sober. I knew I couldn't, and I'd

take another drink. Finally it go so bad the boys told me I had to quit. Even then I didn't stop [field conversation, July 27, 1982].

Alcoholic subjects stand in a bad faith relationship to themselves. Every time they take a drink they act as if they believe what they do not believe for they know they are alcoholics (see Sartre, 1956: 70). They do not want to believe that they are alcoholics; perhaps problematic drinkers, but not alcoholics. They want to believe that this time it will be different.

A music instructor, 49 years old, sober five years, described her drinking in the following words:

I kept telling myself that if I could only drink a little bit before parties, and not talk too loud, that nobody would know that I had been drinking. Except that I'd drink too much before parties because I was nervous about talking too loud. Then I'd talk too loud and people would whisper to my husband that I was drunk [field conversation, December 4, 1982].

A 46-year-old male recovering alcoholic, a biochemist of international fame, with over 2 years of continuous sobriety, described this dilemma as follows:

I had been sober for six months, going to A.A. every Monday night and I was happy. I kept going to those meetings and hearing those sayings and reading those readings and saying I was an alcoholic. Then after six months I stopped going. I was in _____, my old drinking place with some engineers from Japan. They said, "Come on, have a drink." I said, "No, I can't." Then I thought to myself. I have not had a drink for six months. Alcoholics must drink every day. I have not been drinking. Therefore I must not be an alcoholic. Therefore I can drink. So I took a drink. Three months later I called my wife from my laboratory at midnight and said, "I want to kill myself. Did she want to come get me?" She said "No." So I got in my car to drive to my friend's house 300 miles away. I had consumed a bottle and a half of Scotch in two hours. I woke up at 3:00 a.m. outside Detroit. I didn't know how I got there. I came back to A.A. and now I don't drink and now I do believe that I am an alcoholic. I have been all over the world and those meetings and slogans keep me sober today [fieldnotes, November 1, 1983].

A male alcoholic, age 43, an advertising executive, spoke of the relationship between his drinking and his nondrinking self:

When I take a drink it takes control. It's not me talking to me anymore. It's alcohol talking to me and I like what alcohol tells me. It tells me I can drink and control it. If I want to lie to myself and talk myself into a drink all I have to do is to take the first drink. Then alcohol tells me everything will be O.K. But it never is [field interview, November 7, 1983].

By acting as if he accepted what he does not believe about himself the alcoholic subject repudiates any argument that might be advanced against his taking another drink.

The drinking act and alcohol are two adversaries the alcoholic must place before himself so as to overcome them, thereby proving his power and control. He seeks a self and a structure of self-feelings that he believes only alcohol can give. Alcohol becomes, then, another coefficient of adversity the alcoholic subject places in front of himself. By setting the challenge of alcohol in front of himself the alcoholic sets a constraint on his behavior that challenges him to fail (Bateson, 1972a: 322). As he falls back in failure against the barrier that alcohol has set for him the alcoholic locates the adversary, not in alcohol, but in the situation that arose when he drank. The alcoholic flees into the defeated freedom that alcohol gives, claiming victory, when all who know him understand that he has failed once again to control his drinking.

Locating her adversary in others, the drinker seeks to escape the temporal and interactional constraints they place upon her by continuing to drink. Freedom lies in alcohol and in the state of consciousness alcohol produces. Her drinking situation is one that only she understands. That is, no other person can understand the problematic the alcoholic must overcome in order to prove herself to herself. Even failure will be done with a style and a grace that is uniquely hers. This is her challenge and no one else's. The drinker displaces the challenge that alcohol sets by claiming that it is others, not alcohol with which she is competing. In this way the alcoholic flees the facticity of her own drunkenness, blaming others for her failure—not herself and alcohol.

Bad faith allows the alcoholic to lie to himself. Believing what he knows is a lie, in his innermost self the alcoholic knows he is an alcoholic and cannot control either himself or alcohol. I turn next to the thesis of self-control.

THE THESIS OF SELF-CONTROL

The thesis of self-control asserts that the alcoholic believes he is in control of the people, places, and events that constitute his world. He believes as Bateson (1972a: 312) states that "he could be, or, at least, ought to be 'the captain of his soul.'" The alcoholic is in control of herself, her drinking, and her behavior. She believes that she has not acted insanely or irrationally while under the influence of alcohol. The alcoholic believes, rather, that the problematic events that have occurred while she has been drinking were the result of events produced by other individuals who were out of control or were acting irresponsibly.

The alcoholic believes, too, that he or she can overcome, through the force of willpower, self-manipulation, deception, lies, and economic means, the problematic events that have appeared in his or her world. If required to, he or she will move, change jobs, spouses, friends, and even withdraw completely from the world, so as to be able to continue drinking. In such actions the alcoholic will maintain his or her belief in self-control. He or she will give up anything and everything in order to keep on drinking.

In these beliefs the alcoholic clings to the myth of his invincibility in a world that has gone out of control. Positioning himself at the center of that world, the alcoholic looks out upon it as if he were "an actor who wants to run the whole show...forever trying to arrange the lights, the ballet, the scenery and the rest of the players in his own way" (A.A. 1976: 60). He is, as A.A. says, self-centered, full of self-delusion, self-seeking, self-pity, self-will run riot, and a victim of troubles "basically of his (our) own making" (A.A., 1976: 62).

Consider the following statement. The speaker is 39 years old. He has been sober one year and is self-employed in the insurance business.

> I was hospitalized three times with a swollen liver, pancreatitis, malnourishment, high blood pressure, and the D.T.s, was driving on a suspended license, had a trial date coming up. My wife had left me for the third time. I'd been to two detox centers and in treatment two times. I was losing customers hand over fist and the bills weren't paid. I sat at my desk, looked at everything and called a cab to get me a bottle. I drank that bottle and went on a two-week binge. I wrecked the car, damned near ran into my house and still kept on drinking. I thought I could control it. I thought I was having a run of bad luck. All I needed to do was get a change of scenery. That's when I went to South Carolina and tried to start all over again. Trouble was I took myself with me and I just kept on drinking because nothing would go right [field conversation, September 8, 1982].

Our drinker believed that he was in control of his world, of himself, and of his drinking. Through bad faith he continued to talk himself into the position of believing that he could drink successfully.

THE THESIS OF SELF-SURRENDER

This thesis asserts that only through surrender of self does recovery begin. This is A.A.'s first step, which states that "we admitted we were powerless over alcohol—that our lives had become unmanageable" (A.A., 1976: 59). The admission of powerlessness is intended to bring the alcoholics face-to-face with their inability to control their drinking. To state that their lives are unmanageable similarly expresses powerlessness over people, places, and things. Tiebout (1944, 1949, 1953, 1954) argues that the alcoholic's feelings of omnipotence and pure self-centeredness must be punctured and destroyed if he is to admit a power greater than himself into his life. The alcoholic will be unable to accept help for his alcoholism until he admits and surrenders to his powerlessness.

Tiebout (1944) contends that the alcoholic is intent on maintaining at all costs his or her feelings of omnipotence. At the core of the alcoholic's self-system is the myth of self-control, and that myth realizes itself in the self-serving narcissism the alcoholic cherishes. The alcoholic is defiant, and stubbornly persists in believing that he or she has the right to do things in his or her own way. The means to solve his or her problem lie within, in self-will, and in defiance.

The thesis of self-surrender assumes that this defiant structure of self-beliefs, grounded as it is in bad faith, must be demolished. But it can be demolished only by the alcoholic, not by others.

Surrender occurs when the alcoholic hits bottom, that is, when she is no longer able to control herself or the world that surrounds her. Every individual's bottom is unique. It may involve a loss of a husband, a job, income, and home. The drinker may become destitute and be living on the street before hitting bottom. She may hit bottom when the pain of fighting becomes too great. In every case, however, the individual must find what is to her a state of being in the world that is no longer tolerable.

When this state is reached, the alcoholic's theory of problem drinking, his theory of causality, temporality, and structures of bad faith begin to collapse. Indeed, these interpretive structures must collapse in upon him and he must recognize that they have collapsed. Only then will the alcoholic begin to understand that his theories of self-control and denial are myths, built on fabrications, self-deceptions, and self-destructive beliefs.

Surrender is a destructive process that requires a fundamental realignment of every interpretive structure the alcoholic has constructed. She must relinquish her self-centeredness, desire for control, and she must stop drinking. The ego, what Freud termed her "majesty the Baby," must be penetrated so that her systems of denial, false pride, and bad faith are exposed to the critical scrutiny of sober, nonalcoholic thinking.

The process of surrender is threefold, involving first an admission of powerlessness and failure, second, an acceptance of that failure, and third, a deep, inner surrendering to that fact. That is, the alcoholic must come to understand in his inner-most self that he is an alcoholic and powerless over alcohol (A.A., 1976: 30). This is regarded by A.A. as the first step in recovery.

If this last step in surrender is not accomplished, accepted, and repeated over and over again, the alcoholic is likely to become a *verbal convert* and not a *total* convert to A.A.'s point of view. (See Rudy, 1986; Lofland and Stark, 1965.) That is, the alcoholic may well profess his or her alcoholism, but not believe it, because he or she either still wishes to drink, or does not feel totally powerless over alcohol. Verbal converts may become convinced or pure alcoholics, or they may only tangentially accept alcohol as being at the center of their problems. What Rudy (1986: 86) terms pure, convinced, tangential, and converted alcoholics reflect variations on the degree to which the alcoholic has completely surrendered his or her self to alcoholism.

Whether verbal or total, partial or complete, the admission of alcoholism on the part of the drinker is a step toward recovery. Whether that admission occurs prior to coming to A.A. or occurs afterwards is immaterial as far as recovery is concerned. As long as the drinker's admission to himself of his alcoholism stops him from taking the first drink he has successfully taken the first step toward recovery.

Surrender, for A.A., as indicated in Chapter 3, involves more than "fully conceding" to the innermost self the facticity of alcoholism. It requires, as well, the commitment to allow into the alcoholic's life a power greater than himself or herself. Only by being humbled before a power greater than himself or herself, can the alcoholic hope to be relieved of the obsessive compulsion to drink. A.A. states the following:

> The alcoholic at certain times has no effective mental defense against the first drink. Except in a few rare cases, neither he nor any other human being can provide such a defense. His defense must come from a Higher Power [A.A., 1976: 39, 43].

Surrender requires a shattering of self in the face of a power greater than the individual. That power is first understood to be alcohol, that source of friendship, solace, and courage on which the alcoholic has for so long relied. But because that power has failed him or her, another power is inserted in its place: the power of A.A. and the power of a Higher Power, which some call God. The alcoholic finds that recovery, if it is to occur within the confines of A.A., will require a confrontation with spirituality and a reconceptualization of what he or she understands power and control to be in his or her life. These problematics will be taken up in Chapter 7.

CONCLUSIONS

It is now necessary to organize the Six Theses of Recovery (and alcoholism) into a summary statement. I understand alcoholism to be a mode of being in which the human subject places alcohol between himself or herself and the world. Alcoholism is a dis-ease in the world that is temporal, relational, and emotional. It is based on deception, bad faith, and the myth of self-control.

Each of the six theses references structures of experience that are part of the alcoholic circle of existence. Taken together they form a unitary point of view that locks the alcoholic into the self-destructive patterns of conduct that will destroy all that she calls hers. As the alcoholic lives out the six theses she will destroy or irrevocably influence those who come in contact with her on a daily basis. Through her alcohol leaves its destructive imprint on the world.

However, alcoholism is a two-sided phenomenon as designated by the two phrases, active alcoholic and recovering alcoholic. The six theses of alcoholism simultaneously refer to the active and the recovering sides of the phenomenon. Recovery, once surrender in its three phases has been set in motion, reverses the self-destructive consequences of the other five theses. The thesis of surrender exposes the fallacious foundations of the other five interpretive structures that constitute the active alcoholic's worldview.

These theses are not in the immediate reflective range of the alcoholic's consciousness. That is, they are taken for granted and firmly rooted in the cognitive and emotional structures that shape and dictate his or her actions in the world. Because they are so deeply entrenched in the very marrow of his or her interpretive structures, the alcoholic holds to them with a ferocious stubbornness that defies reason and rationality. But within his or her interpretive point of view these theses are perfectly rational and understandable. They are, after all, what sustain him or her in the face of failure, criticism, and pain.

The alcoholic's self, then, is attached firmly to each of the six theses. To let go of even one of these interpretive structures is to experience a loss of self that is severe and felt to be an admission of self-failure. For this reason the alcoholic will cling to these beliefs as he dies before his own eyes. However, this may not be an entirely willful act. The aphasia and amnesia that he suffers from serve to keep him locked within a clouded stream of experience that perpetuates drinking. These disorders in thought, language, and memory organize his self-understandings and support his systems of denial and bad faith.

In the next chapter I take up the problem of the alcoholically divided self. It will be necessary to show how the lay theory of alcoholism and the six theses of alcoholism (and recovery) actually operate in the world of the active alcoholic who must, finally, surrender to the facticity of his or her alcoholism and ask for help—if he or she is to get help, that is.

Part II

THE ALCOHOLIC SELF

6

THE ALCOHOLICALLY
DIVIDED SELF

The alcoholically divided self (and its other) lives two modes of existence, referenced by the terms *sober* and *intoxicated*. These two modes of existence contradict one another, producing deep divisions within the inner and outer structures of the subject's self and the self of the other. Alcohol thickens these divisions, leading the subject to live an emotionally divided self. The subject, like his or her other, is in the grip of negative emotions, including ressentiment, anger, fear, self-loathing, self-pity, self-hatred, despair, anguish, remorse, guilt, and shame (see Denzin, 1984a: 283 on ressentiment and resentment). The alcoholic's self is disembodied. He or she experiences a separation between an alcoholically distorted inner stream of consciousness and a painful, often bruised, bloated, and diseased body he or she lives from within. His or her alcoholic self-pride mobilizes the negative feelings held toward the other.

The following argument organizes my analysis. *The alcoholic and his or her other are trapped within an interactional circuit of progressively differentiated alcoholic and nonalcoholic conduct (schismogenesis) that transforms their relationship into a painful field of negative, contrasting emotional experience. If unchecked, this relationship moves slowly toward self-destruction.* Like the violent family (Denzin, 1984b: 490-491), the alcoholic relationship will move through nine interactional stages: (1) denial of alcoholism and violence; (2)

pleasure derived from alcoholism and violence; (3) the building up of mutual hostility; (4) the development of misunderstandings; (5) jealousy (especially sexual); (6) increased alcoholic violence; and either (7) the eventual collapse of the system; or (8) the resolution of the situation into an unsteady, yet somewhat stable state of recurring alcoholic violence; or (9) the transformation of the relationship into a "recovering" alcoholic situation.

A three-act play titled "A Merry-Go-Round Named Denial" structures this drama of destruction (Kellerman, 1969). Its three acts are (1) the alcoholic situation; (2) violence and the Merry-Go-Round of Trouble; and (3) collapse and surrender. A fourth act, "Recovery," may be added to these three acts. It is the topic of the next chapter. I will present the destructive life story of the alcoholically divided self in terms of this play the alcoholic and his significant others enact. I will analyze each of the above facets and phases of the alcoholic's experiences in terms of its place in this temporal structure. My topic, then, is alcoholism as a relational dis-ease of self, other, temporality, and emotion.

ACT ONE:
THE ALCOHOLIC SITUATION

Four categories of persons are present in Act One: the alcoholic, his family, friends, and coworkers (Kellerman, 1969: 2). In Act One the alcoholic has passed through the stage of being a heavy social drinker into the phases of crucial or chronic alcoholism. As with our drinker in Chapters 4 and 5, the alcoholic still believes that he is in control of his own destiny. The alcoholic lives in a culture that sanctions drinking in a wide variety of contexts, yet he seems to be unable to drink like normal drinkers. He has learned that alcohol makes him feel better, yet he drinks hard and fast, often secretly (Kellerman, 1969: 3). The power to choose whether to drink or not is lost. When drinking, the alcoholic ignores rules of social conduct, often becomes emotionally uncontrollable, and continually embarrasses his significant others. He often creates a crisis that requires that they intercede on his behalf. In the process the drinker becomes increasingly more dependent on them, yet persists in believing that he is independent and in control of the situation. He adopts a reactive stance toward the problems he creates, waiting for others to react to him, while the alcoholic reacts to their reactions.

The alcoholic and his other have built up, through years of heavy drinking, an alcoholic-centered relationship. His spouse, or lover, has supported his drinking. The spouse or lover has denied the problems alcohol has created, and has attempted to control his drinking, all the time maintaining the myth that he is a heavy social drinker.

The following interaction is typical of the experiences the alcoholic and his other confront in Act One. The speaker recounts an experience before he came to A.A.

> I'd gotten mad at my family. They'd come home and found me drunk. They left and went to Burger King for dinner and left me alone. I called a cab, got a bottle of gin, and checked into a hotel under another name. Late that night I called home and said I was going to kill myself. Did she want to do anything? She asked where I was and I wouldn't tell her. I hung up, passed out, and woke up the next morning and called home and asked for a ride to work. They came and picked me up and dropped me off. They looked at me and said "What's going on?" I said, "Nothing, I just needed to get away." Then I got mad. I screamed at them. I said, "Get off my case. You're driving me crazy," and I slammed the door and left them there. That night I took them out for dinner and brought home roses. Everything was "lovey dovey" [field conversation, April 3, 1981].

In Act One the alcoholic and his other coexist in a field of contrasting emotional experiences. Emotional violence, sexual intimacy, physical abuse, gifts offered out of guilt, DUIs, suicide threats, and trips to counselors chart the emotional roller coaster the alcoholic and his other ride in Act One (see following). This act will continue until the alcoholic produces a situation that neither he nor alcohol can handle. That is, he requires the massive assistance of others, including financial aid, legal counsel, medical attention, and help from his coworkers. However, until this occurs, the alcoholic and his others remain within the uneasy interactional space they have created for one another.

Together they have produced *the alcoholic situation* that represents four interactional patterns organized around alcohol and its consumption by the alcoholic. The *open drinking context* displays the drinker with a drink in his hands. The *closed drinking context* references those situations in which the drinker attempts to hide the fact that he has been drinking. The *sober context* is a nondrinking situation in which it is evident that the alcoholic probably is sober. The *normally intoxicated but in control context* references the setting in which the alcoholic is maintaining a level of alcohol intake that others regard as normal and acceptable (see Glaser and Strauss, 1967).

Each time the alcoholic interacts with his other, the other must determine if he has been drinking, and if so, how much. Two interpretive frameworks (Goffman, 1974: 10-11; Bateson, 1972d: 187) compete for attention in the alcoholic situation. The "sober" framework produces one set of definitions regarding accountable and nonaccountable violent, emotional conduct. The "intoxicated," or "he has been drinking" framework produces another set of meanings and interpretations. These two frameworks may exist side by side in the same interactional situation. Drunk, the alcoholic confronts his sober other, attempting to move her into the "intoxicated" framework, or the alcoholic denies his intoxication and attempts to speak to the other from the "sober" framework. The clash of these two interpretive points of view leads to hostility, feelings of anger, and ressentiment. Witness the follwing account, offered by Merryman (1984: 6). The interactants are an alcoholic wife Abby and her husband Martin. Abby has just returned from a weekend escape to the family's cottage on the New England coast. Martin has picked her up from the airport. They are driving home. Afraid of what her husband will say about her drinking, Abby has taken a drink of vodka in the women's restroom at the airport.

> Abby sat silent, waiting, watching, intensely aware of Martin.... She could see right now from his hurt mad expression that the next words from his mouth would be sarcastic hints for self-improvement—unconnected to any tenderness or sensitivity. And then she would defend herself, and they would be at it again, and there would be no real hope.

> Presently, Martin's eyes flicked away from the highway and glanced over his glasses toward Abby. "You look completely burnt out," he said, "Had your nose in the sauce?"

> Abby twisted toward him, hands clenched in her lap, voice controlled. "It so happens I almost missed the plane and haven't had any breakfast. I feel like I've been in a Waring blender set on chop. . . ."

> Martin's eyes remained unswervingly on the road, his face set and grim. When he spoke again, his voice was cutting, punishing. "How much did you drink?"

Reading the Alcoholic

Fearful of the effects alcohol may have upon the alcoholic's conduct, family members, like Martin above, are, as Jackson (1962: 475-477) observes, always alert to what phase of the drinking cycle the alcoholic is in when he or she comes before them. The interaction patterns in the alcoholic-dependent relationship vary, as Steinglass and Robertson (1983: 272) suggest, by whether or not the alcoholic is in a stable or nonstable, sober or "wet" state. The stability of the alcoholic's emotionality, whether predictable or nonpredictable, intentional or nonintentional, whether it is charming or cruel, harsh and aloof, self-pitying and withdrawn, fawning and concillatory, hostile and angry, will be seen to vary by real and imputed states of intoxication. Confronted with the self-fulfilling definition that she has been drinking before she comes into their presence, the alcoholic may, as did Abby above, attempt to mask the effects of alcohol upon her conduct. Or the alcoholic may react with anger and produce the negative experiences family members wish to avoid.

The underlying premise of all interactions in the alcohol-dependent relationship questions the presence or absence of alcohol in the drinker's consciousness. This premise makes problematic the intentionality of the alcoholic's conduct, for her actions and meanings can always be interpreted from within the "she has been drinking" framework. Such a premise diminishes the alcoholic's standing in the relationship, making her dependent on others for the valued self-definitions she seeks. That is, the alcoholic knows and they know—and she knows that they know—that she could have been drinking. Doubt and anger thus cling to every interaction between the alcoholic and her other. Because alcohol has become the central social object in the alcohol-dependent relationship, it—not emotionality or the mutual exchange of selves—becomes the dominant, if not the hidden, focus of all interactions.

Violent Emotionality

The alcoholic and her other live in emotional violence, which I define as negative emotionality turned into active, embodied, hostile interactions with herself and with others. If violence is understood to reference the attempt to regain through force something that has been lost (Denzin, 1984a: 169), then the alcoholic attempts to use emotional and physical force to regain the sense of self-pride she has lost to alcohol and to the other.

The violence the alcoholic engages in may be verbal or physical, or both. It may be sporadic or frequent, and it may involve such actions as the sexual abuse of a spouse or child, the threat to use a weapon (including knives and guns), the actual hitting or beating of another, and the driving of an automobile while intoxicated and killing another. Violent alcoholic emotionality ranges from physical violence, as just indicated, to inflicted emotionality, as well as spurious, playful, real, and paradoxical violent emotional acts (Denzin, 1984a: 185-190). Violent emotionality, in all its forms, is embedded in the daily life of the alcoholic and his or her emotional associates. The interiority of alcoholic existence frightfully illuminates the emotional violence that has been observed in nonalcoholic, violent relationships (Denzin, 1984a: 190-197; 1984b: 483-513). The alcoholic relationship is an emotionally violent relationship.

The Five Forms of Alcoholic Violence

There are five forms of alcoholic violence that are woven through the four interactional-drinking situations the alcoholic and his or her other produce. As indicated above, every time the other interacts with the alcoholic he or she must determine if the alcoholic has been drinking. This master definition then structures the meanings that are applied to the alcoholic's conduct.

The first form of alcoholic violence is *emotional violence.* In emotional violence the alcoholic inflicts his or her emotionality on the other. He or she does this with emotional outbursts and in emotional scenes that get out of control. The following interaction describes alcoholic, emotional violence.

> I came home tired and beat. The house was a mess, the dogs were loose, and she was in the bedroom taking a nap. Supper wasn't even started yet. I fixed a drink, turned on the news. She came out, yelled at me for having that drink. I'd heard it a thousand times before. I couldn't take it anymore. I threw the drink in her face, grabbed her arm and yelled, "Where's my God damned supper! You never do anything around here." She hit back at me, called me no good. She ran and got my wood carving that I'd been making her for Christmas. She laughed at it, called it stupid and dumb. She threw it against the wall. That's when I lost it. I ran at her. She called the police. How can she ever trust me again? How can we start over? I don't know what's wrong with me. I ain't been the same since I got home from Nam. (Denzin, 1984b: 501)

The second form of alcoholic violence is *playful, alcoholic violence.* Here the alcoholic, usually in the open drinking context, plays at being violent, but serious violence is not intended. He playfully slaps his child on the shoulder, or smacks his wife on the cheek, for example. He takes a step away from "literal" reality and makes a play at being violent, but in a nonviolent way. Playful violence is conveyed through winks, smiles, voice intonations, shrugs, hand and shoulder movements, a toss of the head, and so on (Lynch, 1982: 29).

The third form of negative, violent emotionality is *spurious* and/or *accidental alcoholic violence*. As with playful violence, deliberate nonviolence is intended. However, the alcoholic's actions carry the meaning of real, intended violence. His hand slips as he reaches out to touch the other and he slaps her, rather than caressing her. He stumbles, falls, and crashes through a window. He passes out while driving and runs the car through the front door of his house. Though inwardly the alcoholic does not intend to be violent, his outward actions convey violence to the other. Unlike playful violence in which the alcoholic communicates through playful actions that his actions could be interpreted both as violence and nonviolence, in accidental violence, real violent consequences follow from his conduct.

Real alcoholic violence is the fourth form of negative, violent emotionality. Here the alcoholic intends to be violent, is violent, and his or her violent intentions are felt by the other. He or she may hit, hurl an insult, throw a knife, or fire a gun at the other. In real violence the alcoholic embodies a violent line of action from which he or she cannot willfully walk away. Real, alcoholic violence is felt in the bodies of both the alcoholic and his or her other who becomes a victim. It is "naked emotion," often raw and brutal.

The following account illuminates the differences between playful, accidental, and real violence.

> When my husband drank he would do crazy things that he didn't mean. But it got to the point where it didn't matter if he meant it or not. The first time he threw my daughter's teddy bear at me and missed and knocked over the vase of flowers on the dining room table and we both laughed at how absurd it was. We thought something crazy was going on. How could he be mad at me if he threw a teddy bear at me? But it got worse. The next time he knocked me down the stairs and said it was an accident. I knew he was mad at me and he was trying to hit me. He said it was accidental. I never believed him. Finally he got out of hand. He came home slightly drunk. I asked him "How much have you been drinking?" He swore at me. Slammed the kitchen door. I guess he went to the basement and got a drink. He came back up with the drink in his hands and threw it at me. He missed and it went through the front window. Then he came at me, grabbed me by the throat, and started to shake me. He was screaming all the time. He said he hated me and wanted to kill me. I got loose. Ran out of the house. Called the police. They came and arrested him. I filed for separation after that. We're divorced now [field conversation, September 1, 1983, 42-year-old female, occupational nurse].

If violent interactions are to be interpreted as being present, then the other must be able to distinguish between playful, accidental, and real alcoholic mood states. He or she must also be able to understand those moments when *real violence* of a nonalcoholic nature is intended. In this situation the alcoholic is held, without doubt, fully accountable for these actions.

More often, however, alcohol is present in the situation when the alcoholic's violent emotionality erupts. His or her actions occur within the following message frame:

> Because I have been drinking all messages here are untrue.
> I don't want to be violent.
> I want to be violent.

The alcoholic and his other are trapped within this message system. *Paradoxical alcoholic violence* of a "real" order is produced and experienced, but seemingly it is nonintended. This is the fifth form of alcoholic violence. Hence the other must choose whether or not to listen to the alcohol speaking. He or she may discount the alcohol and listen to the words that were not spoken, but would have been spoken, if the alcoholic had not been drinking. If he or she is not willing to suspend disbelief in the words that were in fact spoken, there is no recourse other than to hear what in fact was said. He or she is trapped. If the other knows the alcoholic didn't mean what was said, then how can the other discount the effects of the emotional and physical violence just inflicted upon him or her? Further, if the other feels that the alcoholic has self-control over his or her drinking, then he or she believes that the alcoholic drank in order to be violent. In which case the alcoholic is doubly accountable for his or her actions.

The confluence of playful, accidental, real, and paradoxical violence within the sober and intoxicated interactional contexts that the alcoholic and his or her other produces causes recurring emotional chaos. This situation serves to locate emotional violence, in all its forms, at the center of the alcohol-dependent relationship.

Alcoholic Identities

The alcoholic relationship solidifies into a set of reciprocally expected, alcoholic identities that center on alcohol and drinking. Children may become scapegoats for the family's problems. In reaction to the alcoholic situation, they may become rebellious, withdrawn, or delinquent. They may attempt to become pseudo-parents, taking over the mothering or fathering responsibilities of the alcoholic. They may become family stars, or heroes, and they may become overachievers. What they will become, to use the currently employed phrase, are adult children of alcoholics (Woititz, 1983).

Spouses, family members, friends, lovers, coworkers, employers, physicians, and children become *enablers* and *coalcoholic dependents* in the relationship. These others assist the alcoholic when she gets in trouble. They buy the alcoholic drinks and bring alcohol home for her. They give the alcoholic money when she needs it. They become dependent upon the alcoholic's dependency and mold identities that place them in a "helping" relationship with her. Enablers often become *victims,* for they are victimized by the alcoholic's inability to meet the ordinary demands that have been placed upon her. Victims do the alcoholic's work for her. Victims may also become *provokers.* The provoker becomes the other who feeds back into the alcoholic relationship all the bitterness, resentment, fear, anger, and hostility that is felt when the alcoholic turns against him or her and attacks the provoker for attempting to control the alcoholic's drinking (Kellerman, 1969). Resenting such control, the alcoholic flails out. The victim in turn becomes a *martyr,* bearing the cross of the alcoholic relationship upon his or her shoulders. The victim resents the alcoholic's resentment.

Resenting this attitude, the alcoholic builds a deep hatred toward the victim. He or she provokes the alcoholic's anger. The victim is blamed for everything that goes wrong in the relationship. The alcoholic may drink in order to blot out the painful loss of control experienced from the victim's hands. A recovering alcoholic reported the following angry thoughts he held toward his mother while he was drinking:

> She was domineering and tried to control me. We lived together in a little house trailer she bought. She'd say "Now, Harry, don't drink today." I'd get mad as hell, storm out, go to the bar on the corner and have me a drink. I'd look at her face in the glass and drink to it. I'd say, "Set em up. I'm getting drunk today. She can't tell me what to do!" And I would [field conversation, 36-year-old male, in treatment for the third time, June 22, 1984].

THE ALCOHOLIC SITUATION AS A STRUCTURE OF CONTRASTING EMOTIONS

Contrasting emotional experiences, as first indicated, are layered through the alcoholic relationship. First charming and loving, then cruel and hostile, the alcoholic generates a field of experience that is negative, positive, alienating, ambiguous, ambivalent, and ultimately self-destructive. The alcoholic and his or her others stand at the center of this field of shifting, contrasting emotions. The following account speaks to this feature of their shared life. The speaker is at his first A.A. meeting. He offers the labels Jekyll and Hyde for the two sides of his emotionally divided self. In his mid-forties, he is married, has two children and works for a large accounting firm. His father and grandfather were alcoholics. Before he stopped drinking, seven days earlier, he had been told to leave work because he was drunk. Not believing this, he had checked into a local hospital to have his blood alcohol level tested. The test confirmed that he was, in fact, intoxicated. He speaks the following:

> When I drink I become another person. Like a Dr. Jekyll and a Mr. Hyde (or whatever they're called). I get violent. I swear, I throw things. Last Saturday, a week ago, I threw the kitchen table at my father-in-law. I grabbed my wife (she only weighs 98 pounds) by the throat 'cause she said I was drunk when I came home. My little girls were hanging on my leg, telling me not to hurt Mommy! Christ! What's wrong with me? I'm not violent. I don't swear. I'm quiet. I always wear a smile. I'm easy going. Even when things are going bad I smile and say it'll work out. But I stop and have that first beer and the next thing you know I'm drunk and there till the bar closes. Then the wife's mad. Screaming at me when I come in the door. I feel guilty, mad. Mad at myself. Mad at her. Hell, I know I'm drunk. She don't have to tell me. Why'd she throw it up at me like that? I don't want to be like this any more than she wants me to be drunk. I get crazy, like last Saturday, last week. Then we don't talk. Now she's gone! Took the girls. Told me to get professional help. Are you people professional? I guess you must be cause you're not drinking. You must have something I don't have. Maybe I can get it. I'll be back [field conversation, September 25, 1984].

Self-pride lies behind this alcoholic's anger at his wife. He knows that he is drunk when he comes home. He knows that he has failed to control his drinking once again. His violence represents an attempt to regain a sense of self-worth, or self-pride, in the face of this humiliating situation. He resents her failure to acknowledge this fact. The structures of contrastive experience that are confronted by the alcoholic self and his other revolve around the negative emotions of self-hatred, fear, anxiety, anger, and violence, but most centrally the master emotions of *ressentiment* (Nietzsche, 1897: 35-39, 63-65, 77-78, 90, 110; Scheler, 1961: 39-44, 224-228, 283), and *self-pride* (see Denzin, 1986c).

Negative Emotionality

Restless and uneasy, the alcoholically divided self is always on the move, always seeking new experiences to fill, if only momentarily, the loneliness of self that is felt.

The emotions that divide the self alternate between momentary feelings of positive self-worth, and deep, underlying feelings of doubt, self-hatred, despair, and anguish. Alcoholic drinking, fueled by self-pride and risk-taking, is pursued in a futile attempt to overcome the deep inadequacies that are felt. The alcoholic is unable to sustain over any length of time a positive definition of self.

The following account addresses this aspect of the alcoholic self. The speaker is a 45-year-old advertising executive. He has been in A.A. for over 12 years, but has never had more than 11 months of continuous sobriety. He has been married and divorced. He drives expensive cars, wears expensive, yet casual clothes, and once owned an expensive home. He has been in over five treatment centers and has been exposed to reality therapy, EST, hypnosis, and Individualized Alcohol Behavioral Therapy. He has been addicted to valium and has smoked marijuana on a regular basis. When he starts drinking he begins with very dry Beefeater martinis, but usually ends with sweet liquors, including Southern Comfort and Irish Mist. He has been diagnosed manic-depressive, depressive, an alcohol addict, and a sociopath. He speaks of himself in the following words:

> I have two parts to me. One part wants to take credit for what I accomplish. Like the magazine. Its beautiful. Its one of the best in the country. Best photos. Best layout, best writers. [He had published a monthly magazine for six months, before he lost it during his last binge.] Its just like me. Pretty on the outside, empty, nothing on the inside. Pretty boy, call me. Nothing in here [points to his chest].

> You see, that's why the other part of me wants to destroy what the good part creates. I don't deserve for good things to happen to me. The sick side of me says destroy it all. If that side gets too strong I drink. I want to drink. And I do, and once I have the first drink the alcohol starts to talk to me and it says have another drink. You're rotten. Run, you don't deserve what you have. Blow it all. Run and leave. Kill yourself. You won't live to be 50 anyway. Remember your old man killed himself with this stuff when he was 45.

> These thoughts fill me up. I can't get away from them. I feel guilty if I do well. I'm so damned sick, even when I'm well I'm sick. Pretty Boy on the outside [looks vacantly outside through the windows]. Pretty Boy's sick. Ready to go? [field conversation, April 1, 1983].

Uniqueness and Fear

The alcoholic self cultivates a particular moral individualism that rests on the felt uniqueness of its own alienation. The alcoholic cuts herself off from the rest of society, feeling a profound alienation from all with whom she comes in contact. The alcoholic self nurtures an inner goodness, seeking to hide within a solitude that is solely hers. Rejecting objective experiences with others, the alcoholically divided self lives within the private world of insulated madness that alcohol produces. She assigns a sense of moral superiority to this inner world that is uniquely her own (see Laing, 1965: 94-95). From the unsteady vantage point of this alcoholically produced position, the alcoholic subject directs a world that threatens to come apart at any instant. All the while she lives an inner fear, knowing that the false walls she has built will crumble at any moment.

Consider the following account given by a recovering 44-year-old alcoholic, four years in A.A.

> I felt that nobody else knew how to live their life. I felt that my way was superior; that I knew something other people didn't. It was impossible for me to work or deal with others because I felt this way about them. I lived my life in my studio and in my tiny office where I worked. I stayed at home as much as I could. When I drank I felt that I knew who I was and what was right. In those feelings I gained a strength and a way of thinking that was unique to me. But then I collapsed. Everything came in on me. I went crazy. I came to A.A. and I found out that my way, that all the certainties I had held onto, that all my thoughts were empty too. I didn't know how to live either! I'm still learning [field conversation, June 17, 1984].

ALCOHOLIC RESSENTIMENT

Ressentiment (Scheler, 1961: 39-40) toward the past, toward others, toward the present and the future is felt. The repeated experiencing and reliving of this temporal and emotional attitude toward others and toward time itself characterizes the alcoholic self. The emotional attitude of ressentiment is negative, hostile, and includes the interrelated feelings of anger, wrath, envy, intense self-pride, and the desire for revenge (Denzin, 1984a: 283). Behind alcoholic ressentiment lies alcoholic pride (see below). This emotional frame of reference is fueled by alcohol that elevates the alcoholic's feelings of self-strength and power. However, the power that is felt is illusive and fleeting, always leaving in its wake the underlying ressentiment that the alcoholic drank to annihilate.

The centrality of resentment in the alcoholic relationship is revealed in the following interaction between J, and A. A, the male companion of J, has recently started attending Al-Anon meetings. He has been sponsored by a woman who has been in Al-Anon since 1968. Her name is Mary. J is speaking to C and K, two recovering alcoholics who have come to see him. J has been drinking for 2 days, after having been sober for 30 days. He found a full bottle of vodka in a closet when he was cleaning his and A's house.

> Come in, I'm drunk again. Here, come meet Mary [pointing to A who is seated at the dining room table]. She's been going to Al-Anon. Haven't you, Mary! Oh my, we're so much better now. Aren't we, Mary? Mary knows how to handle me now. Mary taught her "Tough Love." Well, YOU can take your TOUGH LOVE, A, and shove it. Oh, look at him, I hurt his little feelings. I'm so sorry, A, you see, I'm a sick man. You can't get mad at me. You have to love me [field conversation, as reported, September 16, 1984].

The satire, sarcasm, and double meanings that are evident in J's monologue, including his referencing of A with the feminine Mary, while he, J fills the feminine, housewife position in the relationship, speaks to the inability of the alcoholic to form "a true partnership with another human being" (A.A., 1953: 53). Using alcohol to reverse his position in the relationship, J attempts to dominate A through his words and his actions. As he expresses his hurt feelings through retaliatory vindictiveness he drives A further away from him. Resentful over A's attendance at Al-Anon meetings, he blocks and rebuffs any efforts by A to move forward in the relationship.

The return to drinking by J brings to the surface latent ressentiment that exists in his alcoholic relationship with A. Unable, or unwilling, to free himself of the anger, fear, wrath, and envy he feels toward A, his desire for revenge surfaces as he drinks.

Alcoholically induced and experienced emotionality lies at the heart of J's alcoholism. The euphoric and depressive physiological and neurological effects of the drug alcohol magnify the emotional divisions that exist within his self. His relations with A are similarly distorted when he drinks. Alcohol has become a sign, which when brought into the relationship, signifies J's alienation from A.

John Berryman (1973: 102-103) describes the telephone interactions Wilbur, an approximately 60-year-old recovering patient, had with his parents, whom he called two to five times daily from the treatment center:

> "They need me," he said many times. His father, drunk from morning to night was urging him to come home, and Wilbur was anxious to go— although they fought like madmen right through every call and it was perfectly clear to everybody but Wilbur that he got a *bang* out of holding his own against his frightful Dad from a safe telephone distance (Father's

ax, kept in the kitchen where *he* drank: "I'll chop you, Wilbur, late one night, I'll chop you"), reveling in the fact that he himself was not only sober at the moment but being *treated* for the disease that was killing them both. "They need me," he said stubbornly.

The fuel for stubbornly felt ressentiment is present in this account, including Wilbur's desire for revenge. The key to ressentiment is the repeated experiencing and reliving of the emotional feelings that draw the subject to another. Each occasion of interaction between Wilbur and his father becomes an occasion for the production of new feelings of anger, wrath, and perhaps hatred. These new feelings become part of the emotional repertoire that binds the father and son together. They experience the new feelings of ressentiment against the backdrop of all previous negative interactions. Drawn to one another through negativity, they both know that the self-feelings they derive from this relationship can be found nowhere else. The father and son are participants in the classic alcoholic relationship in which both partners are alcoholic. The complexity of their interaction is increased by the fact that they stand in a father-son relationship to one another. They both exist as alcoholically divided selves. The pivotal emotions that join their emotionally divided selves are lodged in the ressentiment they share and produce together.

The anger that the alcoholic feels toward his or her other turns into hatred. That hatred, when reciprocated, as in the case of Wilbur and his father, is increased. It destroys the affection that perhaps once existed between them. Thus it is with alcoholic ressentiment, for hatred and anger are layered upon one another, until the interactants in the social relationship are bound together only through negativity and mutual self-disdain.

Self-Pride

The threats of self-pride that ressentiment magnifies are evidenced in the following statement. The speaker is J, the male homosexual quoted above. He is intoxicated as he speaks. His remarks are directed, as before, to A:

> I hate you. You're cruel to me. You're a pig! You're not half the man W. is. You can't hold a candle to him. You take away my respect. You don't tell me my flowers are nice. You've been mean to me. You undercut me. You make me feel ugly. My sister loves me. My aunt loves me. I don't care if you do hate me. You make me hate myself. When I'm sober you can't do this to me. I feel good about myself. I feel proud to be a man. Why do you make me drink like this? I want to feel good

about myself and have some pride again in what I do [field conversation, July 15, 1984].

Here the speaker blames the other for making him drunk, but he also blames his other for undercutting his self-pride. The ressentiment that flows through his talk masks a desire to regain a sense of self he feels he has lost to A, but also to alcohol. Pride in self, then, organizes and structures the alcoholic's deep-seated feelings of anger and wrath toward the other. The desire for revenge is embedded in this emotional attitude, which is best interpreted within the larger framework of ressentiment toward the other and toward self.

End of Act One

The drinking alcoholic and his or her other(s), to summarize Act One, live inside a recurring structure of negative, contrastive emotional experiences that become self-addictive. Each member of the relationship is trapped in this cycle of destructive emotionality, which becomes, for the alcoholic, nearly as addictive as the alcohol that he or she consumes. The alcoholic and his or her other live hatred, fear, anxiety, anger, and ressentiment. Never far from the next drink, or the next emotional battle with his or her significant other, each day becomes a repetition of the day before. They have stabilized their relationship at this brittle level. Act Two begins with either (1) the eruption of violence that goes beyond emotional attacks on the other; or (2) the alcoholic producing a problematic situation that traps him or her and exposes his or her alcoholism to others. Both of these sequences of action provoke a radical restructuring in the alcoholic's relationship with himself or herself and the significant other.

ACT TWO: VIOLENCE AND THE MERRY-GO-ROUND OF TROUBLE

In Act Two all the key figures in the alcoholic's self-destructive drama are in place. The alcoholic's dependence on alcohol is evident to all of his or her significant others, who have become enablers, coalcoholic dependents, victims, provokers, martyrs, scapegoats, pseudo-parents, family stars, and heroes. Each figure has learned how to adjust to the alcoholic's emotionality, to his or her crises, drunkenness, and unpredictability. Each in their way has rescued the alcoholic from the problems he or she has produced. In so doing they have enabled his or her drinking and dependency upon them and their dependency upon him or her.

The Phases of
Negative Symbolic Interaction

The members of the alcoholic's family have passed through the first five states (as noted above), of negative symbolic interaction that characterize families of violence (Denzin, 1984b: 490). They have (1) denied the alcoholic's alcoholism and violence; (2) seen the alcoholic derive pleasure from drinking, and they derive pleasure from their dependence upon him or her; (3) experienced a buildup of mutual hostility and alienation between themselves and the alcoholic; (4) lived through misunderstandings concerning their respective commitments and responsibilities to one another; and (5) experienced sexual jealousy and violent emotionality because of the alcoholic's conduct (especially the spouse or lover). The alcoholic has placed himself or herself and the significant others in the classic double-bind relationship (Bateson, 1972c: 212). If the alcoholic truly loved them he or she would stop drinking. Because the alcoholic continues to drink he or she must not love them. Yet when the alcoholic drinks and seeks forgiveness, he or she brings gifts and showers them with the positive affection that is missing when he or she is emotionally violent. Trapped in this double bind, the alcoholic's other soon begins to experience a version of the alcoholically divided self that had previously been the sole possession of the alcoholic. That is, the alcoholic begins to drive the other insane.

Witness the following situation. The speaker is a 51-year-old nurse. Her husband is an active alcoholic:

> He's got me going to the psychiatrist. I'm on Valium because I can't sleep or hold my attention at work. He plays games with me. He says he'll cut down and only drink at home. So he keeps beer in the frig and a bottle under the sink. That's supposed to be all he's drinking. Ha! That's a big laugh! He took that new afternoon job, 3-5 delivering prescriptions for the hospital. He gets off the other job at noon. He says he comes home from noon till 3:00 to see me. What a joke. He's passed out on the sofa by 2:30. Says he needs a rest cause of the two jobs. Rest, my foot. He's drunk on his ass at 2:30 in the afternoon. The other day I played a joke on him. I didn't wake him up. Just let him sleep. He woke up at 4:30 and asked what time it was. I said 4:30 dear, are you supposed to be someplace? He knew what I meant. He grabbed one of those beers and left through the back door. Now I mark his bottles and he changes them around. I know he fills them back up after he drinks. Christ, I feel like a God damned kid! Like a child. I can't believe what he's got me doing. The doctor's no help. He just says take the pills and try to relax. Who can relax? I'm ready to check myself in. I don't give a damn what he does anymore. But I love him. Christ, why is he doing this? [field conversation, August 23, 1985].

Thus does the alcoholic relationship stabilize at the end of Act One.

Alcoholic Violence and the
Merry-Go-Round of Trouble

Act Two begins with a sudden shift in the interactional structure the alcoholic and his or her others have constructed. The unsteady, fragile order that had been in place suddenly escalates to a new level. This is often precipitated by an act of violence that gets out of hand. The following episode is representative. The speaker is a 32-year-old, in treatment for the second time. His wife is in the process of divorcing him. He is under a court order not to see his wife or children. He describes how this occurred:

> I'd come home drunk on my ass. Ain't nothin different 'bout that. Done it a thousand times before. Don't know what got in her damned head. I threw her up 'gainst the kitchen wall. Told her to get off my fuckin' case. I didn't need her shit anymore, I said. Give me space, I said. Kids was screamin all 'round. My teenage girl was havin' a party in the front room. They was dancin' to that God damned punk music. I told 'em to turn it down. Man got to get some peace. Then the bitch (my old lady) turned on me. Said this was enough. She wasn't taking this shit anymore. She grabbed the kitchen knife and told me to get my ass out of the house and be gone for good. Said she didn't want to see me again. Fuck, I didn't want to stick around if I wasn't wanted. I'm no dummy, you know. But, Christ she'd drove me out of my house. Told me to get. That's my house, you know. She'd throwed the beer out after me. So I went, and I went mad. I broke the door when I left. I climbed in my new truck, went to town and got me a six-pack. Then I drove back home, drinkin' it and gettin' madder as I went. I drove that truck on the front steps of the house, laid back on the horn and kept her and kids up til one o'clock. She called the sheriff and they came and took me off. I had a gun on the front seat, but I'd never of used it. Just wanted to scare her. It ain't that I can't drink and it ain't that I don't get crazy when I drink. I just want her to talk to me when I get like that. 'Cept she gets scared, runs away from me. I just get madder and all hell breaks loose. I guess I'm an alcoholic. I sure can't control what the damned stuff does to me and what I think when I get to going [field conversation, April 1, 1983].

The drinker in the above account seeks to force his way violently into an understanding relationship with his wife. He does not drink so that he can be violent, as some have claimed (Gelles, 1972, 1979). Nor does he become violent because alcohol necessarily releases aggressive behavior that is pent up inside him, as others have argued (Hetherton and Wray, 1964; Carpenter and Armenti, 1972). The ressentiment he feels is exaggerated and highlighted in his stream of experience as he drinks. Furthermore, as he drinks he calls out in his wife negative, hostile feelings she has toward him when he drinks. The drinker is not pathologically violent, as others have suggested (Mark and Ervin, 1970).

This drinker, instead, craves and seeks a sense of self and a relational involvement of intimacy with his other that he has lost through his drinking. His violence, then, is not necessarily a display of an underlying pathology, nor is he using the "time-out" period of drinking (MacAndrew and Edgerton, 1969) as an excuse to be violent. He knows, his wife knows, and his culture has told him, that violence is not an appropriate line of action to be taken when intoxicated, especially toward a family intimate. If he forgot this, the sheriff jogged his memory for him.

Our drinker was trapped within a line of action that built upon itself. As his anger got out of hand, it turned to violence. The violence was fueled by his drinking, and his drinking was fueled by his violent emotionality. In a circle of violent, drinking emotionality, he acted out his feelings of despair and frustration by driving the truck up the front steps of the house.

The outcome of the above event was to bring this alcoholic into a treatment center. His display of emotional and physical violence moved his relationship with his family into stages six and seven of the violent family. That is, the increased violence shifted his alcoholism out of the private arenas of his home into the public sphere where the police, the courts, and now a treatment center have become involved. His relationship with his wife will either (1) collapse, (2) be stabilized at this somewhat stable state of recurring violence, or (3) be transformed into a "recovering" relationship wherein he and his family seek assistance for their jointly experienced alcoholism. His actions brought others into his alcoholic situation in ways that had never occurred before. He had finally produced an episode of violence that could no longer be denied. Although he saw his violence as being no different from his actions a thousand times before, his wife took a different view. This was real violence; violence for which he must be held accountable. It no longer mattered if he was drunk or sober, or whether his actions were playful or accidental. Somehow, in a previously unnoticed fashion, their relationship moved into a new phase of interaction. What they had before had suddenly slipped through their fingers.

Alcoholic Troubles

The key to Act Two, as suggested, is the sudden eruption of a new problematic that can or no longer will be handled within the interpretive, accomodative structures the alcoholic and his or her other have previously constructed. Violence of a new order is one form this problematic may assume. But other alcoholic troubles will also occur. A DUI, causing an automobile accident, killing a person while intoxicated, having a love affair that comes to the attention of the alcoholic's spouse, failing to deliver a work assignment at the appointed time, becoming intoxicated at a family dinner, abusing one's in-laws, getting fired, being hospitalized for an alcohol-related illness or injury, making obscene telephone calls during a blackout, firing a gun at a neighbor's house, or setting fire to a spouse's clothing in the front yard of one's home may be the event that produces the radical alteration in the alcoholic's interactional situation that is the key to Act Two. Whatever the event is, it will produce the following consequences.

First, it will shatter the significant other's denial system, leading the other to finally begin to understand that an alcoholic inhabits his or her life. He or she must come to understand that they are enabling the alcoholic's alcoholism. If the other does not come to this recognition, he or she will continue to come to the alcoholic's assistance when he or she confronts the round of troubles just outlined.

Second, this event must bring home to the alcoholic the point that he or she has problems with alcohol. If this does not occur, and if he or she continues to deny that alcoholism, Acts One and Two will continue. That is, the alcoholic will continue to drink, denying that a drinking problem exists, that he or she is an alcoholic, and that alcohol is causing him or her trouble (Kellerman, 1969: 7). The alcoholic will deny also that he or she has caused the family any harm. The alcoholic may even blame the family for the problems they have caused him or her (Kellerman, 1969: 7).

Third, this event will serve to discredit the alcoholic in his or her own and in the other's eyes. It will leave a memory of failure, self-disgust, embarrassment, and self-pain. He or she will fall back on alcoholic pride in an attempt to deny that the event occurred. Or, if he or she accepts the occurrence of the event, he or she will not take responsibility for it.

Fourth, the alcoholic and his or her other will vow that what happened will never happen again. The alcoholic may promise never to drink again, and the other will state that he or she will never help the alcoholic again.

If the other and the alcoholic continue to deny the alcoholic's troubles, the latter's dependency will only increase. Act Two will continue with the alcoholic having been saved once again by his or her enablers. He or she will end up back at home, in a safe place. The alcoholic will have been propped up in his or her job and restored to his or her usual place in the family. Kellerman (1969: 6) states:

> As everything has been done *for* him and not *by* him, his dependency
> is increased, and he remains a child in an adult suit. The results, effects
> and problems caused by his drinking have been removed by others....
> The painful results of the drinking were suffered by persons other than
> the alcoholic. This permits him to continue drinking as a way to solve
> his problems. In Act One the alcoholic killed his pain and woe by getting
> drunk; in Act Two the trouble and painful results of drinking are
> removed by other people. This convinces the alcoholic he can go on
> behaving in this irresponsible way.

The following situation describes these reactions of the alcoholic
and his other to the problematic events that structure Act Two. The
speaker is an engineer. He describes how he came to burn his wife's
clothing in the front yard of their home:

> We'd had another of those damned fights over my drinking. I'd come
> home drunk again, yelled and screamed as always. She stonewalled me.
> Turned her back on me. Got the kids, got the suitcases, took the car
> keys, walked out of the front door and drove off. I was flabbergasted.
> What an insult. But she hadn't taken everything. Her winter clothes were
> all there in the closet. I went in, took them off the hangers, real neat-
> like, stacked them up, got a laundry basket, carried them to the front
> yard, took four trips. I made a cross out of them. Then I got the gasoline
> can for the lawnmower, and the bag of charcoal. Put that charcoal in
> the shape of a cross, on the top of the clothes, then I poured gas on
> everything. Then I went and called her and told her please come home.
> I'd never drink again. She fell for it. She was back from her folks in
> 20 minutes. I turned the lights off when she drove up, stepped outside,
> waved to her and the kids, dropped a match on the clothes, and the
> whole front yard went up in flames. I stood at the top of it and screamed
> "Here I am, here's your God damned alcoholic. Do you want to crucify
> me?" All hell broke loose after that. I passed out drunk on top of the
> clothes, she had to call the fire department and take me to the hospital
> for burns. When I came to she told me everything. The neighbors in
> the street, the police and fire department, the story in the newspaper.
> Everything. I vowed I'd never drink again. She swore this was the last
> time she was coming back. Course we were both lying. I drank again,
> she left again, but the next time she was gone for a year and when she
> came back that time I'd been in A.A. for three months [field
> conversation July 22, 1985].

End of Act Two

The alcoholic in the above account is at the end of Act Two. He
and his spouse have passed through the sixth and seventh stages of

the violent, alcoholic family. All the structures of denial, violence, pain, ressentiment, and alcoholically produced troubles are out in the open for public inspection. Rescued once again, the alcoholic stands ready to enter Act Three, in which his interactional situation will either be completely destroyed, or he will collapse and surrender to his alcoholism.

ACT THREE:
COLLAPSE AND SURRENDER

Act Three returns to Act One, for the alcoholic drinks again. This time, however, it is different. A past history of not being able to control drinking is by now common knowledge, as are the troubles and violence the alcoholic has just produced in Act Two. From the end of Act Two onward all of her drinking and conduct are interpreted within the "alcoholic" framework, even though she still may deny her alcoholism. The transition from Act Two to Act Three is critical. This is the most strategic moment for intervention. As Kellerman (1969: 9) notes, Act Two (and I add the beginning of Act Three) is the only act in which the destructive course of alcoholism can be changed.

Three factors are pivotal to Act Three. The first is the withdrawal of support from the alcoholic's other. The second is a collapse in the alcoholic's world of interaction, often accompanied by an act of insanity, an accident, or the onset of an alcohol-related illness. The third factor is surrender, which, as noted earlier (Chapter Five) is threefold: the admission of alcoholism, acceptance of this fact, and an inner surrender to this situation.

The following two cases summarize the above analysis of the alcoholic's situation as Act Three begins. Indeed they may be said to encapsulate all of Act Three, insofar as they both involve dramatic changes in action on the part of the alcoholic and his or her other.

The first case involves an *intervention,* which is the "process by which those close to the alcoholic—family, employer, friends, and coworkers—confront the alcoholic. The goal of the intervention is to force the alcoholic to seek treatment" (Wholey, 1984: 227).

The speaker, H, describes how he got into a treatment center.

J [the woman he had been living with] kicked me out. I guess I was drunk, anyway I'd been drinking, even tho' I'd said I was sober. I packed everything up and went to a friend's house. I really gave him no choice. I started going crazy. I heard sounds, I couldn't sleep, I stayed up talking to my friend and his wife all night. The next day I was in no shape

to go to work. They called my supervisor who got somebody else to
cover for me. It kept getting worse. I was afraid to leave the basement
where I was staying. I thought I was going crazy. Then they called some
people from A.A. and two of them came over, along with a relative,
my supervisor, and somebody else from work who is in A.A. There I
was, up against the wall, holding my head. The room was filled with
all of these people. They told me how I hadn't been able to do my work.
How I was worse off than the last time. How I had to do something.
"What was I going to do?" That's what they kept saying. I couldn't
hear it. Didn't want to hear it. I kept saying I wanted to stop drinking
but didn't know how. They asked me if I wanted to go to detox. I said
no. They asked me if I wanted to get sober. I said yes. They said, "How
are you going to do it?" Finally I agreed. I didn't want to, but I did
[field conversation, September 20, 1985, 38-year-old researcher, in
treatment for the third time in nine months].

As of this writing this individual is in his third week of treatment. He
calls himself not an alcoholic, but an alcohol abuser. Whether or not
he remains sober and fully surrenders to his alcoholism (see discussion
below) remains problematic at this time. This case reflects the three
key factors in Act Three. His significant others withdrew support. His
world collapsed in upon him, and he surrendered, if only begrudgingly,
to his alcoholic situation and entered a treatment center. The goal of
the intervention was accomplished.

The next case is more clear-cut in terms of outcome. The speaker
has been sober nearly five years. He is 41 years old, and is an elec-
trician. He attends five A.A. meetings a week, and is the treasurer
of one A.A. group. He talks of how he got to A.A.:

The wife backed off. Damned if she didn't go to Al-Anon over at the
Catholic Church. They told her to let me drink. She did. I went at it
free as hell for six weeks. Got up one Friday morning. Sat at the kitchen
table. Sun coming in. She'd gone into town to work. I'd called in sick.
By myself, all alone. I looked at them six empty bottles of beer in front
of me on the table. I'd finished the Peppermint Schnapps. I felt empty,
sick, scared. What was I doing? I called A.A. and they said they had
a noon meeting. I went, scared as hell. Been coming ever since.

Its funny, bout the wife. She'd gone to see the priest. He'd told her
that there was nothing she could do. He said men drink. It was her lot
to take care of me. And she did. She'd buy the stuff for me. Hold my
head when I was sick. Turn the other way when I was drunk. Even have
sex with me sometimes. The boss was O.K. too. I think he knew
something was wrong but he never said anything when I called in sick.

Course I was hell to live with all this time. I was never happy, could never get high from the booze. Depressed all the time, drinking to stay even. God I'm glad that's over. Haven't had a drink today. Thank God! [field conversation, November 4, 1981].

This alcoholic and his wife lived out all three acts of the alcoholic's play. She was his enabler, his victim (as was his boss), his provoker, his source of comfort. They lived denial. When she stopped attempting to control his drinking his illness moved quickly to the point at which he was forced to confront the problematics of his drinking situation. He surrendered and reached out for help. It is now necessary to discuss briefly the phenomenon of collapse and surrender and reaching out for help.

Collapse and Surrender

The "help" the alcoholic reaches out for is of two varieties. A request for *enabling help,* characteristic of Acts One and Two, is a cry for assistance to get the alcoholic out of his or her troubles. There is not a sincere desire to stop drinking, although the alcoholic may declare verbally that he or she is an alcoholic and will never drink again. It is an inauthentic declaration of alcoholism. His or her alcoholism will be used as an excuse to continue drinking. When trouble again occurs the alcoholic will fall back on his or her disease as an excuse for what he or she has done.

A request for *sincere help,* on the other hand (which appears in Act Three), represents a call for help that is accompanied by the alcoholic's initial authentic surrendering to his or her alcoholism. The drinker openly confronts the problems produced by his or her drinking. He or she asks for help in order to stop drinking. The alcoholic expresses this plea for help with the words of a total convert to alcoholism (see Lofland, 1977: 57; Rudy, 1986). He or she cries out for help and sincerely means what is said or so the alcoholic and the significant others believe. The first two steps of surrender are passed through. The alcoholic has admitted an inability to control his or her drinking and appears to accept this failure.

It is nearly impossible to distinguish inauthentic from authentic statements of alcoholism by the words the alcoholic speaks, just as it is impossible to distinguish clearly a request for enabling help from a request for sincere help. The proof of the difference lies in the actions the drinker takes, once he or she has made the request for help.

Hitting Bottom

In order for the alcoholic to surrender he or she must "hit bottom."
Two "bottoms" are distinguished by A.A.: "high bottom" and "low
bottom." In A.A.'s early days its cofounder Bill Wilson stated:

> Those of us who sobered up in A.A. had been grim and utterly hopeless
> cases. But then we began to have some success with milder alcoholics.
> Younger folks appeared. Lots of people turned up who still had jobs,
> homes, health, and even good social standing. Of course, it was necessary
> for these newcomers to hit bottom emotionally. But they did not have
> to hit every possible bottom in order to admit that they were licked
> [A.A., 1967: 209].

When an alcoholic will hit bottom can never be predicted in advance.
An A.A. member with 15 years in A.A. and a veteran of 12 Steps (an
act that carries A.A.'s message of recovery to an alcoholic who requests
help) states: "You never know when it will happen. I've taken one
man to detox 14 times. He's still drinking. Someday he'll get it. You
never know. It's a gift. You never give up on anybody [field conversation, October 3, 1983].

The bottom that is hit is emotional, economic, physical, personal,
and social. The drinker must find the situation intolerable and confront
the fact that the life he is living is not the life he imagined. He also
must come to see that all the reasons he gave to himself for drinking
are no longer working. His theory of successful drinking must be
demolished. The structures of bad faith that stood in the way of the
drinker confronting his alcoholism similarly must be destroyed.

Collapse

Collapse coincides with "hitting bottom." It takes three forms:
physical, interactional, and phenomenological or psychological. Physical collapse refers to the physical deterioriation of the drinker's body,
which often requires hospitalization for alcohol-related illnesses.
Interactional collapse points to the withdrawal of support from
significant others. As her others draw away, the drinker finds herself
alone in the world. Without a theory to explain her conduct, the drinker
experiences phenomenological or psychological collapse. She
experiences an "insanity of self" (see the account of H above and M
below) that may lead to suicidal thoughts. In such a state she may
surrender and reach out for help.

Surrender

The thesis of self-surrender asserts that only through surrender does the recovery process begin. The alcoholic cries out for help and her cry may be sincere. There is no one to turn to. Nobody will buy her a drink, loan her money, drive her to a bar, pay the bills, or call her employer and say she is sick and won't be in today to work. Her enabling system has collapsed. Surrender is a threefold process: She must admit failure, accept this failure, and concede to her innermost self that she believes this fact.

Confronting the Alcoholic Label

At this point the alcoholic must, at some level, confront the fact that she is an alcoholic and no longer a problem drinker. She cannot hide behind the label, use the label, or run away from it. She must accept the facts that confront her. She cannot drink like ordinary people. Further, she must understand that no amount of will power or self-knowledge will keep her from taking that first drink. This has been proven time and time again, yet in the past she has denied this fact. The stigma that she has placed on the label *alcoholic* must now be understood to be no greater than the degradation experienced at her own hands. That is, if she is not an alcoholic, then whatever is wrong with her has created a situation that could be no worse than calling herself alcoholic. If the drinker does not understand this about herself she will continue to deny her alcoholism.

The following account, given by a 43-year-old middle-level management executive in his second week of treatment, illustrates the dilemma the alcoholic confronts:

> I don't think I'm a real alcoholic. Sure I drank too much, but it was the work, the house payments, the kids in college, the wife's bills. When I had that DUI and passed out and hit the light pole I had a heart attack. That's what my doctor said. He said you're overweight, you need to exercise, take a good rest, stop drinking for awhile. That's why I'm here. This is good for me but I don't think I'm an alcoholic [field conversation April 16, 1981].

This man changed his name while in treatment, refusing to allow the staff or the other patients to call him by his real name. He was still in a denial phase.

The following speaker has been in contact with A.A. for over 12 years, making annual calls to A.A. asking for help. He has never gone through treatment nor attended more than five A.A. meetings (by his words). He is dressed in a green hospital gown, 62 years old, over six feet tall, yet he weighs less than 135 pounds. Retired from the Air Force, now on pension and social security, he lives in a trailer with his wife who is not alcoholic. His teenage daughter left home several months ago because he sexually abused her. He speaks the following:

> Hell, I'm an alcoholic, but I don't want to stop. I got all those good "old boy" friends. They know I can't hold the stuff anymore. Just as I get sobered up they come over with a case of beer and a bottle of whisky. I woke up from a blackout and there was two six packs of beer next to me in bed. They'd brought it to me. What can I do? Hell, it'd kill me to pour it out! [field conversation, October 2, 1984].

This drinker is in a detoxification unit to dry out so that he can go home to drink again. He uses the alcoholic label to continue his drinking.

The following drinker used A.A. and treatment to deal with a problem of wife battering. Drunk one night, he beat up his wife. She filed charges. Three days prior to his court hearing he entered treatment. He completed his treatment. The court dropped the charges. He drank the next day. He has not attended an A.A. meeting since treatment.

> Sure I'm an alcoholic. I can't hold the stuff. But I like it. I like the stuff. I ain't got time to come to these here meetings though, I got to get me a job. You folks got a good thing here, though [field conversation, December 15, 1981].

The above drinkers have made insincere calls for help. They have made a verbal, inauthentic surrender to their alcoholism. They have passed through the first two phases of surrender, but not the third.

Complete, Inner Surrender

The following two alcoholics have surrendered authentically to their alcoholism and have been sober since that time. The first speaker has been sober three years, the second five years.

M is 41 years old, an academic, twice married. In this field conversation (November 28, 1982), he is speaking to two recovering alcoholics (O and R) who have been called to his house by M's wife (B), after he attempted suicide.

> M [to O and R]: I want to die. I tried to kill myself last night. See [points to his slashed wrists], but it didn't work. You know I was in A.A. before. I don't believe in God. I stopped thinking I was an alcoholic. I think Albert

	Camus was correct. Suicide is the ultimate act of freedom. I tried to be free and failed.
O [to M]:	I think Camus changed his mind in his later work. Have you read *The Plague?*
M [to O]:	No. Doesn't matter. I'll have to think about that though. When I stopped going to A.A. things started to get worse. I was invited to a conference in Berlin. My host offered me a drink. I knew that I shouldn't take it. I debated with myself. I didn't want to hurt his feelings. I took it. Nothing happened. I drank every day after that when I was on my trip. When I got home I started buying wine and having it with dinner. Then I had to have it with lunch. Then wine wasn't strong enough and I started buying gin. See [points to half gallon of gin], that would last not quite two days. Last June I was at a conference in Paris. I fell in love. I want to marry that woman. I've told my wife about it. She doesn't know what to think. I've been writing this woman since June and I started drinking more heavily. I guess I went crazy. Last night we had company for dinner. After they left I started drinking gin. I got more and more depressed. I went into the bathroom and tried to kill myself. I still want to. See the blood on the floor [takes O and R into the bathroom and points to the blood stains on the floor].
R [to M]:	M, do you think we should go to the fifth floor [the local psychiatric ward]?
M [to O and R]:	Yes. I know I'm crazy right now. I also know I can't drink. I'm an alcoholic. I belong in A.A. Will you take me? Can we get rid of the gin?
O [to M]:	Yes, M, come on, let's put it outside for the garbage men. Are you ready to go?
M [to O and R]:	Yes, just let me kiss the kids goodbye. B, where are they?
B [to M]:	They're on the table, dear [points to three stuffed teddy bears on the dining room table who are positioned in front of a small television screen, which is on, without the sound].
M [to teddy bears]:	Bye kids, you be good while Daddy's gone. He's going to the hospital to get well. He's sick. He's an alcoholic.

M spent two weeks on the psychiatric ward. He attended A.A. meetings during that time and told his story at an open A.A. meeting. When he left the hospital he entered a treatment center for three weeks. He has been sober since November 28, 1982. At the time of this writing he is in Europe with the woman he fell in love with in the summer of 1981. He is again divorced. His suicide attempt was his bottom. Sometime during the day and evening of November 28, 1982, M authentically surrendered to his alcoholism.

The second alcoholic is R, age 48, who was with O when they called upon M. Sober five years, he describes his moment of surrender in the following words:

S [his wife] and I had gone to Detroit to visit her family. I was drinking heavily. We had a fight and I went to a hotel. I took two six packs with me. I got drunk. I was in my underpants. I went out in the hallway and closed the door to the room. I passed out, blacked out. I came to in the hotel lobby, in my underpants, asking the hotel clerk for my room key. There I was, practically naked. My God! What was wrong with me? I knew then that I was an alcoholic. I'd called A.A. six months earlier. Somebody on the answering service told me about the meetings and said I should sober up. I got mad. Who the hell were they to tell me to sober up? I stayed drunk off and on for six months, trying to control it. I'd drink vodka in half pints and beer. I hid the half pints in the bedroom closet behind my clothes. Once S was looking for something and a bottle fell out and hit her on the head! Prior to this six months I'd had 3 DUI's, rolled the car once and spent three nights in the drunk tank. I knew I was an alcoholic. But I thought I could control it. After that night in Detroit I knew I couldn't control it any longer. I called A.A. when we got home. I've been going ever since. That first year I went every night to a meeting. S and my daughter go to Al-Anon three to four times a week now [field conversation March 10, 1983].

R surrendered to his alcoholism that evening in the hotel in Detroit. He hit his low bottom when he found himself in the hotel lobby in his underpants.

End of Act Three

Act Three has one of two basic endings, given in the terms *authentic* and *inauthentic surrender*. For the alcoholic who inauthentically surrenders to his or her alcoholism and returns to drinking the scenario is as follows. His or her destructive drama stabilizes into one of three variations on Acts One and Two. The first variation repositions the alcoholic and his or her other in an alcohol-centered relationship. They carry on as if nothing had happened or been accomplished as a result of his surface surrendering to his or her alcoholism. The relationship settles in the final stages of the violent, alcoholic relationship. It is an uneasy truce, in which the alcoholic continues to drink and his or her other continues to enable.

The second variation witnesses the collapse of the marriage or relationship with the other. The alcoholic and his or her other go their separate ways; the alcoholic to continue drinking, and the other perhaps to form a new relationship, often with another alcoholic. The third variation places the other in treatment for the alcoholism he or she experienced with the alcoholic, and the alcoholic continues drinking. In this case the spouse or other joins Al-Anon, or a similar self-help group for spouses, friends, and family members of alcoholics. In the case of immediate (or near immediate) authentic surrender, both the alcoholic and his or her other enter treatment. The alcoholic goes to A.A. and the spouse to Al-Anon.

The following case encompasses these three variations on Act Three. The speaker is 51 years years old, a successful salesman. He has been sober one year, although he has been in and around A.A. for 12 years.

> T [his wife] and I separated 12 years ago. We've been back together for two years. She'd been raising hell about my alcoholism back then. I'd gone to a few meetings. She'd gone to Al-Anon. I said I was an alcoholic, but I didn't believe it, and she knew I didn't believe it. Anyway, one night I came home drunk, as usual, and she had all my clothes in grocery bags by the front door. She told me to get out. So I left. I stayed away 10 years. Moved out west, found a friend, kept drinking. T stayed here, with the kids, I sent money off and on, not much though. We kind of lost touch with one another. She stopped going to Al-Anon, made friends with somebody from the A.A. side who went back out [started drinking again]. That didn't last. My new friend was a drunk, too. She's still drinking, far as I know. Anyway, 2 years ago I'd finally had it. Still loved T. Knew she wouldn't take me back if I was drunk. So I went into A.A., got sober, came back, we got set up again, I slipped once or twice, but I got a good sponsor and he made me go to meetings. I've got a year tonight [of sobriety] and I think we're going to make it. T's back in Al-Anon and we're trying [field conversation, November 2, 1982].

This case represents a happy conclusion to the alcoholic's three-act play. It must be remembered, however, that this drama took over 12 years to reach this position. Other alcoholics reach this point but do not remain there, as the following case reveals. Here the alcoholic takes back the act of surrender.

Angel

Angel was 53 years old when he killed himself on January 23, 1982, by asphyxiation. He had closed the door to his garage at approximately 8:30 p.m., started his car, and left a suicide note to his wife leaving all of his money to her and his daughter. Angel was a recovering alcoholic who had been sober six years. He was a regular attender of A.A. meetings. Six months prior to his death he left his wife and started drinking. His small business had gone bankrupt. He became more and more depressed. He made repeated attempts to make contact with his wife. Every time he contacted her he was intoxicated. He stopped attending A.A. meetings, but he kept up regular telephone conversations with friends in A.A. One month before he committed suicide he bought a gun and went to his wife's home. He asked to see her and to talk with her, but she refused to let him in the house. He pulled his gun out and threatened to shoot her. She slammed the door and called the police. A court injunction was issued against his coming onto the premises of his wife's home. He began to call her at all hours of the day and night. Each time he talked to her he was drinking.

The night that Angel killed himself he had gone to his wife's house. He said goodbye to her and tried one more time to get into the house to talk to her. She again refused to see him. Leaving her he said that "it was all over." She repeatedly tried to call him at his house but the phone was busy. She called the police. They went to Angel's house and found him dead, slumped over the steering wheel of his car.

Angel's death was reported as "death by reasons of heart failure." Although his earlier surrender to alcoholism had produced a happy conclusion to his version of the alcoholic's three act play, his return to drinking shattered all of that. The facts of Angel's case are kept alive in the A.A. community I studied.

The second basic ending to Act Three is produced by authentic surrender. In complete authentic inner surrender, the alcoholic sets in motion a process that carries the potential of changing him from an active, drinking alcoholic, to an alcoholic seeking recovery. The meanings he holds toward himself, alcohol, alcoholism, and alcoholics are slowly tranformed. Alcohol becomes a poison, a liquid that can kill him or drive him crazy. The drinking act, long the center of his life, is now defined in negative terms. Alcoholics and alcoholism slowly are given new meanings, now that he has defined himself as being an alcoholic. In his surrender the alcoholic begins to turn his back on the drinking self of the past. Perhaps unwittingly he seeks a new self, not knowing, however, what this self will feel like, or how it will comport itself in the world. His act of surrender has brought him to the edge of a new life.

Authentic surrender also alters the alcoholic's relationship with his or her other. By surrendering to alcoholism and entering treatment or A.A. (or both), the alcoholic makes a move that destabilizes the alcohol-centered relationship with the others in his or her life (see the case of R above). He or she and the other enter a new interactional space that alcohol and drinking previously filled. The alcohol-centered identities that he or she and the other had earlier shared must now be reconstructed, if not destroyed, and replaced by new identities that focus on the "recovery process." The end of Act Three for the alcoholic who authentically surrenders sets the stage for Act Four, which is "Recovery," the topic of the next chapter.

CONCLUSIONS

I have analyzed the drama of destruction the alcoholically divided self experiences. The three acts of this drama, (1) the alcoholic situation, (2) violence and the merry-go-round of trouble, and (3) collapse and surrender, were discussed in detail. The various scenarios that flow from the original alcoholic situation, with its denial and enabling structures, were sketched. I have shown how the alcoholic and his or her other live contrasting, negative emotionality on a daily basis.

I also examined the centrality of emotional and physical violence in this drama. Although it has not been my intention to offer a full-scale analysis of the relationship among alcohol, alcoholism, and violence, my observations warrant the following conclusions. First, the relationship between alcohol and violence in the alcoholic family is not spurious as some have suggested (Berk et al., 1983: 120; Gelles, 1979: 173). The alcoholic marriage does not give the alcoholic a license to hit his or her spouse, and he or she does not become drunk so that in this time-out period he or she can be violent.

Second, I concur with Steinglass and Robertson (1983: 299), who argue that "the preponderance of research evidence suggests the existence of some relationship between alcohol abuse and family violence." Third, this relationship perhaps can be best interpreted from within the framework I have offered in this chapter. That is, violence is woven through every interactional structure of the alcoholic relationship. It is emotional and physical, real and spurious, paradoxical and playful. It is also indicative of the "insanity of self" that the alcoholic experiences when he or she drinks. In her intoxication the alcoholic holds violent thoughts toward herself and her other. If the alcoholic continues far enough in her drinking she may, as in the case of Angel, kill herself, and threaten to kill her family. Drinkers such as Angel drink and become violent in an attempt to regain something that has been lost. What they have lost is self-pride and the intimacy the other can offer. Alcohol produces for these drinkers those forms of behavior American society defines as violent, criminal, insane, and alcoholic. Until the forms of insanity that alcoholism produces are better understood, the relationship between alcoholism and violence will remain misunderstood.

The alcoholically divided self and his or her other have played out the three crucial stages of alcoholism. As recovery begins they find themselves in a drinking culture that has victimized them. How to adjust to that fact is one of the major problems they must confront jointly in recovery. The following alcoholic, a female with over one year of sobriety phrases this problem as follows:

> We bought the whole thing. They told us to drink and be happy. So that's what my ex-husband and I did. Boy did we drink and try to be happy. Now he's my ex and I'm an alcoholic trying to recover. And everywhere I look there's an ad or a sign telling me to drink and have a good time. We were sold a bill of goods and we bought it! It's no wonder I don't trust them anymore. This is a fucked up society we live in! [field observation, October 14, 1985].

I turn now to the topic of recovery, offering an outline of the major steps in the recovery process. A detailed analysis of this process is reserved, however, for the second part of this study, *The Recovering Alcoholic.*

7

THE RECOVERING ALCOHOLIC SELF

M [a female alcoholic] never got it. She'd been through treatment twice. She had three years one time, then her husband divorced her and she went back. She'd come to this Friday night meeting drunk on vodka and say she was a crazy, grateful alcoholic. And she was drunk. She loved all of us, would do anything for anybody. When she died in the hospital everybody cried. It was a cold day in February when we buried her. Her memory helps me stay sober today. They say no alcoholic dies in vain. M didn't. God bless her [male alcoholic, speaking at a meeting, 10 years sobriety, 65 years old, retired].

I turn now to the topic of recovery. My point of departure is the alcoholic who has reached the end of Act Three in the play called "A Merry-Go-Round Named Denial." Authentic and inauthentic surrender have brought the alcoholic into the social world of recovery A.A. and treatment centers provide. He or she now enters Act Four, which is "Recovery." However, this act is better conceptualized as a new three-act play for it represents a radical break or rupture in the life experiences of the alcoholic and his or her other. As such, it may be interpreted in terms of three interrelated acts, or phrases, which I term (1) sobriety, (2) becoming an A.A. member, and (3) two lives. My analysis focuses on the individual's experiences in A.A. I will not examine the process of recovery that begins in treatment centers (see future volumes). The recovery that I describe in this chapter is understood properly as a relational, interactional, and often family-based process. Because of the complexity of this process my analysis focuses primarily on the alcoholic, not on his or her other. (See future volumes for a fuller discussion of the other's place in the recovery process.)

Transformation of Self

The recovering alcoholic undergoes a radical transformation of self (see Travisano, 1981: 244). Not only does he or she become sober, but a new language of self is acquired, as are a new set of meanings concerning alcohol, alcoholism, alcoholics, and the drinking act. By becoming a part of the lived history of A.A. the individual is transformed into a "recovering alcoholic" within a society of fellow alcoholics. At the same time the individual becomes an outsider (Becker, 1973) to the larger society that continues to sanction the cultural and interactional use of alcohol on a regular basis.

If, during the active stages of her alcoholism, the alcoholic also stood outside the boundaries of society, then now, in recovery, she is doubly outside that society. That is, by no longer drinking, the alcoholic can now pass as a "normal" within society. But this is a duplicitous "normalcy," for the recovering alcoholic carries the previous label of having been an alcoholic. And, knowing this, she looks somewhat askance at the normal world that previously judged her, knowing that it does not understand alcoholism as she does. Furthermore, the alcoholic now looks differently at herself, for attempting to be "normal" was what caused her, in part, to become an active alcoholic. Hence, she desires not to be normal as others understand being normal. She desires, rather, to be a recovering alcoholic, with all the meanings A.A. gives to that identity. The alcoholic has, then, not undergone an alternation in personal identity. She has experienced what Travisano (1981: 242-244), James (1904), Burke (1954), Berger and Luckmann (1967), Thune (1977), Wallace (1982), and Strauss (1959) would term a radical transformation of personal identity that signals a conversion and commitment to a new way of life (Becker, 1960, 1964). How this deep transformation in the alcoholic's identity is accomplished is the central topic of this chapter.

The Alcoholic's Other

It must be noted that the alcoholic's other is more likely to experience an alternation, but not a transformation, in personal identity (although this may occur). That is, the other undergoes a transition in identity from being the spouse or lover of an active alcoholic, to being the spouse or lover of a recovering alcoholic. The other's changes in identity are contingent, in large part, on the actions the alcoholic takes or does not take. Although the other may become an "Al-Anon," or a member of a group of significant others of alcoholics, or join a group of "Adult Children of Alcoholic Parents," he or she (1) does not have to stop drinking, or have a desire to stop drinking in order to do so; and (2) will not have been ordered by the court to attend such meetings, or sent through treatment, as is often the case for the alcoholic. In short, the other's changes are more voluntary, less a matter of societal knowledge or concern, and the identity that is assumed is less deviant, or stigmatized, than is the label of "alcoholic" that the alcoholic assumes. The other, like the alcoholic, will find, though, a social group that fosters and supports the changes in identity that are sought. Recovery for the other is a wholly different process and it is not well understood.

Structural Constraints on the Alcoholic's Recovery

Racial, ethnic, gender, family, economic, and cultural factors intervene in the recovery process. If the alcoholic is a male, black or Hispanic, he is likely to live in a culture that encourages heavy drinking as a sign of manhood. Economic frustrations, including lack of work, coupled with peer pressures, increase the rewards that are found in heavy alcohol consumption. Indeed the black or Hispanic male may find himself in a totally alcohol-centered environment (see Kane, 1981; Cahalan, 1970). These factors work against recovery. The alcoholic who wishes to stop drinking finds little support for the new transformation in identity he wishes to pursue.

If the alcoholic is female (Gomberg, 1976), she lives in a culture that has a double standard toward alcoholism and alcohol consumption. The tolerance for drunkenness in women is low in our culture. The female alcoholic carries a double stigma. She is (1) a female who is alcoholic and (2) one who has been a secret alcoholic, having lived out her alcoholism in the private confines of the family home. Because her society has positioned her in the protective position of the home, the normal excuses for becoming an alcoholic have been removed, that is, pressures of work or peer pressure. She may carry also the stigma of sexual abuse in childhood (Vander Mey and Neff, 1986).

American society, then, has produced four basic classes of alcoholics: male, female, white, and nonwhite. Not surprisingly, the recovery probabilities are highest for white males (see Kane, 1981). However, recent trends (*Time*, 1985: 68-78) indicate changes in this situation. That is, as American society becomes less alcohol- and drug-centered, and as the social worlds of recovery expand and become more and more a part of the collective consciousness of the society, the stigmas from alcoholism are likely to decrease. At the same time the recovery rates for alcoholics from the other three classes noted above also should increase. However, the factors that structure alcohol consumption in adolescence, when drinking is learned, must also undergo change, for problem drinking first erupts in the early and mid-twenties for both males and females (Mandell and Ginzburg, 1976). I turn now to the first act of the three-act play called "Recovery."

ACT ONE:
BECOMING SOBER

Becoming sober involves living a nondrinking self into existence. This involves the following interrelated process that may be repeated several times before the alcoholic establishes a stable sobriety trajectory (that is, a period of continous sobriety defined within A.A. in terms of 1, 3, 6, 9, and 12-month sequences). These phases, or processes are (1) hitting bottom; (2) reaching out for help; (3) making contact with A.A. and presenting one's self to an A.A. group; (4) announcing one's self as an alcoholic in an A.A. meeting; (5) slipping and returning to A.A.; (6) maintaining contact with A.A. and learning how not to drink on a daily basis; (7) becoming a regular member of A.A.; (8) learning A.A.'s Twelve Steps; and (9) becoming integrated into an A.A. network, getting a sponsor, and working the Steps, especially Steps Four and Five. (On A.A.'s steps see, A.A., 1953, 1976; Leach and Norris, 1977; Maxwell, 1984; Kurtz, 1979.)

Phases One and Two were analyzed in the last chapter. They will be relived in A.A. as the alcoholic learns to talk and tell his or her story. Phases Three, Four, and Five are the proper subject matter of Act One for they speak directly to how A.A. teaches the alcoholic not to drink (in practice Phases Three and Four are often combined, see below). Steps Six through Nine constitute the focus of Act Two, "Becoming an A.A. Member," and will be dealt with in the discussion of that act.

It is important to point out that the recovering alcoholic may move through all nine of these phases and still return to active alcoholism. The case quoted at the outset of this chapter establishes this fact. What occurs is a progressive funneling process that slowly solidifies the alcoholic's recovery program. It may take several movements through these phases before a solid recovery trajectory, or career, is secured.

A recovering alcoholic phrases this process in the following words:

It is like an elevator that keeps going down to lower levels and lower floors until it hits bottom. I have stopped drinking, surrendered, come to A.A. and worked the Steps, but each time before it was at a level that still allowed me to drop lower. I started at too high a level. It took me a long time to hit the lowest level. I have finally hit what I hope is the bottom floor for me. But I don't know. I thought this before, too. There's always a new bottom for me to hit. Last time it was a DUI. But I've had those before too. It has taken me a long time, a long time, to learn this program. I just pray that I have it today [field observation, December 5, 1984; recovering alcoholic, 37-year-old graduate student].

An alcoholic may abstain from alcohol and not move through these eight phases. An alcoholic within A.A. may work only a portion of the Steps and also maintain sobriety. But for the alcoholic to be defined as working an A.A. program these nine phases will be experienced.

A recovering alcoholic with 11 years of sobriety speaks to the distinctions implicit in the above paragraph:

You can get sober on just the First Step. You can stay sober and never go to meetings. You can get sober but you'll go crazy. You may be dry, and somewhat sober, but you won't have any peace of mind. You might as well be drinking. I know. That's what I did for the first four years of my sobriety. I went back to drinking. Life was just hell. You have to work all of the program. I do, anyway [field observation, July 15, 1984].

The First A.A. Meeting and Presenting an "Alcoholic" Self

Making contact with A.A. by attending one's first meeting is, of course, a basic step in the recovery process. This is Step Three in the recovery trajectory of the alcoholic. It must be followed up by subsequent A.A. meetings if the alcoholic is to learn the A.A. way of life. When an alcoholic attends his or her first A.A. meeting, by custom and tradition the meeting is turned into a *First Step Meeting*. (A.A.'s First Step states: "We admitted we were powerless over alcohol—that our lives had become unmanageable.") This means that each member at the meeting will speak to the processes of hitting bottom, surrendering, and coming to his or her first A.A. meeting. In these dialogues each member tells a story that will not be unlike the story the person at their first meeting will tell. This sharing of stories immediately joins the new alcoholic with a group perspective that has been constructed out of each individual's experiences with alcoholism before he or she got to A.A.

The following alcoholic is at his first A.A. meeting. He has been asked if he wants to speak by the chair of the meeting. Dressed in blue jeans, a heavy woolen shirt, hands shaking, face ashen and unshaven, eyes blurred, and tearing, he stated:

> I couldn't find the place. Walked by four times before I saw the A.A. sign on the front door. 'Fraid to come in. Guess that's why I'm here. My name's G, guess I'm an alcoholic. Can't stop by myself. God its good to be here. You make me feel good. Don't like to talk, though. I'm a loner. That's why I go to the bars. For the company. Never talk there either. Just drink and listen to people. Live by myself. Afraid of people. Been doin' this for 20 years. Keep gettin' into trouble when I drink. Don't even drive to the bar anymore. Walk. Can you people help me? Please [field observation, as reported, October 30, 1984].

Here the drinker presents an "alcoholic self" to the group. He asks for help, as he relates a portion of his story as a problem drinker. He calls himself an alcoholic and expresses an awareness that there must be help for alcoholics at A.A. This suggests that he knows that there are two kinds of alcoholics: his kind and those to whom he is speaking. This alcoholic has found his way to his first A.A. meeting. The group to which he presented his "alcoholic self" has since become his "home group" and he now attends three or more times a week. Having not yet announced a "dry date" for himself, he has become, in the eyes of the regular group members a "regular" at this group.

After G had spoken, the 14 A.A. members present at the meeting talked and told their stories involving the First Step. Each member spoke briefly, no longer than two to three minutes. The following comments are typical:

> My name's M and I'm an alcoholic. It took me 12 years to get to my first A.A. meeting. I came at just the right time. A day earlier and I wouldn't have been here. A day later and I wouldn't have come. It took me 18 months to get one year of sobriety. I'd been drinking for 20 years. Drunk the first time I drank, drunk every day after. I lost 3 wives, 14 cars, 2 houses, but kept the same job. I went to treatment and still drank. I came to A.A. meetings drunk and I drank after I left A.A. meetings. I didn't want to quit. I didn't want to give up. I finally surrendered. Today my miracle goes on. I didn't have to have a drink. So G, you're in the right place. Keep coming back. At least you didn't have to die before you got here [field observation, as reported, October 30, 1984; recovering male alcoholic, 52 years old, upper-level manager].

The next alcoholic speaks more directly to G:

> My name's L, I'm an alcoholic. Welcome to your first meeting. I'm
> glad to see you here. Its newcomers like you who help me stay sober.
> I know what kind of hell you've been through. I drank in bars, too.
> I was afraid to drive, too. I was in the emergency room at the hospital
> so many times they knew my clinic number. They told me if I drank
> again, I'd die. And I drank again. I had to come and keep coming.
> They told me to keep coming until I wanted to. They said come to a
> meeting every day. Some say 90 meetings in 90 days. I just go to a meeting
> every day. They said get a *Big Book*. Learn the Steps. Find a sponsor.
> Clear away the wreckage of your past. You're not a bad person, you
> are a sick person trying to get better. I have a disease called alcoholism
> and I can't drink. My medicine is A.A. and the poison is alcohol. I
> come here for my medicine. I get a little bit better everyday. Get involved
> with these people. You've got friends here you never knew you had
> [field observation, as reported, October 30, 1984, recovering male
> alcoholic, 44-years-old, chemist].

In the comments of these two speakers, G, the newcomer, was
exposed to the A.A. theory of alcoholism, alcoholics, and alcohol.
A process of socialization was at work. A new view of self, other,
language, and meaning was being communicated. Of course the
"new" self the alcoholic presents contains the term "alcoholic." In
presenting this "alcoholic" self to the group the speaker announces
a verbal (at least) commitment to the identity of alcoholic. Placing
his name before or after the word alcoholic locates the speaker,
for himself and for others, in the identity of alcoholic (see Stone, 1962,
on identity placement).

Presenting Self

This simple speech act (Searle, 1970) which states "I am an
alcoholic," carries manifold implications for the speaker. Not only
does it mean more than the speaker intends, but it means exactly what
is said: The speaker is an alcoholic. But more is given in this simple
utterance. In a frightening sense it reflects an attempt on the part of
the speaker to convince himself that he is, in fact, an alcoholic. The
utterance is both an expression of a self-affirmation, and a request
the speaker makes to himself, asking himself to, in fact, believe what
he has just said.

The sincerity of this speech act also must be considered, for the
speaker may utter the phrase "I am an alcoholic" and not believe
it. He makes the utterance because others expect it or because one
part of him believes it to be true and another part denies this label.

In these senses the speaker commits an act that connects him to a line of action that is produced by the effects of the utterance itself. In short, to himself and to others, the alcoholic publicly has defined himself as an alcoholic. This speech act signals, then, a conversion to an identity the speaker has heretofore gone to great lengths to avoid, if not deny. But having once made the statement, "I'm an alcoholic and my name if Bill," the speaker has crossed the verbal line from denial to surrender. He or she has begun the move from active alcoholism to recovery from alcoholism.

The following speakers display in their utterances these three attitudes toward the meaning of the phrase "I am an alcoholic."

The first speaker is at his first A.A. meeting. He states the following:

> My name's _____ and I'm an alcoholic. I guess. I hope, I'm afraid to say the word. I must be, I can't stop drinking. On New Year's Eve I got drunk and beat up my girlfriend because she left her apartment and locked the door. I don't want to do this anymore. I am an alcoholic [field observation, January 8, 1985].

This speaker fearfully pronounces the word "alcoholic," distancing himself from the word as he draws near to it. Commanding himself to believe what he has uttered, he offers the evidence he needs to make himself believe that he is, in fact, an alcoholic.

The next speaker describes his relationship to the word "alcoholic" in the following words:

> I've said I was an alcoholic for four years at these meetings. But deep down, inside, I didn't believe it. I still wanted to drink. I came here and said what you wanted me to say. Today I believe, as deeply as I can, that I am an alcoholic. It's a miracle that I haven't had a drink today. The reason I haven't, in part, is because I believe and know that I am an alcoholic and I can't take the first drink. You people have taught me that [field observation, October 27, 1983].

Here the speaker moves from insincerity to sincerity. He describes the transition he made from not believing in what he said and what he meant when he said he was an alcoholic, to the position of belief.

This simple speech act is the alcoholic's verbal ticket into the A.A. experience and into the A.A. meetings. What she does with it is wholly up to her. But if she chooses to follow through with this self-presentation at an A.A. meeting she must return. This new self that she has defined for herself and presented to others has been waiting for her.

The first A.A. meeting sets in motion, then, a process of socialization that will put the alcoholic on a sobriety trajectory, if that trajectory is desired. The socialization process turns on four levels of interpretation that move from the abstract to the specific. The first, and most abstract, level of interpretation is given to the object *alcohol* which is defined as "poison" for the alcoholic. The second level of meaning is given to the term *alcoholism,* which in A.A. is defined as a disease or an illness. The third level of meaning references the *alcoholic,* who is seen as suffering from an obsession to drink that is physical, mental, and spiritual. The fourth interpretive level speaks directly to the *problem drinker* who believes herself to be an alcoholic. A.A. tells the drinker that she is an alcoholic if she says so. And, if the drinker agrees, then she has come to the right place, for they will help her not to take a drink today.

Slipping and Returning to A.A.

It is nearly axiomatic that an alcoholic will drink after attending the first or second A.A. meeting. Slips, or returns to drinking, may be planned or accidental—that is, the alcoholic takes a drink with no prior plan of doing so. In order for recovery to occur within A.A. the alcoholic must, after slipping, return to A.A. He or she must grasp the idea that for A.A. not drinking is the key to recovery. The following speaker makes this point. After attending his first A.A. meeting, he was sober for three months, then he drank three beers at a party. He states the following:

> I feel so bad I want to cry. You know I didn't get drunk. But I did drink. I guess for you people that counts as a drink, right? I'll just have to start all over again. I don't know why I did it. Control I guess [field conversation, September 12, 1985, 46-year-old painter].

This alcoholic slipped and returned to A.A. He is struggling not to drink. He still keeps alcohol in his house. He still socializes with drinking friends. His A.A. attendance is erratic. His attendance at A.A. confirms, however, the A.A. adage that "If you drink after you come to A.A. it will never be the same again."

Reasons for Slips: Becker's Model

Slips are caused by the following factors: (1) the alcoholic's belief that he or she can once again control alcohol; (2) a desire to return to old drinking contexts in which sociability and fun were experienced (Bateson, 1972a: 328-329); (3) a phenomenological craving for alcohol coupled with a high stress situation in which drinking, in the past, was used as a means of reducing stress and anxiety; and (4) a failure to commit fully to the A.A. program. (See Denzin, 1986a, Chapters 4 and 5 for a more detailed discussion of slips and relapse.)

Two kinds of "slips" are defined by A.A. First, there are the slips experienced by the newcomer who is starting to "get" the program. These are regarded as normal and to be expected. The second kind of "slip" is experienced by the member who has had a period of continuous sobriety and is defined as a failure in the program. This return to drinking is often regarded as deliberate and not appropriately termed a slip. A.A.'s speak of these as planned drunks.

Slipping may be explained in terms of Becker's (1960, 1964) model of situational adjustments to problematic situations. That is, alcoholics slip when the transformation of self that has occurred in the early stages of recovery has not been complete. If it has produced only an alternation, but not a transformation, in identity (Travisano, 1981), then a return to drinking is likely. A complete transformation in identity, including a commitment to A.A., to the First Step, to A.A.'s concept of a Higher Power, and to the A.A. meeting structure, appears to secure the alcoholic's sobriety for that length of time that the commitment is sustained. If the alcoholic withdraws from A.A., drinking will be taken up again. His or her sobriety was, then, just a situational adjustment to a momentary problematic situation in life. He or she did not make the commitments and side bets into A.A. that would have anchored the recovering self in the A.A. way of life.

Situational adjustments to A.A. are likely when the alcoholic is forced to attend meetings, either because of pressures from work, home, or the courts. He or she will learn how to talk at an A.A. meeting, will call himself or herself an alcoholic, and may even put together a long list of attended meetings, with dates and places duly recorded. If, however, the commitment to A.A. is produced externally, a transient "alcoholic" identity is likely to be created. This will often occur for large "classes" of alcoholics, that is, those who go through a treatment center together. In this case situational adjustment becomes a collective phenomenon, shared within a group perspective.

The process of commitment to A.A. (see below) will work against slips. The alcoholic will have built up consistent lines of action toward not drinking that crisscross through the many life situations he or she might confront. He or she will have learned how to reject situational alternatives or contingencies that might provide an excuse for drinking. He or she will, that is, no longer regard not drinking as a temporary situational adjustment to a problem situation in life.

A.A. offers a social structure in which these commitments and side bets can be made. If the alcoholic chooses to anchor himself or herself in the A.A. way of life, sobriety can be secured. That is, he or she will become a member of a society of recovering alcoholic selves. In this case recovery becomes both a collective and an individual phenomenon. Slips—returns to drinking—will, for such an individual, be momentary and short lived. For the alcoholic who has not made these commitments slips may be permanent. He or she may never return to A.A.

A.A. phrases this position as follows:

> Why all this insistance that every A.A. must hit bottom first? The answer is that few people will sincerely try to practice the A.A. program unless they have hit bottom. For practicing A.A.'s remaining Eleven Steps means the adoption of attitudes and attitudes that almost no alcoholic who is still drinking can dream of taking. Who wishes to be rigorously honest and tolerant? Who wants to confess his faults to another and make restitution for harm done? Who cares anything about a Higher Power, let alone mediation and prayer. Who wants to sacrifice time and energy in trying to carry A.A.'s message to the next sufferer? No, the average alcoholic, self-centered in the extreme, doesn't care for this prospect—unless he has to do these things in order to stay alive himself [A.A., 1953: 24].

A.A.'s position is clear. In Becker's language, commitments and side bets into A.A. will not be made until the alcoholic hits bottom.

The next alcoholic makes this clear. After four and a half years of sobriety he returned to drinking.

> I still liked the taste of that damned stuff. I stayed on top of your A.A. bus for more than four years. I came to you folks so I could learn how to drink socially. After four years I told myself I could drink again. In three months I was crazy again, back on the mental ward. When I came back I got inside the A.A. bus. I learned how to rub shoulders with you people. I got involved [field observation, October 16, 1984].

This alcoholic has passed through stages one through five. After four and a half years he is ready to enter Act Two. He is ready to commit himself to A.A.

ACT TWO:
BECOMING AN A.A. MEMBER

As indicated earlier, Act Two, "Becoming an A.A. Member," has four phases; (1) maintaining contact with A.A. and learning how to not drink on a daily basis; (2) becoming a regular member of A.A.; (3) learning the Steps; (4) becoming integrated into an A.A. network, finding a sponsor, and working Steps Four and Five. (Because Steps Four and Five reference the transition between the old and the new life the alcoholic learns to live, I will discuss them under Act Three, below.) I begin with phase one of Act Two, giving it the title "Building Sobriety." (See Leach and Norris, 1977: 483-484, and Rudy, 1986, for alternative views of "becoming an A.A. member.")

Building Sobriety

A.A. recognizes two types of sobriety: continuous and interrupted. Individuals who become A.A. members endeavor to build a continuous sobriety trajectory measured, after the first days and months of sobriety have been obtained, by years. On the other hand, sobriety is measured on a one day at a time model, which is given in A.A.'s often repeated statement "Who ever got up first this morning has the most sobriety in this room." As the member builds sobriety he or she accumulates medallions or tokens, which symbolically mark the length of time he or she has been sober. Each person is responsible for announcing a "dry date," or a birthday date. Their sobriety is measured, henceforth, from this date. On the occasion of the first year of continuous sobriety the member has a birthday party with one candle on a cake, signifying the first year of his or her new life.

Becoming a Regular

As the member builds a sobriety career within A.A. he or she begins to be recognized around the tables. They become a regular at one or more A.A. groups. They will find a "home" group, often the first group they attended. In this group they will become regular "readers" of the A.A. materials that are read at the outset of every meeting (that is, "How It Works," "The Twelve Traditions," and "The Thought for the Day," for the groups I studied). He or she also may become a temporary chair of the group, agreeing to lead its meetings for a month or more. Later an elected position within the group may be obtained. The member may become the group's General Service Representative or its treasurer, although this probably will not happen until after a year or more of sobriety. The member also may be asked to tell his or her story at an open A.A. meeting. The key to becoming a group-recognized, responsible regular is continuous sobriety.

Learning the Steps

A.A. describes the importance of its Twelve Steps for recovery:

> Many of us had long been booze-fighters. Time after time, we had stopped drinking and tried to stay stopped, only to return to drinking sooner or later.... But those Twelve Steps of A.A. mark our road to recovery. Now, we do not have to fight any more. And our path is open to all comers [A.A., 1976: 85].

> A.A.'s Twelve Steps are a group of principles, spiritual in nature, which, if practiced as a way of life, can expel the obsession to drink and enable the sufferer to become happily and usefully whole [A.A., 1953: 15].

The discourse between the following two A.A. speakers, both female, gives meaning to the Steps as they are applied to the member's recovery program.

The following speaker, a 37-year-old musician, has been sober 10 months. Her husband is an active alcoholic.

> I don't know, I don't know, you know, it's like, it's like, you know what it's like, like when you make a long distance telephone call and talk in the receiver to somebody and nobody answers, it's like there's no connection. My husband's like that. He'll make plans, get drunk, forget the plans, make new plans, get drunk, and never get anywhere. Now he's got me doing it. It's like, I don't know how I'm going to pay the bills. You know on New Year's Eve it was the greatest night of my life. I was with old friends, musicians, they were drinking and I wasn't. There was so much love there. It's like, do you know what I mean, it's like there was all that love there all around and I missed all of it because I was always drunk. I went home and cried. How could I have done that to myself? You know I think I might still be crazy, I just can't make any connections anywhere. Can anybody help me? [field observation, January 10, 1985].

A speaker with four years sobriety came forth in the meeting:

> Have you tried the Steps? Have you tried turning your life over? Have you done the Fourth and Fifth Steps? Do you do daily prayer and meditation? How many meetings do you go to? You know I was just like you my first year. I was all crazy. Then my sponsor told me to get to work on the Steps and stop feeling sorry for myself. It worked

for me [field observation, January 10, 1985, 39-year-old female, middle-level executive].

Two modes of sobriety are expressed in these statements. The first speaker is sober with A.A.'s First Step, but not the other Steps. By her own words she is not sane. The second speaker suggests that this is because she hasn't used the Steps. But more is at issue. The first speaker has not committed herself fully to the A.A. program. She attends meetings so as to stay sober, but she has gone no farther into the transformations in self that A.A. prescribes.

A.A.'s Steps may be understood as guidelines for self-transformation. They suggest a clearing away of the alcoholic's past (Steps Four and Five), so that the program of recovery A.A. offers may be embraced fully. If the Twelve Steps are followed the identity of alcoholic is made a central part of the alcoholic's self.

Speaker L, in the above account of G's first A.A. meeting, addresses the major points in learning the Steps. These turn on regular meeting attendance (90 meetings in 90 days), which ensures that the alcoholic will hear, over and over again, A.A.'s Twelve Steps read and discussed. In the community I studied the alcoholic also could attend regular Step Meetings that devoted 12 weekly meetings in a row to each one of the Steps. Thus, over the course of 12 weeks the alcoholic would be exposed to an in-depth discussion of each Step. At the end of Step Twelve the group would then start over with Step One.

The following alcoholic speaks to the place of these meetings in her recovery:

> I went to the Sunday night Step Meeting for one year. Never missed a Sunday. We went over every Step four times that year. We read from the *Twelve and Twelve*. That's how I learned the Steps. Then I went to the *Big Book* Meetings on Saturdays and we read every chapter and story in the *Big Book*. By the end of my first year I felt like I had learned the basics of A.A. It took repetition, listening, and hearing other people read and discuss the Steps before I finally began to understand how they all fitted together [field interview, August 5, 1985].

In addition to regular meeting attendance, the alcoholic is encouraged to learn the disease concept of A.A., to make friends within A.A., to work the Steps and to find a sponsor. He or she also is told not to question why he or she became an alcoholic. In this way the newcomer is taught a new interpretive theory of alcoholism. He or she learns, through modeling, imitation, and repetition (Bandura, 1977) how to become a recovering alcoholic. The alcoholic learns how to take the attitudes of the generalized community of recovering alcoholics, and apply those attitudes and their interpretations to his or her conduct (Mead, 1934). The Steps within A.A. become significant symbols, in Mead's language, that call out interpretations toward self, alcoholics, and alcoholism that are consensual and geared toward maintaining sobriety. As significant symbols that signify lines of action to be taken in the recovery process, the Steps become integral parts of the alcoholic's self-system.

A recovering alcoholic with 30 years sobriety states the following:

> I'd be nothing today without the Steps. With them I regained self-respect, got my family back, got rid of the guilt and shame about my past and learned to live like a normal human again. I became a new kind of person. The Steps were my guide posts to a new life [field conversation, July 5, 1984].

Maxwell (1984: 128) quotes a recovering alcoholic who echoes the position of the above speaker:

> A.A. gave me a whole new way of life, so that I am still continuing on with the things that A.A. taught me—this philosophy I found in A.A. I still apply it daily as I go along. *I feel like I'm still growing....* I now have a positive outlook on life, and I understand myself. I can recognize my limitations, but I have respect for myself, and I'm much happier [Italics in original].

These accounts reference the kind of reflective self-awareness A.A.'s Steps create when they are followed and become a part of the alcoholic's life. I turn now to sponsorship.

Phase Four: Finding a Sponsor

As the alcoholic becomes a member of A.A., becomes sober, and begins to learn the Steps, a sponsor will be found. A.A. (1975: 27) defines a sponsor as "a sober alcoholic who can help solve only one problem: how to stay sober. And the sponsor has only one tool to use—personal experience, not scientific wisdom." A sponsor may, as in the early days of A.A., "sponsor" a man or woman into A.A. and into the recovery process. This may include taking an alcoholic to detox (or treatment), visting him or her regularly, meeting the alcoholic's family members, taking the alcoholic home, and then to an A.A. meeting. At his or her first meeting the sponsor will introduce the newcomer to other recovering alcoholics (A.A., 1975: 26).

A sponsor becomes a friend with whom the alcoholic shares problems that may not be discussed at A.A.'s meetings. A.A. culture recommends that sponsors not be of the same sex. A sponsor may be someone who knows secrets about the alcoholic's past. A sponsor is also someone who may take the member through Steps.

These features of the sponsor are summarized in the following account.

When I got off the crazy ward after my last drunk I picked a sponsor who was someone I hated. I picked him because he was staying sober and I knew I could talk to the sonofabitch. I had done that plenty of times when we used to drink together at "Eddies." He even used to work for me. Then I worked for him. He took me through the Steps and I shared things with him that I never shared with nobody else. When he died I had to get someone else cause I had to have another living human being who knew this particular thing about me [field observation, June 2, 1981].

The sponsor may also become a focal point in the alcoholic's daily recovery. The following member speaks to this point:

For 18 months I called my sponsor almost on a daily basis, sometimes more than once a day. He helped me with everything. He told me I would become a new human being. He told me I wouldn't know the old person I used to be. He taught me how to read the *Big Book*. He had me do a daily inventory (the 10th Step) and he made me commit to five or more meetings a week. I did and what he said would happen happened. He took me through the 4th and 5th Steps too [field conversation, July 2, 1984].

The sponsor is a socializing agent within the A.A. culture. The relationship he or she forms with the newcomer is purely voluntary and works only as long as both parties continue their commitment to it. Such relationships often last years. Witness the following statement:

N was my friend for 26 years. We stayed in touch all this time. He stood up with me at my wedding. He was the Godfather for my kids. He was a friend, a family member, a confidant. He was everything you could ask of another human being. I would never have met this man, or found him, if it hadn't been for my alcoholism and A.A. [field conversation, August 22, 1983].

As the member acquires a sponsor, he or she may also become a sponsor to a newcomer. The newcomer, in turn, if he or she stays, may become a sponsor. Thus, a network of sponsors exists within any A.A. community, for behind every recovering alcoholic stands a sponsor. This dyadic relationship lies at the heart of the A.A.

experience (see Maxwell, 1984: 110-113). I turn now to Act Three of Recovery, "Two Lives."

ACT THREE:
TWO LIVES

Act Three has four distinct phases that do, however, overlap. These are (1) taking Steps Four and Five; (2) acquiring a "spiritual" program as part of recovery; (3) learning how to live sober; and (4) coming to see that one has, in fact, led two lives: before A.A. and after A.A.

Steps Four and Five

A.A. tells the alcoholic that "self, manifested in various ways, was what had defeated us. Resentment is the 'number one' offender" (A.A., 1976: 64). From resentment stems the spiritual disease from which, according to A.A., all alcoholics suffer. In order for the alcoholic to recover, resentments must be dealt with, and this is the topic of the Fourth and Fifth Steps. The alcoholic is told to list his or her resentments, to identify the persons, places, and institutions that have produced them, and to locate how these resentments have affected his or her self-esteem, financial situation, and relations (including sexual) with others. A thorough review of the alcoholic's life is thus suggested. Once this searching, moral inventory is taken, the alcoholic is told to share this with God and another human being (Step Five). Having taken these two Steps the alcoholic is told to ask God (as this Higher Power is understood) to remove these defects of character that have produced these resentments and harmful actions toward others (Steps Six and Seven). Finally, A.A. suggests that the alcoholic make amends to those who were harmed before and during the active phases of alcoholism (Steps Eight and Nine).

In these moves A.A. separates the alcoholic from the past. It offers a new life with the resentments and misdeeds of the past laid to rest. At the same time A.A. locates the alcoholic within a new social world wherein other alcoholics are engaging in the same process. Recovery becomes a collective, group phenomenon.

A member with over five years sobriety speaks to the importance of Steps Four and Five for the alcoholic's recovery:

> They don't think there's anything wrong with them, except that they drank too much. They don't think the Fourth and Fifth Steps apply

to them. They just think they drank a little too much. They come in, get dried out, sobered up, stay three months, make big speeches, and then they leave, never to be seen again. They may be too successful. I know three well-known businessmen, big money. They came for a while. They're all out now, drinking. They said A.A. wasn't for them. They didn't have problems like those drunks they saw at the meetings. They weren't willing to do the hard work the program asks. They didn't have anything in their pasts they had to share with anybody else. They were "successes" [field conversation, January 31, 1985].

Steps Four and Five cut to the core of the alcoholic's self-system. They suggest an illumination of the hidden corners of the alcoholic's self that he or she has kept from others. The good-me, bad-me, and not-me components of the self are thus addressed in these two steps.

A member speaks to the importance of these Steps for her recovery:

It was like a giant weight was lifted from my shoulders. The past slowly began to drift away. I felt free for the first time in years. Everything fell into place, my father's alcoholism, my mother's death, my divorce, my alcoholism, what happened to me as a child sexually, why I'd had trouble with new relationships, how I was raising my son. I felt like a new woman with a new life in front of me. My sponsor took me through these steps. I trusted him and without him and what he taught me I wouldn't be here today [field conversation, April 4, 1983, female alcoholic, administrator, 4 years sober, 37 years old].

The importance of the sponsor for these two Steps is underscored in these remarks. At the same time this woman speaks to how the Steps allow the past to become understandable, as a new life within and outside A.A. is entered

Acquiring a Spiritual Program: Serenity

As indicated previously, A.A.'s Twelve Steps are organized by a set of spiritual principles (see Kurtz, 1979) that are intended to remove the alcoholic's obsession to drink. Embedded within these spiritual structures is a concept called "serenity," or "peace of mind," which carries two meanings for the A.A. member. The first meaning is the absence of negative emotion in the alcoholic's life, including anger, fear, jealousy, and resentment (A.A., 1967: 48). The second meaning is spiritual. It references a concept of "rebirth," and a peace of mind that comes when the alcoholic admits a Higher Power into his or her life (A.A., 1967: 104).

Only A.A.'s First, Fourth, Eighth, and Ninth Steps omit reference to a spiritual program or a Higher Power. Thus to enter into A.A.'s program of recovery is to enter into a spiritual program. This part of the program forgives the alcoholic for misdeeds of the past and offers a set of practices that will produce serenity or peace of mind.

These practices are situated in the A.A. meetings, wherein the Serenity Prayer opens every meeting and the Lord's Prayer closes every meeting. At the same time A.A. encourages individual meditation through the prayers that are associated with the Third, Seventh, and Eleventh Steps. Many members of A.A. also read *The Twenty-Four Hour a Day Book,* a publication of Hazelden (1954), and other meditation books, including *Each Day a New Beginning, The Promise of a New Day* and *Today's Gift* (Hazelden, 1982, 1983, 1985). In the following paragraph members discuss serenity and its meaning for them. They make reference to self-feelings that are associated with this state of mind.

The first speaker is a female, with 13 months of sobriety. Married, she is an account executive, and 53 years old:

> When I come in here everything slips away. The tension, the anxiety, the fear. The pent-up anger goes away. Today, this morning I was a fright. Just in a state. My head was like a nest of cobwebs; thoughts were crisscrossing every which way, nothing made sense. I was in a corner of my mind and couldn't get out. I think my boss set me off. I needed to come here. I feel better already. I have a tiny bit of peace of mind now that I can carry back with to work this afternoon. Thank you all for being here. I needed you today! Thank you [field observation, April 2, 1982].

In the next paragraph a member elaborates on the feelings that are experienced during a meeting. This member has been away from meetings (by choice) for five months. Sober 14 months, he is 21 years old. He states the following:

> I was afraid to come back. I don't know why. I just was. Now that I'm here I feel the peace and serenity of the group. It's just seeping into me. I'm relaxing. My fear is goin' away. I don't know why I stayed away so long. I didn't drink, but I don't know why. I need to be here every day. I remember now what it was like when I came every day. These good feelings stay with you after you leave. You carry them with you and that's why I always came every day. I need to get back to doing that. Thank you for being here when I finally got myself together to get back [field observation, February 5, 1985].

The next speaker refers to meetings he had with his group when he was in Mexico City.

At noon everyday I'd say the Serenity Prayer to myself and repeat the Eleventh Step. Then I'd put myself at the tables for the noon meeting and I'd look at everybody, just as I remembered you. Then I'd select a topic and imagine what you would be talking about and saying. Then I'd say what I would say if I was at the meeting. This would calm me down and give me a moment of peace when I was in that crazy Mexico City trying to find my way around [field observation, August 26, 1982, 49-year-old male, two years sobriety, employed as a copy editor].

These three accounts are descriptions of personal, spiritual experiences. Modifying William James (1961: 299-301), they may be seen as having the following characteristics. First, they reference definable, self-feelings that are relational. The members speak of having to be in the presence of others (real and imagined) in order for these feelings to be produced. Second, these feelings cannot be sustained for long periods of time, but when they are recalled, they are remembered with a depth of feeling that brings the member back to the A.A. meetings. Third, the serenity, or peace of mind, the alcoholic feels and experiences in meetings, although transitory and fleeting, is grounded in an interactional context. The knowledge that these feelings will be felt when members go to a meeting draws them back to the A.A. structure of experience. The alcoholic comes to define a central part of sobriety as residing in serenity, or the peace of mind that comes from attending meetings.

Having once attempted to find this self-feeling in alcohol, the member now finds it in interactions with other recovering alcoholics. The A.A. meetings become the setting for the production of a state of mind that is both shared and entirely personal.

James (1961) stressed the importance of spiritual experiences for the self that found itself divided against itself. A.A. is more specific in regard to the centrality of spiritual experiences. Such experiences are basic to the attainment and maintenance of sobriety. The second and third speakers (above) refer directly to this point.

A.A. thus works within a conceptual structure that is circular. Taking the position that a spiritual experience is basic to the attainment of sobriety, A.A. argues that serenity, which comes, in part, from meetings, is necessary in order for sobriety to be maintained. Furthermore, sobriety without serenity, which for A.A. takes the form of "dry drunks" and negative emotionality, is to be avoided at all costs. Dry drunks lead to wet drunks. Hence, serenity stands at the center of the A.A. experience. It is both the "cause" and the "effect" of becoming and being sober. It is also the sought after state of mind that replaces intoxication. And, it is the state of mind that can be obtained best through participation in the social worlds of A.A.

Living Sober

The test of a member's program is given in the ability to confront a problematic situation and not drink. A.A. (1975) offers the recovering alcoholic a number of "tips" or protective measures that can be followed when the occasion to drink arises. These include (1) staying away from the first drink; (2) becoming active within A.A. and making commitments to A.A.; (3) calling the sponsor when the desire to drink returns; (4) not getting too tired, hungry, angry, or lonely; (5) reading the A.A. literature; and (6) being careful of drinking situations.

The probability of living sober is increased if the member's commitment to A.A.'s spiritual program is sustained (see above). At the same time, as the alcoholic becomes more committed to the identity of a recovering alcoholic, a redefinition of self in relationship to problems and drinking occurs. That is, problems that were previously defined as justifying a drink are now defined as occasions for personal, spiritual growth. This massive conceptual reordering of the alcoholic's thought patterns is accomplished through the working of the Steps, the use of the sponsor, and regular attendance at A.A. meetings.

The following alcoholic addresses this problematic:

I don't have an excuse to drink today. A.A. took every one of them away from me. I used to think, what if my wife died, or my daughters were killed, or I lost my job, or my house burned down? What if? What if? I knew I'd drink if that happened. Today I know I'd come to a meeting and talk about it. I'd pray and ask God's guidance. I'd call my sponsor. I'd do anything I had to not to drink. A drink would not solve one of my problems today. I've finally learned what that cliché about problems being occasions for personal growth really means. I thought it was bullshit at first! They're right. I've got no excuse to drink. If I drink it's because I talk myself into it. Period [field conversation, February 2, 1982, 35-year-old male, carpenter, sober 5 years].

This alcoholic has made the transition between the two lives that a recovering alcoholic experiences. He indicates how problematic situations are redefined within A.A.'s interpretive theory. Thus far he has been successful for he has been sober over five years.

Two Lives

As the alcoholic learns how to deal with the past and as the A.A. program is internalized, he or she comes to think of his or her past life as something that happened long ago. At this point in recovery the alcoholic will have learned how to talk at A.A. meetings, will have worked the Fourth and Fifth Steps, and will have become an A.A. regular in one or more groups. (See Denzin, future volumes, for a more detailed discussion of this process.) The next two speakers make reference to this transition in self-hood that occurs.

Raymond Carver (1983: 196-197), the poet and novelist, makes the following observations regarding his alcoholic past:

> It's very painful to think about some of the things that happened back then.... Toward the end of my drinking I was completely out of control and in a very grave place. Blackouts, the whole business.... I was at Duffy's on two different occasions; in the place called DeWitt, in San Jose, and in a hospital in San Francisco—all in the space of twelve months. I guess that's pretty bad.

In these words Carver is describing how it was at the end of his drinking. Any alcoholic could give a similar story, although the details would vary, of course. In the following passage Carver describes his relationship to this past life.

> I can't change anything now.... That life is simply gone now, and I can't regret its passing. I have to live in the present. The life back then is gone just as surely—it's as remote to me as if it happened to somebody I read about in a nineteenth-century novel. I don't spend more than five minutes a month on the past. The past really is a foreign country, and they do do things differently there. Things happen. I really do feel I've had two different lives [Carver, 1983: 207].

Finally, Carver (1983: 196) speaks to the meaning of recovery. When asked by an interviewer, "How long since you quit drinking?" he replied:

> June 2, 1977. If you want the truth, I'm prouder of that, that I've quit drinking, than I am of anything in my life. I'm a recovered alcoholic. I'll always be an alcoholic, but I'm no longer a practicing alcoholic.

Carver's remarks reveal four basic features of the alcoholic's recovery story. First, the date of his last drink is fixed vividly in his memory. Second, the details of his last days of drinking are fresh in his memory. Third, he takes pride, as do all alcoholics who are recovering, in the fact that he has stopped drinking. Fourth, he now sees himself as living a new life. He has distanced himself from the old self of the past. He feels at home with the new, recovering self. He has made the full transition from the active alcoholic self of the past to the recovering self of the present.

The following speaker, the same speaker who opened Chapter 2, now sober 72 days, glimpses what Carver has seen:

> I feel that there are two me's. The old Frank of the past and the new Frank of today. The drunk Frank and the sober Frank. I don't never want to see that drunk sonofabitch again. I hope, I pray to God that he's gone away and died. I hope to meet the new Frank again in heaven when I see my maker. I pray to God I'll be sober the day I die. Last summer you never could have said that about me. I just wanted to curl up and die. I wanted to hook up one of them hoses we got at work to the back of the tailpipe of the old Chevy I got and drive down an old country lane with a pint, leave the motor runnin, maybe play some bluegrass music and jest die. Jest die. Kill myself, that's how low I felt. Lower than low, beneath a damned snake. Thank God I ain't afeelin' that way today. Thank God! Its me, the a, a, a, a. Its the New Frank a 'speakin' today. Thank God! [field observation, January 28, 1985, 53-year-old recovering alcoholic, printer].

Now 72 days away from his last drink, Frank still feels the pain of the old self that was an active alcoholic. Carver, over 6 years sober, spends less than "five minutes a month on the past." Frank is divided between the past and the present. These two alcoholics speak to the experiential distance that is traveled by the recovering alcoholic once recovery is securely in hand. Were they to sit together in the same meeting, Carver, if Frank were to hear him, would show him how much a part of his past the old Frank can become, if he stays sober.

Accepting the Alcoholic Identity

The difference between these two alcoholics is more than temporal, or their length of time in A.A. It is conceptual, moral, and lies deep within the self of each of them. Carver has accepted his alcoholic identity. He is committed fully to and invested in it, emotionally, personally, temporally, and interactionally. Frank still is learning and accepting his identity. They are in differing places in their moral careers as recovering alcoholics.

As the member makes the moves that bring this transition between the "two lives," he or she has come full circle in the A.A. experience. Starting as a newcomer at the first A.A. meeting, perhaps barely able to speak, he or she is now a recovering alcoholic. The emotionally divided self of the past has been dealt with. The horrors and traumas of the destructive alcoholic play called "Denial" have now become a part of the past. Yet that past is kept alive, as newcomers come into A.A. meetings and remind the regular where he or she used to be.

CONCLUSIONS

I have mapped the radical transformations of self that accompany the recovery process. I have structured my interpretations, as in the previous chapter, in terms of a three-act play. The phases of recovery—sobriety, becoming an A.A. member, and living two lives—represent dramatically different phases of experience. Each phase has a different focus. Phase three presumes the first two. The first two phases work back and forth upon one another, as becoming an A.A. member solidifies the member's sobriety, but one can hardly become sober within A.A. without desiring to become an A.A. member.

The key players, or figures in recovery are, of course, the alcoholic, his or her network of significant others, and recovering alcoholics in A.A. As the alcoholic becomes connected to A.A., a sponsor will be selected out of the universe of recovering alcoholics he or she comes to know. The dyadic, personal relationship that is built up between these two individuals becomes the cornerstone for the alcoholic's recovery. This dyadic structure stands, I have suggested, at the heart of the A.A. experience. From it flows the alcoholic's grasp and working of the Fourth and Fifth Steps. As the alcoholic moves beyond these steps the spiritual side of A.A. becomes more apparent. Serenity and peace of mind become sought after states of consciousness that replace the old obsession to drink that brought the alcoholic to A.A. in the first place. With spirituality comes a healing of the alcoholically divided self of the past.

The alcoholic's relationship with the other also structures the recovery process. The other may support or be negative about the new life the alcoholic wishes to lead. The other may complain about over-involvement in A.A. meetings and may miss the control he or she once exerted when the alcoholic was drinking actively. Resentment and anger may appear in the spaces that alcohol previously filled. The alcoholic and his or her other may find that nothing holds them together now that the drinking has stopped. Or they may find a new foundation for their relationship and grow more closely together (A.A., 1976: Chapter 9).

The alcoholic's recovery turns on a dialogue between two self-structures: the old self of the past and the new self of recovery. In order for recovery to begin working in the alcoholic's life a firm commitment to meetings and the A.A. Steps must be made. If this commitment is withheld, the alcoholic assumes a "transient" alcoholic identity, which represents only a situational adjustment to the problems his or her active alcoholism produced.

The new, committed "alcoholic" self that the alcoholic assumes becomes an interpersonal process (Sullivan, 1953) that is woven into the structures of experience A.A. offers. Transformed into a recovering alcoholic who is a storyteller, the member learns how to talk about the self of the past from the standpoint of humor and dramatic irony. By radically transforming himself or herself, the alcoholic transforms the world he or she lives in.

Limits of the Dramatic Metaphor

A note on the dramatic metaphor that has been employed in the last two chapters is in order. Elsewhere (Denzin, 1985a) I have criticized the use of this model because it too often produces a static, structural view of interaction. I have attempted to avoid this bias by treating the overlap that occurs between the several acts that make up the alcoholic's two plays.

With Goffman (1959: 254-255), my concern is with finding a framework that will aid in the understanding of how persons go about structuring and maintaining definitions of situations. The dramatic language of the stage is one way in which this process can be understood metaphorically. My problem has been to interpret how alcoholics and their others struggle to make sense out of a world that has gone out of control. Like actors on a stage, these individuals act out parts that they hope will make them appear (to themselves and others) to be normal. Attempting to act as normals they sink farther and farther into the destructive worlds of interaction that alcoholism produces. Like the characters in O'Neill's *Long Day's Journey Into Night* (1955), they experience ruptures and breaks in interactions that move them from one phase of experience to another. These ruptures and the new phases of experience they produce take the form of acts in a play. Different actors, different lines of action, different audiences, and different scripts are played out. Yet, in the main, it is the same set of individuals throughout. They have simply experienced new definitions of who they are in relation to one another. I turn now to reflections on the foregoing analysis.

8

CONCLUSION
Self, Temporality, and Alcoholism

> The real cause of alcoholism is the complete baffling sterility of existence as sold to you [Malcolm Lowry, 1984: xxx].

> The moral, then, is this. Since societies, like individuals, get the kinds of drunken comportment that they allow, they deserve what they get [MacAndrew and Edgerton, 1969: 173].

The alcoholic self has been my topic. A victim of a course of action he or she helps construct, the alcoholic and his or her other live through the three-act play I have, following Kellerman (1969), called the "Merry-Go-Round Named Denial." The alcoholic who collapses and surrenders to alcoholism then enters the regions of experience called recovery. I have briefly sketched the stages of recovery the alcoholic passes through.

It is now necessary to reflect on the alcoholic experience as I have presented it. I shall discuss briefly, in turn, the following topics: (1) alcoholism, science, and American society; (2) the alcoholic self; (3) self, temporality, and existence; and (4) the alcoholic as social critic.

ALCOHOLISM, SCIENCE,
AND AMERICAN SOCIETY

American society, through its mass media, cultures, schools, laws, and institutions of social control teaches individuals how to drink and use alcohol. People, as MacAndrew and Edgerton (1969: 172) suggest, learn about drunkenness from what their societies teach them. Members of a culture also learn how to identify problem drinkers. Their society also makes available to them a variety of interpretations concerning how and why it is that certain people become alcoholics and others do not. If a society is contradictory, ambivalent, or less than clear-cut on the patterns of drunken comportment that it allows (Pittman, 1967), then what individuals do when they drink will vary enormously. Furthermore, if a society teaches, as ours does, that "the state of drunkenness carries with it an 'increased freedom to be one's other self' " then the variety of selves that a society produces when it encourages its members to drink will also vary enormously (MacAndrew and Edgerton, 1969: 172). American society thus gets the kinds of alcoholic selves it deserves, for it encourages the use of alcohol in the pursuit of a self that is valued, cherished, and celebrated in everyday discourse (Madsen, 1974: 107).

Modern behaviorial science aids in this pursuit of a desired self that is produced in and through the drinking act. It does so in the following ways. First, it offers evidence on the drinking patterns of "normal" drinkers (Beauchamp, 1980). Second, it offers causal theories and explanations of problem, alcoholic drinking. Third, it offers theories and methods for turning problem, alcoholic drinkers into social drinkers. Fourth, it aids in the production of scientific texts that hold out hope for alcoholics and their families, suggesting in these texts that science may one day remove the specter of alcoholism from the American scene (see Franks, 1985). Fifth, by questioning the scientific and medical status of the term "alcoholism," modern science suggests that the "alcoholism" problem it has helped create may, in fact, not exist at all (Beauchamp, 1981). In this manner, science turns the lived problems of alcoholic drinking back on the drinker and his or her family. It suggests in the process that drinkers have become victims of a scientific or folk myth. They, in fact, do not have alcoholism. They have something else.

Driven by the causal question "Why does the 'alcoholic' drink alcoholically?" this literature often has gone in circles as it debates the reality of the phenomenon it supposedly has committed itself to eradicating. Periodically a "new" cause of alcoholism is discovered. Most recently the activities of the enzyme called P-450 and the opiate compounds in the central nervous system called TIQs have been located as the causes of alcoholism (Franks, 1985).

Such discoveries by science of course cannot be discounted. They offer new narrative texts that, as just suggested, hold out hope for the suffering problem drinker and his or her significant others. They of course do not speak to the alcoholic who has been defined, by himself or herself and others, as alcoholic. For the alcoholic has something that he or she and others believe has caused the alcoholic to act in ways that society defines as deviant, abnormal, or alcoholic. Whether that something happens to be TIQs or the enzyme called P-450 really is irrelevant.

These discoveries, then, serve to divert attention away from the lived experiences of alcoholics. Indeed it is unlikely that the phenomenon called alcoholism will disappear. It will be with us as long as our society persists in holding on to the ambivalent, contradictory attitudes toward alcohol and self-hood that it now values. We will have, that is, a phenomenon with the characteristics of alcoholism long after science has discovered and secured an undebatable, verifiable cause of it. This is so because alcoholism is a disease of living that is produced, in part, in its modern forms, by societies that do not provide alternative, nonalcoholic answers and solutions to selfhood, meaning, and every-day existence.

American Society

Our society, then, provides the arenas for the production of alcoholic selves. It produces the language for describing such selves (narcissistic, self-centered, divided against itself). It creates a need for a mass media that reports on the conduct of these selves and others like them (that is, those who are spiritually bankrupt, alienated, or schizophrenic). Our society also creates the alcohol that persons defined as alcoholic drink. It creates the laws that such persons violate when they, for example, drink and drive (Gusfield, 1981). Our society pro-vides the treatment centers that treat these selves. A new class of bureaucratic personalities (or selves) has been created also. They go by various titles: DUI instructors, alcoholism counselors, Certified Alcoholism Professionals, and so on.

At the same time American society has created a social and moral space for the emergence of Alcoholics Anonymous (see Kurtz, 1979; Maxwell, 1984; Rudy, 1986). A.A. also produces alcoholic selves of the recovering variety. I have outlined how A.A. works in Chapters 3 and 7. It is apparent that societal attitudes toward the existence of the alcoholic self are drastically changing. In the 1980s the problem drinker cannot escape the labels of alcoholic and recovering alcoholic (see *Time,* 1985).

Alcoholism as a
Dis-ease of Conduct

Given the foregoing preconceptions, I have decided to examine the alcoholism that the alcoholic in the 1980s experiences as a dis-ease of conduct. Alcoholism is an uneasiness of self that draws the subject into a vicious circle of addictive, destructive drinking. Alcoholism touches nearly every area of the alcoholic's life, as I have attempted to show in Chapters 4, 5, and 6. At the heart of alcoholism lies a fear of temporality. Locked in the past, the alcoholic fearfully confronts the present and future through the temporal consciousness alcohol creates. Alcoholism becomes a dis-ease of time. This uneasiness with time is manifested in the divided self the alcoholic experiences. Trapped within the negative emotions that alcoholism produces, the alcoholic dwells within the emotions of the past. The alcoholic approaches the present and the future with an anxious, self-fearfulness that undermines the ability to generate positive, emotional feelings toward self or others.

THE ALCOHOLIC SELF

My concern in this text, accordingly, has been to examine, in a variety of ways, the same question: "How do ordinary men and women experience that form of conduct modern society calls alcoholism?" This experience, I have suggested, is structured by an alcoholic self. This self is divided against itself (see Laing, 1965). Narcissistic and self-centered, the alcoholic self uses alcohol as a mirror, seeking in the self-reflections that alcohol offers a truer picture of itself. Yet alcohol, for the divided self, fuels a resentment toward others and an inner hatred of self. The unstable, inner self of the alcoholic runs to violent emotionality, madness, insanity, and imaginary fears. The emotional and sexual relations the alcoholic has with others are similarly distorted by alcohol's effects. The alcoholic is unable to present a "true" picture of self to the other, for he or she always sees the other through alcoholically clouded streams of consciousness. Hampered by alcoholic amnesia and alcoholic aphasia, the alcoholic lives within a distorted world of self-other relations. Symbolically and interactionally attached to dominating emotional associates from the past, the alcoholic lives out a maddening inner self-drama that is scripted by resentment and hatred. I have traced the major contours of this drama in Chapter 6.

Telling the Alcoholic's Story:
The Six Theses

There are, Henry James (1920) suggests, 5 million ways to tell the same story. I have distilled the stories alcoholics tell about themselves into the Six Theses of Alcoholism as given in Chapter 5. These theses organize the alcoholic's experiences with alcoholism and recovery. They refer to an interaction process that organizes the alcoholic's relationship to alcohol, drinking, self, emotionality, meaning, temporality, action, and the other.

They do not, however, always operate at the level of conscious, interpretive strategies. Rather, they structure the alcoholic's existence at a taken for granted, habitual, often preconscious level. They may, on occasion, however, evolve into consciously developed, well thought-out interpretive systems, as is the case of the alcoholic's theory of denial.

The concepts of time, social relationships (real and imagined), emotionality (positive and negative), bad faith, denial and self-deception, and beliefs in self-control and surrender reference the inner and outer forms of experience that constitute the essential structures of alcoholism (and recovery). As such they reflect an interpretive theory of self and conduct in the world.

ALCOHOLICS AND "NORMALS"

These theses also apply to the world that is taken for granted by nonalcoholics. That is, active alcoholics take to the extreme the assumptions and principles that structure the lives of ordinary people. Ordinary individuals live bad faith, lie and deceive themselves and others, and engage in distorted human relationships. Ordinary individuals also experience negative emotions, hold onto resentments, experience time inauthentically, and believe in willpower and self-control. Such persons also develop divided selves and live out imaginary self-ideals that have little to do with the worlds of the "real."

What sets the alcoholic off from the "normal" are the lived experiences that accompany his or her self-definitions. The individual's divided self leads him or her into the world of alcoholic dreams and fantasies; that world soon takes over the alcoholic's life. As the alcoholic moves farther and farther into it, his or her distance from normals and normal everyday life increases. The alcoholic becomes an outsider to society, almost by choice (Becker, 1973).

In telling the alcoholic's story I have repeatedly focused on the universal singularity of each alcoholic's experiences. I have assumed that each alcoholic is unique, yet in his or her uniqueness lies a universal generality that describes the experiences of all persons who become alcoholic during this particular period of American history. Although there are as many stories of alcoholism as there are alcoholics, the outline of every story is the same, and each can be interpreted within the structures that the Six Theses reference.

Alcoholic Time and "Normal" Time

In Chapter 5, I compared alcoholic time with normal time. I suggested that "normal" time (1) is grounded in the present, (2) is not experienced fearfully, (3) is reflectively grasped as being part of ongoing purposive action, (4) is not lodged in the past or the future, and (5) does not give rise to feelings of self that are located in the past. Normal time informs the present in a purposively useful fashion. Alcoholic time demolishes the present.

I then suggested that modern societies have produced large classes of individuals who share certain features of the alcoholic's dis-ease of time. Following Scheler (1961), I argued that the elderly, women, members of racial and ethnic minorities, the recently divorced, students, and the unemployed all experience a resentment that is grounded in time. Alcoholism, then, is just one version of the dis-ease of time that grips the modern situation.

SELF, TEMPORALITY, AND EXISTENCE

Consider the following self-statements given by alcoholics.

I don't know who the fuckin' hell I am. It's been eight months that I've been sober and I still don't know myself. Nothin's right. I'm messin' up everything I touch and even the things I leave alone are fucked up. I come to meetings every day and I want to leave early. I talk and nothin' works. I hear the sound of my voice and I don't know what I'm sayin'. I feel like there's no space for me. No space in my head. No space where I am. I'm in the middle of nothing.

Last night I decided to take action. Fix the frozen drainpipe on the house I said to myself. Went outside. The fucker was frozen all to Hell. Nothin' I could do. Went back to go inside and the damned door was locked. I thought maybe I could take out a window, real gentle-like. Instead I smashed it to pieces. Went all over my living room. Got inside and there was glass all over. I didn't want to be there. So I left. But I didn't know where to go. Too dumb to go to a meeting I just drove around by myself [field observation, February 8, 1985, recovering alcoholic, 35 years old, accountant].

In this account, or story, the member speaks to a loss, or emptiness of self. Indeed as he speaks he is searching for a self to which he might anchor himself.

Compare the previous account to the following. The speaker is 43 years old. He is still intoxicated, after two days of not drinking. He is at his second A.A. meeting.

> I've got everything. A good wife. A good job. A new car. Great kids. Great groups of buddies. Sure I maybe drink too much. But what the hell, who doesn't? Some days I can go with just one drink, then I stop and stay till closing time. I feel something you people got here but I'm not sure it's for me. I think I can handle this deal by myself. Don't know. Nothing makes sense. Thanks for letting me talk [field observation, October 13, 1983].

This member talks with a self-confidence that is absent in the account of the first speaker. He has a self firmly attached to material and personal things, including a wife, a job, children, a car, and friends. He speaks as if he knows who he is. The first speaker does not know who he is.

The following speaker is reflecting back on his "using days." A dentist, 29 years old, he has been "clean and straight" for three months. He has been in A.A. for over four years. He has gone through three threatment centers.

> I would get up, depressed as hell. Roll a joint and grab a beer, lay back. Get in touch with the universe. I'd fly off, out of my apartment, into space, in tune with the world. No worries, no fears. I knew everything. I had all the answers. Turn the music on high, the Stones, mellow out. No depression. I called it getting in touch with the universe. Today that all sucks. I get high with you people [field observation, January 2, 1985].

This speaker references two modes of experiencing self: the first is produced by drugs and alcohol, the second by A.A. interaction.

The following speaker is more explicit. Sober 12 years, he is 68 years old. A retired barber, he states the following:

> A.A. will be here after I'm gone. People who are still out there drinking will take my place in this fellowship. And like me they will find a peace of mind, a serenity, and a God of their understanding that I could never get with that damned booze. They will find out who they are and they will learn that they belong here, if they want to be here. They will help others find what I have found. This has been a very good way of life for me. I am just glad I found it before it was too late [field observation, October, 13, 1983].

Our barber has found himself. He speaks of a place in a fellowship that will go on after he dies. He has experienced a self-transcendence that is unlike the negativity of the first speaker. He has transcended, as well, the material foundations of self the second speaker is still attached to.

Problematics of Self
and Alcoholism

Smith (1957: 279) has described the alcoholic in the following paradoxical words:

> The [A.A.] member was never enslaved by alcohol. Alcohol simply served as an escape from personal enslavement to the false ideals of a materialistic society.

These four accounts by alcoholics speak directly to Smith's position, for each alcoholic locates himself within a materialistic culture that is somehow found empty or lacking. Each, in his way, is criticizing that culture. These statements reference three problematics of self that are displayed in the alcoholic experience. These problematics may be termed (1) self as loss, (2) self as false or illusive subjectivity, and (3) self as transcendent experience.

Self as loss references the experiences of the first speaker. He is sober but his life has no meaning for him. He can feel his inner subjectivity, but he feels an emptiness of self as he speaks. His selfhood is illusive. He is haunted by a sense of self that escapes his grasp.

Self as false subjectivity is given in the account of the second speaker. He has everything: wife, job, new car, friends, house. Yet he drinks more than he wants to and suspects that he may be an alcoholic. The meaning of self he seeks in material things has failed him.

Self as transcendent is given in the accounts of the third and fourth speakers. The third speaker seeks self-transcendence in drugs and alcohol, the fourth in the A.A. experience. The transcendent-self seeks to be part of something larger than itself that is not materialistic. It seeks an immanence in a structure of experience that is both enveloping and, in a Durkheimian sense (1912), collective, and perhaps ritualistic, spiritual, or religious (Bateson, 1972a: 319, 333). The self that is transcendent is processual, outside itself objectively, but subjectively aware of its own relationships with the world. It seeks to transcend direct empirical experience in the search for a broader and larger meaning of self and existence (James, 1961: 399-400).

The transcendence that is found in drugs and alcohol is a chemical transcendence. This is a personal, unshareable selfhood that is isolating, alienating, and individualistic. This inner state of experience is not immanent in a structure larger than itself, although such an immanence is sought. Interactional self-transcendence is given in the A.A. experience as described by the fourth speaker. He has found a non-competitive, complementary relationship with a world that is larger than he is (Bateson, 1972a: 335).

These three problematics of self are woven through every alcoholic's experiences. They reference modes of self-experiencing that move from the individual to the group. As the alcoholic becomes embedded in A.A., a shared, group conception of self is acquired. A.A.'s move, which is truly sociological, locates transcendence of self in the group, not the person. The active alcoholic had, of course, the opposite position. He or she located individuality, subjectivity, and transcendence in alcohol, drugs, and in the self. A.A.'s self is in the group, not the person.

THE ALCOHOLIC
AS SOCIAL CRITIC

There is a third mode of self as transcendent. It is given in the texts of Malcom Lowry, especially *Under the Volcano* (1984). It can be located also in the discourse of nearly any practicing alcoholic. In the quotation cited at the beginning of this chapter, Lowry locates the cause of alcoholism in "the complete, baffling sterility of existence." In the transcendent mode of *self as critic,* the active alcoholic believes that she sees a sickness in society that no one else sees. In the alcoholic's transcendent critique and dreams she believes she is above the problems of society. She displays an attempt to escape and transcend a society that is seen as crumbling and falling apart from within. She searches for an alternate set of ultimate values that will locate and anchor self in a structure of experience that is eternal, transcendent, and not purely subjective. The alcoholic attempts, however, to discover the purely transcendent in the depths of her own alcoholically produced consciousness. Like our third speaker, the alcoholic seeks *in vino veritas* (Bateson, 1972a: 311). But unlike our third alcoholic, Lowry's narrator sees his vision revealing an inner structure and meaning to life that is partially reflected only in the fragmentary pieces of personal experience (Spender, 1984: ix). That is, Lowry's alcoholic Honorary Consul finds, having transcended his own existence, that the vision of life below is empty and hollow. He finds ultimate meaning only in himself. In his moment of death this shattering view of reality is finally given. He states the following:

> And now he has reached the summit. Ah, Yvonne, sweetheart, forgive me! Strong hands lifted him. Opening his eyes, he looked down, expecting to see below him, the magnificent jungle, the height...like those peaks of his life conquered one after another before the greatest ascent of all had been successfully, if unconventionally, completed. But there was nothing there: no peaks, no climb. Nor was this summit a summit exactly: it had no substance, no firm base. It was crumbling too, whatever it was, collapsing, while he was falling, falling into the volcano, he must have climbed it after all...yet no, it wasn't the volcano, the world itself was bursting, bursting into black spouts of villages catapulted into space, with himself falling through it all, through the inconceivable pandemonium of a million tanks, through the blazing of ten million burning bodies, falling, into a forest, falling [Lowry, 1984: 327-328].

Out of his own consciousness Lowry's Consul has discovered an eternal nothingness in existence. In that discovery he has become the ultimate social critic who has illuminated and revealed the eternal meaning to life by inspecting his own personal experience.

The Alcoholic's Dis-ease

The alcoholic as critic is the modern antihero "reflecting an extreme external situation through his own extremity. His neurosis [alcoholism] becomes diagnosis, not just of himself, but of a phase of history" (Spender, 1984: ix). The alcoholic's dis-ease of conduct thus is justified because it is no longer just one individual's case history or life story. Within the context of history it becomes the "dial of the instrument that records the effects of a particular stage of civilization upon a civilized individual" (Spender, 1984: ix).

The alcoholic's transcendent vision of his or her culture and times thus becomes a symbolic statement concerning the breakdown of the modern world. This expression affects other individuals in ways that they may only dimly understand or accept (see Spender, 1984: ix). But the alcoholic as critic registers feelings and insights that in some senses apply to all members of the culture at large. The alcoholic is thereby accorded a place in the culture because his or her situation speaks to everyone. And it is not just because of the alcoholic's deviance that this place is given. He or she does more than reveal the boundaries of the acceptable or the unacceptable (Durkheim, 1895). The alcoholic signals a doubt about the inner, felt truth of the culture and its times. By living that doubt into existence, and by taking it to its extremes, the alcoholic becomes the symbolic representation of every modern individual who also doubts the meaning of modern existence. Understanding this, the alcoholic as critic justifies alcoholism in the name of a higher cause. He or she buys into the place culture has accorded him or her.

Lowry's alcoholic sought transcendent insight through the analysis of his own personal experience. The fourth speaker, by contrast, searches for an alternate set of ultimate values that will locate and anchor self in a structure of experience that is not purely subjective and introspective. He finds his values in the rituals, traditions, and interactions of Alcoholics Anonymous. Like a "postmodernist" (Spender, 1984: ix; Habermas, 1983; Jameson, 1983; Updike, 1984; Lyotard, 1984), the recovering alcoholic discovers a universality of tradition (and spirituality) that is barely revealed in the distorted structures of modern life. But this approach is not purely rational or nonpersonal, it is emotional, subjective, and historical. At the deepest level, the transcendent meanings the recovering alcoholic discovers are found in the self and in a reading of the past which is taken as evidence of the failure of previous modes of self-understanding. Out of this rereading of the self appear the "shadows" of the past (Jung, 1939) that have haunted the subject. And these are shadows that haunt every modern individual, for the alcoholic has positioned doubt at the center of modern existence. From this confrontation with the past may emerge a joining of the personal consciousness of the individual with the collective, shared consciousness of Alcoholics Anonymous. And, in this process, the individual is reinserted into his or her culture as a new subject. This subject is the topic of the next book in this series, *The Recovering Alcoholic* (Denzin, 1986a).

The alcoholic, drinking or recovering, thus brings before us new possibilities of existence. He or she shows us how far we may have to go before we are forced to change our lives and the social structures that we live in. In studying the alcoholic we study ourselves.

Glossary

A.A. member Any person who calls himself or herself an A.A. member.

A.A. meeting Two or more alcoholics meeting together for the purposes of sobriety. Types: *Closed,* attended only by individuals who have a desire to stop drinking; *Open,* attended by those who have an interest in alcoholism and A.A.; *Speaker,* one A.A. member tells his or her story to others in an open meeting; *Discussion,* a topic of discussion (that is, resentment, anger) is discussed by each member in turn; *First Step,* a meeting (usually closed) devoted to a discussion of A.A.'s First Step, by tradition any meeting attended by a "newcomer" or a person at his or her first meeting becomes a First Step Meeting; *Step Meeting,* a meeting devoted to a discussion of each of A.A.'s twelve Steps.

Ambivalent alcohol culture The cultural attitude toward alcohol usage conflicts between use and nonuse (Pittman, 1967).

Abstinent alcohol culture The cultural attitude is negative and prohibitive toward any type of ingestion of alcoholic beverage (Pittman, 1967).

Adult child of an alcoholic parent An adult with an alcoholic parent.

Alcoholic rhythm A regular pattern of drinking, established in the critical and chronic phases of alcoholism, usually involving drinking on a four-hour cycle.

Alcoholic A person who defines himself or herself as alcoholic. Characterized by an inability to control drinking, once the first drink is taken, and an inability to abstain from drinking for any continuous period of time.

Alcoholism I A self-destructive form of activity involving compulsive, addictive drinking, coupled with increased alcohol tolerance and an inability to abstain for long periods of time from drinking. Phases: prealcoholic, prodomal, crucial, chronic. Types: Types: alpha, beta, gamma, delta (see Jellinek, 1960).

Alcoholism II American Medical Association definition: An illness characterized by preoccupation with alcohol and loss of control over its consumption such as to lead usually to intoxication if drinking is begun; by chronicity; by progression; and by tendency toward relapse. It is typically associated with physical disability and impaired emotional, occupational, and/or social adjustments as a direct consequence of persistent and excessive use of alcohol.

Alcoholism III   Alcoholics Anonymous definition: The manifestation of an allergy, coupled with the phenomenon of craving for alcohol, producing an illness that is spiritual, mental, and physical.

Alcoholic aphasia and amnesia   Thought disorders associated with the critical and chronic stages of alcoholism; Wernicke's disease and Korsakoff's psychosis are types.

Alcohol-centered relationship A relationship between an alcoholic and an other in which alcohol has become the center or focus of interaction. Alcohol displaces intimacy, love, or conversation as the previous focus, or center, of the relationship.

Alcoholic as social critic   A mode of self-transcendence in which the alcoholic locates himself or herself outside society, seeing in society a sickness or illness that no one else sees.

Alcoholic identity   Coming to define one's self as alcoholic. There are two forms (1) *transient or situational alcoholic identity,* when one assumes the alcoholic identity so as to overcome a problematic situation. This is a situational adjustment to the problems alcoholism produces; (2) *committed alcoholic identity,* when one invests and commits one's self in the identity of recovering alcoholic as defined by A.A. Produced by a transformation of self, whereas a transient identity is produced by an alternation of identity.

Alcoholic other   An emotional-interactional associate of the alcoholic. May be spouse, friend, relative, employer, co-drinker. This other becomes a member of an alcohol-centered relationship.

Alcoholic pride Also called false pride, which is mobilized behind the alcoholic's belief that alcohol can be controlled. Leads to "risk-taking" in drinking (Bateson).

Alcoholic risk-taking   Taking a drink when the probabilities of success are minimal and the likelihood of failure is high (Bateson).

Alcoholic self   A self divided against itself, trapped within the negative emotions that alcoholism produces. Key emotions are ressentimant and self-pride. Characterized by denial, bad faith, and emotional and physical violence.

Alcoholic situation There are two forms: (1) act one of the three-act play called "A Merry-Go-Round Named Denial"; (2) a descriptive term used to reference four interactional-drinking patterns the alcoholic and his or her other become embedded in: open-drinking context, closed-drinking context, sober context, in-control, normally intoxicated context.

Alcoholic understanding   The process of interpreting, knowing, and comprehending the meaning intended, felt, and expressed by another alcoholic.

Alcoholic violence   Refers to attempts by the alcoholic to regain through emotional and physical violence a sense of self that has been lost to alcohol and his or her other. There are five types: emotional, playful, spurious, real, and paradoxical.

Alternation of identity   Changes in identity that do not require transformations or a radical restructuring of self. Evidenced in alcoholics who do not remain in A.A. and in the self-changes the alcoholic's other often experiences.

Bad faith   A lie to oneself in an attempt to escape responsibility for one's actions. A denial of one's situation and one's place in it. A fleeing from what one is—that is, alcoholic.

Big Book   A.A.'s name for *Alcoholics Anonymous: The Story of How Many Thousands of Men and Women Have Recovered from Alcoholism: The Basic Text of Alcoholics Anonymous,* 3rd ed., 1976.

Blackout   "Amnesia, not associated with loss of consciousness, for all or part of the events that occurred during or immediately after a drinking session" (Keller and McCormick, 1968).

Bottom   Confronting one's alcoholic situation, finding it intolerable and surrendering to alcoholism. Accompanied by collapse and sincerely reaching out for help. May be high or low.

Circuit of selfness   The moving field of experience that connects the person to the world.

Codependent   An alcoholic other who has become dependent on the alcoholic's alcoholism.

Craving   Overwhelming desire for alcohol. There are two forms: (1) *physiological,* or *nonsymbolic,* located in the withdrawal effects felt as the body detoxifies alcohol; and (2) *psychological, symbolic,* or *phenomenological,* felt as a compelling need for alcohol in the absence of any withdrawal symptom.

Denial   Refusing to accept one's alcoholism; closely akin to being in "bad faith."

Dis-ease   An uneasiness, or disorder in health, body, or manner of living. Alcoholism is a dis-ease of conduct in the world, involving an uneasiness with self, time, emotion, and relations with others.

Drunken comportment   Culturally and socially patterned forms of behavior that occur after an individual has been drinking. Situationally, culturally, and historically determined and defined (MacAndrew and Edgerton, 1969).

Dry drunk   When an A.A. member displays all of the characteristics of being drunk, or hung-over, that is, self-centered, emotional, self-pitying, angry, resentful, and so on, he or she is said to be in a dry drunk.

DUI   Driving under the influence of alcohol.

Emotion   Self-feeling.

Emotionality   The process of being emotional.

Emotional account   Justification of a self-feeling.

Emotional associate   A person who is implicated in the subject's emotional world of experience.

Emotionally divided self A self turned against itself, disembodied, characterized by self-loathing and ressentiment.

Emotional understanding Knowing and comprehending through emotional means, including sympathy and imagination, the intentions, feelings, and thoughts expressed by another.

Emotional practice An embedded practice that produces anticipated and unanticipated alterations in the person's inner and outer streams of emotional experience.

Enabler An alcoholic other who enables, or assists, the alcoholic in his or her drinking career.

Field of experience The temporal structure of meanings, definitions, and feelings that surround and situate the person in the world.

Gamma alcoholic Jellinek's term: involves excessive drinking, acquired increased tissue tolerance to alcohol, withdrawal symptoms, craving due to physical dependence on alcohol, and an inability to stop drinking once it is begun. This type is most like A.A.'s alcoholic.

Grapevine A.A.'s international monthly magazine.

Home group The A.A. group an A.A. member calls his or hers. Often the first group ever attended, but not necessarily. The member will become a regular in this group.

"How It Works" A section of *The Big Book* (pp. 58-60), which is read at many A.A. meetings as it contains A.A.'s Twelve Steps.

Ideal-self Self-ideal individual selects for self, but often fails to achieve.

Imaginary The inner world of symbolic, imaginary conversations the person locates himself or herself within.

Integration hypothesis A social group will have lower rates of alcoholism when it has clear rules concerning how alcohol is to be used, that is, when drinking is ritually integrated into the group's way of life (Ullman).

Lay theory of alcoholism A threefold interpretive structure that contains theories of time, causality, denial, and successful drinking.

Loss of control Any drinking of alcohol starts a chain reaction that is felt as a physical and psychological demand for alcohol. Typically experienced as (a) an inability to stop drinking after one drink, (b) and an inability to predict one's behavior once drinking begins.

"Merry-Go-Round Of Trouble." A continuous circuit of negative symbolic interaction, involving the alcoholic and his or her other in an endless round of problems and troubles, that is, DUI's, unpaid bills, loss of work, divorce, violence, and so on.

Narcissism The individual acts as if he or she were in love with himself or herself. The state of self-love and admiration of oneself. In A.A. the phrase "His or her majesty" is taken to refer to this form of narcissism from which alcoholics believe they suffer.

Negative symbolic interaction An interaction process characterized by violence, contrasting, negative emotions, and destructive schismogenesis.

Newcomer A person early in A.A.'s program of recovery; usually with less than three months sobriety.

Normal social drinker A drinker who can control alcohol and not become alcoholic.

Oldtimer An A.A. regular with 10 years or more continuous sobriety and A.A. membership.

Overpermissive alcohol culture The cultural attitude is permissive toward drinking, to behaviors that occur when drinking, and to drinking pathologies (Pittman, 1967).

Permissive alcoholic culture Cultural attitude toward ingesting alcohol is permissive, but negative toward drunkenness and other drinking pathologies (Pittman, 1967).

Pigeon An A.A. term for a newcomer with whom an oldtimer is working.

Program An A.A. reference to the Twelve Steps and the Twelve Traditions and the spiritual program contained in the Steps.

Relapse Also called a "slip." A return to drinking by a recovering alcoholic.

Ressentiment The repeated experiencing and reliving of a particular emotional reaction against another. The emotion is negative, hostile, and includes a cluster of interrelated feelings—anger, wrath, envy, intense self-pride, and desire for revenge.

Schismogenesis The genesis of divisions and conflicts within a relationship such that more of one kind of behavior by one member produces more of a counter-behavior by the other member, that is, attempts to control the alcoholic's drinking produce more drinking (Bateson).

Self That process that unifies the stream of thoughts and experiences the person has about himself or herself around a single pole or point of reference; not a thing, but a process. It is consciousness conscious of itself, referring always to the sameness and steadiness of something always present to the person in his or her thoughts, as in "I am here, now, in the world, present before and to myself." Involves moral feelings for self, including all the subject calls his or hers at a particular moment in time, such as material possessions, self-feelings, and relations to others. Also includes the meaning the person gives to himself or herself as a distinct object and subject at any given moment, involving the meaning of the person as he or she turns inward in reflection. The self is not in consciousness, but in the world of social interaction. It haunts the subject.

Self as false subjectivity Living self through material things and experiencing a loss of self as a result.

Self as loss Experiencing the absence of an inner sense of selfness, or positive being.

Self as transcendent Seeking a mode of self-understanding and awareness that is located in a structure outside the self. May be produced by drugs and alcohol, or by interaction in a group.

Self-feelings Sequences of lived emotionality having self-referents, including a feeling for self, a feeling of this feeling, and a revealing of the moral self to the person through this feeling.

Self-ideal Ideal self set before person by others.

Serenity A.A. term for peace of mind, emotional sobriety, and the absence of negativity in one's life.

Serenity prayer Said at the beginning of every A.A. meeting: "God grant me the serenity to accept the things I cannot change, courage to change the things I can, and wisdom to know the difference."

Six Theses of Alcoholism Six points of interpretation in the structures of experience that constitute the alcoholic circle. They refer, in turn, to temporality, self, relations with others, emotionality, denial and bad faith, self-control and surrender.

Slip A return to drinking by a recovering alcoholic. May be planned or unplanned. Also called relapse.

Sobriety date The date of an A.A. member's last drink.

Social phenomenological method That mode of inquiry that returns to the things of experience and studies them from within. Involves five phases: deconstruction of previous theories of the phenomenon, capture, reduction, construction, and contextualization.

Sponsor An older A.A. member who assists a newcomer in getting sober and working the Steps.

Steps A.A.'s Twelve Steps (see A.A., 1976).

Surrender A threefold process: (1) admitting alcoholism, (2) accepting alcoholism, (3) surrendering in the inner self to alcoholism.

Tables A.A.'s name for the tables around which all A.A. meetings occur.

Time-out period An universal societal phenomenon in which the everyday demands for accountability over one's actions are suspended, or set aside. Drunken comportment is typically structured within these moments, as drinking commonly is associated with time-out periods of experience (MacAndrew and Edgerton, 1969).

Traditions A.A.'s Twelve Traditions (see A.A., 1953).

Transformation of self Radical restructuring of self and its basic beliefs, evidenced in recovery from alcoholism.

Twelve and Twelve A.A.'s name for its second basic text, *The Twelve Steps and the Twelve Traditions.*

Victim An alcoholic other who becomes victimized by the alcoholic's alcoholism.

References

Alcoholics Anonymous

1985   Eastern United States A.A. Directory. New York: Alcoholics Anonymous World Services.

1984   "Pass It On": The Story of Bill Wilson and How the A.A. Message Reached the World. New York: Alcoholics Anonymous World Services.

1980   Dr. Bob and the Good Oldtimers: A Biography with Recollections of Early A.A. in the Midwest. New York: Alcoholics Anonymous World Services.

1976   Alcoholics Anonymous. New York: Alcoholics Anonymous World Services. (1939)

1975   Living Sober: Some Methods A.A. Members Have Used for Not Drinking. New York: Alcoholics Anonymous World Services.

1973   Came to Believe: The Spiritual Adventure of A.A. as Experienced by Individual Members. New York: Alcoholics Anonymous World Services.

1967   As Bill Sees It: The A.A. Way of Life—Selected Writings of A.A.'s Co-Founder. New York: Alcoholics Anonymous World Services.

1963   "The Bill W.-Carl Jung letters." Grapevine (January): 26-31.

1957   Alcoholics Anonymous Comes of Age: A Brief History of A.A. New York: Alcoholics Anonymous World Services.

1953   Twelve Steps and Twelve Traditions. New York: Alcoholics Anonymous World Services.

Al-Anon Family Groups

1985   Al-Anon Faces Alcoholism. New York: Al-Anon Family Group Headquarters.

1977   Lois Remembers. New York: Al-Anon Family Group Headquarters.

American Medical Association

1968   Manual on Alcoholism. New York: American Medical Association.

Armor, D. J., J. M. Polich, and J. B. Stambul

1976   Alcoholism and Treatment, Report #R-1739-NIAAA. Santa Monica, CA: Rand Corporation.

Bacon, M. K., H. Barry III, and I. L. Child

1965   "A cross-cultural study of drinking, II: relations to other features of culture." Quarterly Journal of Studies on Alcohol, Supplement No. 3: 29.

Baldwin, John W.

1984   "Comment on Denzin's 'Note on emotionality, self and interaction.'" American Journal of Sociology, 90: 418-421.

Bales, Robert F.

1946   "Cultural differences in rates of alcoholism." Quarterly Journal of Studies on Alcohol, 6: 480-499.

Bandura, Albert

1977   Social Learning Theory. Englewood Cliffs, NJ: Prentice-Hall.

Barnes, Gordon E.

1983   "Clinical and prealcoholic personality characteristics," pp. 113-196 in Benjamin Kissin and Henri Begleiter (eds.) The Biology of Alcoholism, Vol. 6:

Psychosocial Factors. New York: Plenum.

Bateson, Gregory
    1972a "The cybernetics of self: a theory of alcoholism," pp. 309-337 in G. Bateson,
          Steps to an Ecology of Mind. New York: Ballantine.
    1972b "The logical categories of learning and communication," pp. 279-308 in
          G. Bateson, Steps to an Ecology of Mind. New York: Ballantine.
    1972c "Double bind," pp. 271-278 in G. Bateson, Steps to an Ecology of Mind.
          New York: Ballantine.
    1972d "A theory of play and fantasy," pp. 177-193 in G. Bateson, Steps to an
          Ecology of Mind. New York: Ballantine.
    1972e "Toward a theory of schizophrenia," pp. 201-227 in G. Bateson, Steps to an
          Ecology of Mind. New York: Ballantine.

Baudrillard, Jean
    1983 "The ecstasy of community," pp. 126-134 in Hal Foster (ed.) The Anti-
         Aesthetic: Essays on Postmodern Culture. Port Townsend, WA: Bay Press.

Beauchamp, Dan E.
    1980 Beyond Alcoholism: Alcohol and Public Health Policy. Philadelphia, PA:
         Temple University Press.

Becker, Howard S.
    1973 Outsiders. New York: Free Press.
    1967 "History, culture and subjective experience." Journal of Health and Social
         Behavior 8: 163-176.
    1964 "Personal Change in Adult Life." Sociometry 27: 40-53.
    1960 "Notes on the Concept of Commitment." American Journal of Sociology
         66: 32-40.

Beecher, Henry K.
    1959 Measurement of Subjective Responses: Quantitative Effects of Drugs. New
         York: Oxford University Press.

Benson, Michael
    1985 "Denying the guilty mind: accounting for the involvement in a white collar
         crime." Criminology 23: 583-607.

Berger, Peter and Thomas Luckmann
    1967 The Social Construction of Reality. New York: Doubleday.

Bergson, H.
    1947 Creative Evolution. New York: Modern Library.

Berk, Richard A., Sarah Fenstermaker Berk, Donileen R. Loseke, and David Rauma
    1983 "Mutual combat and other family violence myths," pp. 197-212 in D.
         Finkelhor, R. J. Gelles, G. T. Hotaling, and M. A. Straus (eds.) The Dark
         Side of Families: Current Family Violence Research. Beverly Hills, CA: Sage.

Berryman, John
    1973 Recovery: A Novel. New York: Farrar, Straus and Giroux.

Bertaux, Daniel
    1981 "Introduction," pp. 1-22 in D. Bertaux (ed.) Biography and Society. Beverly
         Hills, CA: Sage.

Biegel, Allan and Stuart Ghertner
    1977 "Toward a social model: an assessment of social factors which influence prob-
         lem drinking and its treatment," pp. 197-234 in Benjamin Kissin and Henri
         Begleiter (eds.) The Biology of Alcoholism, Vol. 5, Treatment and Rehabilita-
         tion of the Chronic Alcoholic. New York: Plenum.

Blane, H. T.
    1968 The Personality of the Alcoholic: Guises of Dependency. New York: Harper
         & Row.

Blumer, Herbert
   1969   Symbolic Interactionism. Englewood Cliffs, NJ: Prentice-Hall.
Burke, Kenneth
   1954   Permanence and Change (rev. ed.). Los Altos, CA: Hermes.
Caddy, G. R., H. J. Addington, and D. Perkins
   1978   "Individualized behavior therapy for alcoholics: a third year independent double-blind follow-up." Behavior Research and Therapy 16: 345-362.
Cahalan, Don
   1970   Problem Drinkers. San Francisco: Jossey-Bass.
Cahalan, Don and Robin Room
   1974   Problem Drinking Among American Men. New Brunswick, NJ: Rutgers Center of Alcohol Studies.
   1972   "Problem drinking among American men aged 21-59." American Journal of Public Health 62: 1473-1482.
Cahalan, Don and I. H. Cisin
   1976   "Drinking behavior and drinking problems in the United States," pp. 77-115 in B. Kissin and H. Begleiter (eds.) The Biology of Alcoholism, Vol. 4: Social Aspects of Alcoholism. New York: Plenum.
Cappell, H. and C. P. Herman
   1972   "Alcohol and tension reduction—a review." Quarterly Journal of Studies on Alcohol 33: 33-64.
Carpenter, J. A. and N. P. Armenti
   1972   "Some effects of ethanol in human sexual and aggressive behavior," pp. 509-543 in B. Kissin and H. Begleiter (eds.) The Biology of Alcoholism, Vol. 2: Physiology and Behavior. New York: Plenum.
Carver, Raymond
   1983   Fires: Essays, Poems, Stories. New York: Vantage.
Catanzaro, Ronald J.
   1967   "Psychiatric aspects of alcoholism," pp. 31-44 in David J. Pittman (ed.) Alcoholism. New York: Harper & Row.
Cavan, Sheri
   1966   Liquor License: An Ethnography of Bar Behavior. Chicago: Aldine.
Chafetez, Morris E., and Robert Yoerg
   1977   "Public health treatment programs in alcoholism," pp. 593-614 in Benjamin Kissin and Henri Begleiter (eds.) The Biology of Alcoholism, Vol. 5: Treatment and Rehabilitation of the Chronic Alcoholic. New York: Plenum.
Charmaz, K. C.
   1980   "The social construction of self-pity in the chronically ill," pp. 123-146 in N. K. Denzin (ed.) Studies in Symbolic Interaction, Vol. 3. Greenwich, CT: JAI.
Chomsky, N.
   1959   "A review of B. F. Skinner's Verbal Behavior." Language 35: 26-58.
Clough, Patricia T.
   1979   "Sociability and public behavior in a mid-sized city," pp. 359-376 in N. K. Denzin (ed.) Studies in Symbolic Interaction, Vol. 2, Greenwich, CT: JAI.
Cockerham, William
   1981   Sociology of Mental Disorders. Englewood Cliffs, NJ: Prentice-Hall.
Conger, J. J.
   1956   "Alcoholism: theory, problem and challenge, II: reinforcement theory and the dynamics of alcoholism." Quarterly Journal of Studies on Alcohol, 17: 291-324.

1951   "The effects of alcohol on conflict behavior in the albino rat." Quarterly
       Journal of Studies on Alcohol 12: 1-29.
Davies, D. L.
1962   "Normal drinking in recovered alcoholics," Quarterly Journal of Studies on
       Alcohol 23: 94-104.
Davis, Fred
1961   "Deviance disavowal: the management of strained interaction by the visibly
       handicapped," Social Problems, 9: 120-132.
Denzin, Norman K.
1986a The Recovering Alcoholic. Beverly Hills, CA: Sage.
1986b Treating Alcoholism. Beverly Hills, CA: Sage.
1986c "A phenomenology of the emotionally divided self," forthcoming in Krysia
       Yardley and Terry Honess (eds.) Self and Identity: Psychosocial Perspectives.
       New York: John Wiley.
1985a "Review essay: signifying acts: structure and meaning in everyday life."
       American Journal of Sociology 91: 432-434.
1985b "Emotion as lived experience." Symbolic Interaction 8: 223-239.
1984a On Understanding Emotion. San Francisco: Jossey-Bass.
1984b "Toward a phenomenology of domestic, family violence," American Jour-
       nal of Sociology 90: 483-513.
1984c "Reply to Baldwin," American Journal of Sociology 90: 422-427.
1983a "A note on emotionality, self and interaction," American Journal of Sociology
       88: 943-953.
1983b "Interpretive interactionism," pp. 129-146 in G. Morgan (ed.) Beyond Method.
       Beverly Hills, CA: Sage.
1982   "Notes on criminology and criminality," pp. 115-130 in H. E. Pepinsky (ed.)
       Rethinking Criminology. Beverly Hills, CA: Sage.
1981   "Frame Analysis Reconsidered" (with Charles Keller). Contemporary
       Sociology 10: 52-59.
1980   "Towards a phenomenology of emotion and deviance." Zeitschrift für
       Soziologie 9: 251-261.
1979   "On the interactional analysis of social organization." Symbolic Interaction,
       2: 59-72.
1978   "Crime and the American liquor industry," pp. 87-118 in N. K. Denzin (ed.)
       Studies in Symbolic Interaction, Vol. 2. Greenwich, CT: JAI.
1977a "Notes on the criminogenic hypothesis: a case study of the American liquor
       industry." American Sociological Review 42: 905-920.
1977b Childhood Socialization. San Francisco: Jossey-Bass.
Derrida, Jacques
1981   Positions. Chicago: University of Chicago Press.
1978   Writing and Difference. Chicago: University of Chicago Press.
1976   Of Grammatology. Baltimore, MD: Johns Hopkins University Press.
1973   Speech and Phenomenona. Evanston, IL: Northwestern University Press.
1972   "Structure, sign, and play in the discourse of the human sciences," pp. 247-272
       in Richard Macksey and Eugenio Donato (eds.) The Structuralist Controversy:
       The Languages of Criticism and the Sciences of Man. Baltimore, MD: Johns
       Hopkins University Press.

Dewey, J.
  1922 Human Nature and Conduct: An Introduction to Social Psychology. New York: Henry Holt.
Duhman, Bob
  1984 "The curse of the writing class." Saturday Review, (January-February): 27-30.
Durkheim, Emile
  1982 The Rules of Sociological Method. New York: Free Press. (1895)
  1973 "Elementary forms of religious life," in R. Bellah (ed.) Emile Durkheim on Morality and Society. Chicago: University of Chicago Press. (1912)
  1964 The Division of Labor in Society. Glencoe, IL: Free Press. (1893)
  1961 The Elementary Forms of Religious Life. New York: Collier. (1912)
  1951 Suicide. Glencoe, IL: Free Press. (1897)
Faulkner, William
  1981 "Mr. Acarius," pp. 435-448 in Joseph Blotner (ed.) Uncollected Stories of William Faulkner. New York: Vantage.
Foucault, M.
  1982 "Afterword: the subject and power," in H. Dreyfus and P. Rabinow (eds.) Michael Foucault: Beyond Structuralism and Hermeneutics. Chicago: University of Chicago Press.
  1980 Power/Knowledge: Selected Interviews and Other Writings 1972-1977 (C. Gordon, ed., C. Gordon, L. Marshall, J. Mepham, K. Soper, trans.). New York: Pantheon.
  1977 Discipline and Punish. New York: Pantheon.
  1970 The Order of Things: An Archaeology of the Human Sciences. New York: Random House.
Fox, R.
  1957 "Treatment of alcoholism," pp. 163-172 in H. E. Himwich (ed.) Alcoholism: Basic Aspects and Treatment. Washington, DC: American Association for the Advancement of Science, 47.
Franks, David
  1984 "Role-Taking, social power and imperceptiveness: the analysis of rape," pp. 123-147 in N. K. Denzin (ed.) Studies in Symbolic Interaction, Vol. 6. Greenwich, CT: JAI.
Franks, Lucinda
  1985 "A new attack on alcoholism." New York Times Magazine (October 29): 46-48, 50, 61-65, 69.
Freedman, Samuel G.
  1984 "Fugard traces a dark parallel on film." New York Times (Section 2): 1, 19.
Freud, S.
  1965 The Interpretation of Dreams. New York: Avon.
  1954 The Standard Edition. London: Hogarth.
  1938 The Basic Writings of Sigmund Freud. New York: Random House.
Gadamer, H. G.
  1976 Philosophical Hermeneutics (D. E. Linge, ed. and trans.). Los Angeles: University of California Press.
  1975 Truth and Method. London: Sheed and Ward.
Garfinkel, H.
  1967 Studies in Ethnomethodology. Englewood Cliffs, NJ: Prentice-Hall.
Geertz, C.
  1983 Local Knowledge: Further Essays in Interpretive Anthropology. New York: Basic Books.

1973   The Interpretation of Cultures. New York: Basic Books.
Gelles, Richard J.
1979   Family Violence. Beverly Hills, CA: Sage.
1972   The Violent Home: A Study of Physical Aggression Between Husbands and Wives. Beverly Hills, CA: Sage.
Glaser, Barney and Anselm Strauss
1967   "Awareness contexts and social interaction." American Sociological Review 29: 669-679.
Goffman, E.
1956   "Embarrassment and social organization." American Journal of Sociology 67: 264-271.
1959   The Presentation of Self in Everyday Life. New York: Doubleday.
1961a   Asylums. New York: Doubleday.
1961b   Encounters. Indianapolis, IN: Bobbs-Merrill.
1963a   Behavior in Public Places. New York: Free Press.
1963b   Stigma. Englewood Cliffs, NJ: Prentice-Hall.
1967   Interaction Ritual. New York: Doubleday.
1971   Relations in Public. New York: Basic Books.
1974   Frame Analysis. New York: Harper.
1981   Forms of Talk. Philadelphia: University of Pennsylvania Press.
1983   "The interaction order." American Sociological Review 48: 1-17.
Gomberg, Edith S.
1976   "Alcoholism in women," pp. 117-166 in Benjamin Kissin and Henri Begleiter (eds.) The Biology of Alcoholism, Vol. 4: Social Aspects of Alcoholism. New York: Plenum.
Gomberg, Edith, L. Helene R. White, and John A. Carpenter
1982   Alcohol, Science and Society Revisited. Ann Arbor: University of Michigan Press and New Brunswick, NJ: Rutgers Center of Alcohol Studies.
Goodwin, Donald
1979   "Alcoholism and heredity: a review and hypothesis." Archives of General Psychiatry 36: 57-61.
1976   Is Alcoholism Hereditary? New York: Oxford University Press.
Goodwin, Donald W. and Samuel B. Guze
1974   "Heredity and alcoholism," pp. 37-52 in Benjamin Kissin and Henri Begleiter (eds.) The Biology of Alcoholism, Vol. 3: Clinical Pathology. New York: Plenum.
Goshen, Charles E.
1973   Drinks, Drugs, and Do-Gooders. New York: Free Press.
Grove, William M. and Remi J. Cadoret
1983   "Genetic factors in alcoholism," pp. 31-56 in Benjamin Kissin and Henri Begleiter (eds.) The Biology of Alcoholism, Vol. 7: Biological Factors. New York: Plenum.
Gusfield, Joseph R.
1981   The Culture of Public Problems: Drinking-Driving and the Symbolic Order. Chicago: University of Chicago Press.
Guze, S. B., V. B. Tuasvon, M. A. Stewart, and B. Picken
1963   "The drinking history: a comparison of reports by subjects and their relatives." Quarterly Journal of Studies on Alcohol, 24: 249-260.
Habermas, Jürgen
1983   "Modernity—an incomplete project," pp. 3-15 in Hal Foster (ed.) The Anti-Aesthetic: Essays on Postmodern Culture. Post Townsend, WA: Bay Press.

Hall, Peter M. and John P. Hewitt
    1973   "The quasi-theory of communication and the management of dissent," Social Problems 18: 17-27.
Hazelden Foundation, Inc.
    1985   Today's Gift. Center City, MN: Hazelden Foundation.
    1983   The Promise of a New Day. Center City, MN: Hazelden Foundation.
    1982   Each Day a New Beginning. Center City, MN: Hazelden Foundation.
    1954   Twenty-Four Hours a Day. Center, MN: Hazelden Foundation.
Hegel, G. W. F.
    1910   The Phenomenology of Mind (J. B. Braillie, trans.) London: Allen & Unwin. (trans. 1931)
Heidegger, Martin
    1982   The Basic Problems of Phenomenology. Bloomington: Indiana University Press. (originally published 1975)
    1962   Being and Time. Harper & Row. (originally published 1927)
Hetherton, E. M. and N. P. Wray
    1964   "Aggression, need for social support and human preferences." Journal of Abnormal Sociology and Psychology 68: 685-689.
Hewitt, John P. and Peter M. Hall
    1973   "Social problems: problematic situations and quasi-theories." American Sociological Review 38: 367-374.
Hewitt, John P. and Randall Stokes
    1975   "Disclaimers." American Sociological Review 40: 1-11.
Hochschild, Arlie
    1983   The Managed Heart: Commercialization of Human Feeling. Berkeley: University of California Press.
Horton, Donald
    1943   "The functions of alcohol in primitive societies: a cross-cultural Study. Quarterly Journal of Studies on Alcohol 4: 199-320.
Husserl, E.
    1962   Ideas: General Introduction to Pure Phenomenology. New York: Collier. (originally published 1913)
Isbell, H.
    1955   "Craving for alcohol." Quarterly Journal of Studies on Alcohol 16: 38-42.
Jackson, Joan
    1962   "Alcoholism and the family," pp. 472-493 in D. J. Pittman and C. R. Snyder (eds.) Society, Culture, and Drinking Patterns. New York: John Wiley.
Jakobson, Roman
    1962   Selected Writings, Vol. 1: Phonological Studies. The Hague: Mouton.
    1956   "Two aspects of language and two aspects of aphasic disturbances," pp. 69-96 in R. Jakobson and Morris Halle (eds.) Fundamentals of Language. The Hague: Mouton.
James, Henry
    1920   "Letter to Mrs. Humphry Ward," pp. 332-336 in Percy Lubbock (ed.) Henry James: Letters. London: Hogarth.
James, William
    1961   The Varieties of Religious Experience: A Study of Human Nature. New York: Collier. (originally published 1904)
    1955   Pragmatism and Four Essays from the Meaning of Truth. New York: Humanities. (originally published 1910)

Jameson, Fredric
   1983   "Postmodernism and consumer society," pp. 111-125 in Hal Foster (ed.)
           The Anti-Aesthetic: Essays on Postmodern Culture. Port Townsend, WA:
           Bay Press.
Jellinek, E. M.
   1962   "Phases of alcohol addiction," pp. 356-368 in D. J. Pittman and C. R. Snyder
           (eds.) Society, Culture, and Drinking Patterns. New York: John Wiley.
   1960   The Disease Concept of Alcoholism. New Haven, CT: Hillhouse Press.
Jessor, R., T. D. Graves, R. C. Hanson and S. L. Jessor
   1968   Society, Personality and Deviant Behavior: A Study of a Tri-ethnic Com-
           munity. New York: Holt, Rinehart, and Winston.
Johnson, Bruce Holley
   1973   "The alcoholism movement in America: a study in cultural innovation."
           Ph.D. dissertation, University of Illinois, Urbana-Champaign.
Johnson, Dianne
   1983   Dashiell Hammett: A Life. Boston: Little, Brown.
Jung, Carl G.
   1939   The Integration of Personality. New York: Farrar and Rinehart.
Kane, Geoffrey P.
   1981   Inner-City Alcoholism: An Ecological Analysis and Cross-Cultural Study. New
           York: Human Sciences Press.
Keller, Mark
   1978   "A nonbehaviorist's view of the behavioral problem with alcoholism," pp.
           381-398 in Peter E. Nathan, G. Alan Marlatt, and Tor Løberg (eds.)
           Alcoholism: New Directions in Behavioral Research and Treatment. New
           York: Plenum.
   1976   "The Disease Concept of Alcoholism Revisited." Quarterly Journal of Studies
           on Alcohol 37: 1694-1717.
Keller, Mark and Mairi McCormick
   1968   A Dictionary of Words About Alcohol. New Brunswick, NJ: Rutgers Center
           of Alcohol Studies, Publications Division.
Kellerman, Joseph L.
   1969   Alcoholism: A Merry-Go-Round Named Denial. New York: Al-Anon Family
           Group Headquarters.
Kemper, Theodore D.
   1981   "Social constructionist and positivist approaches to the sociology of emo-
           tions." American Journal of Sociology 86: 336-362.
Kissin, Benjamin
   1977   "Theory and practice in the treatment of alcoholism," pp. 1-52 in Benjamin
           Kissin and Henri Begleiter (eds.) The Biology of Alcoholism, Vol. 5: Treat-
           ment and Rehabilitation of the Chronic Alcoholic. New York: Plenum.
Knight, R. P.
   1937   "The psychodynamics of chronic alcoholism." Journal of Nervous and Mental
           Diseases 86: 538-548.
Kohut, H.
   1984   How Does Psychoanalysis Cure? Chicago: University of Chicago Press.
Kristeva, Julia
   1974   La Révolution du Langage Poétique. Paris: Editions du Seuil.
Kuhn, Manford H. and C. Addison Hickman
   1956   Individuals, Groups and Economic Behavior. New York: Dryden.

Kurtz, Ernest
    1979   Not-God: A History of Alcoholics Anonymous. Center City, MN: Hazelden
           Educational Materials.

Lacan, J.
    1982   Feminine Sexuality. New York: W. W. Norton.
    1978   The Four Fundamental Concepts of Psycho-Analysis. New York: W. W.
           Norton.
    1977   Ecrits: A Selection (A. Sheridan, trans.). New York: W. W. Norton.
    1968   Speech and Language in Psychoanalysis (A. Wildon, trans.). Baltimore, MD:
           Johns Hopkins University Press.
    1966   Ecrits. Paris: Edition de Seuil.
    1957   "The agency of the letter in the unconscious or reason since Freud,"
           pp. 146-178 in Lacan (1977).
    1949   "The mirror stage as formative of the function of the I as revealed in
           psychoanalytic experience," pp. 1-7 in Ecrits: A Selection (A. Sheridan, trans.).
           New York: W. W. Norton.

Laing, R. D.
    1965   The Divided Self: An Existential Study in Sanity and Madness. Harmonds-
           worth, England: Penguin.

Lasch, C.
    1985   The Minimal Self: Psychic Survival in Troubled Times. London: Picador.
    1983   The Culture of Narcissism. New York: Doubleday.

Leach, Barry and John L. Norris
    1977   "Factors in the development of Alcoholics Anonymous (A.A.)," pp. 441-519
           Benjamin Kissin and Henri Begleiter (eds.) The Biology of Alcoholism:
           Vol. 5: Treatment and Rehabilitation of the Chronic Alcoholic. New York:
           Plenum.

Lemert, Edwin M.
    1967   Human Deviance, Social Problems and Social Control. Englewood Cliffs,
           NJ: Prentice-Hall.
    1964   "Drinking in Hawaiian plantation society." Quarterly Journal of Studies on
           Alcohol 25: 689-713.
    1958   "The use of alcohol in three Salish Indian tribes." Quarterly Journal of Studies
           on Alcohol 19: 90-107.

Levine, Harry Gene
    1978   "The discovery of addiction." Journal of Studies on Alcohol 39: 143-174.

Lewontin, R. C., Steven Rose and Leon J. Kamin
    1984   Not in Our Genes: Biology, Ideology, and Human Nature. New York:
           Pantheon.

Lindesmith, Alfred R., Anselm L. Strauss, and Norman K. Denzin
    1977   Social Psychology. New York: Holt, Rinehart & Winston.
    1975   Social Psychology. New York: Holt, Rinehart & Winston.

Lindesmith, Alfred R.
    1975   "A reply to McAuliffe and Gordon's 'test of Lindesmith's theory of addic-
           tion,' " American Journal of Sociology 81: (July): 147-153.
    1968   Addiction and Opiates. Chicago: Aldine.
    1947   Opiate Addiction. Bloomington, IN: Principia.

Lisansky, E. A.
    1960   "The etiology of alcoholism: the role of psychological predisposition."
           Quarterly Journal of Studies on Alcohol 21: 314-324.

Lofland, John
    1977   Doomsday Cult: A Study of Conversion, Proselytization, and Maintenance
            of Faith. Enlarged Edition. New York: Irvington.
Lofland, John and Rodney Stark
    1965   "Conversion to a deviant perspective." American Sociological Review 30:
            862-875.
Lowry, Malcolm
    1984   Under the Volcano. New York: New American Library. (originally published
            1947)
Ludwig, Arnold M.
    1983   "Why do alcoholics drink?" pp. 197-214 in Benjamin Kissin and Henri
            Begleiter (eds.) The Biology of Alcoholism, Vol. 6: Psychosocial Factors. New
            York: Plenum.
Lynch, R.
    1982   "Play, creativity, and emotion," pp. 45-62 in N. K. Denzin (ed.) Studies in
            Symbolic Interaction, Vol. 4. Greenwich, CT: JAI.
Lyotard, Jean-Francois
    1984   The Postmodern Condition: A Report on Knowledge. Minneapolis: The
            University of Minnesota Press.
MacAndrew, C. and H. Garfinkel
    1962   "A consideration of changes attributed to intoxication as commonsense rea-
            sons for getting drunk." Quarterly Journal of Studies on Alcohol 23: 252-266.
MacAndrew, Craig and Robert B. Edgerton
    1969   Drunken Comportment: A Social Explanation. Chicago: Aldine.
McAuliffe, William E. and Robert A. Gordon
    1974   "A test of Lindesmith's theory of addiction: the frequency of euphoria among
            long-term addicts." American Journal of Sociology 77: 795-840.
McClearn, Gerald E.
    1983   "Genetic factors in alcohol abuse: animal models," pp. 1-30 in Benjamin
            Kissin and Henri Begleiter (eds.) The Biology of Alcoholism, Vol. 7: Biological
            Factor. New York: Plenum.
McClelland, David C., William N. Davis, Rudolf Kalin, and Eric Wanner
    1972   The Drinking Man. New York: Free Press.
McCord, W., J. McCord, and J. H. Mendelson
    1960   Origins of Alcoholism. Palo Alto, CA: Stanford University Press.
Madsen, William
    1974   The American Alcoholic: The Nature-Nurture Controversy in Alcoholic
            Research and Therapy. Springfield, IL: Charles C Thomas.
Maisto, Stephen A. and Janice Boon McCollam
    1980   "The use of multiple measures of life health to assess alcohol treatment out-
            come: a review and critique," pp. 15-76 in Linda Carter Sobell, Mark B.
            Sobell, and Elliot Ward (eds.) Evaluating Alcohol and Drug Abuse Treat-
            ment Effectiveness. New York: Pergamon.
Mandall, Wallace and Harold M. Ginzburg
    1976   "Youthful alcohol use, abuse and alcoholism," pp. 167-204 in Benjamin Kissin
            and Henri Begleiter (eds.) The Biology of Alcoholism, Vol. 4: Social Aspects
            of Alcoholism. New York: Plenum.
Mann, Marty
    1968   New Primer on Alcoholism 2nd ed. New York: Holt, Rinehart and Winston.

Mark V. H. and F. R. Ervin
1970   Violence and the Brain. New York: Harper & Row.
Marshall, Shelly
1978   Young, Sober & Free. Center City, MN: Hazelden.
Marx, K.
1983   "From the eighteenth brumaire of Louis Bonaparte," in E. Kamenka (ed.)
        The Portable Karl Marx. New York: Penguin. (1852)
Maxwell, Milton A.
1984   The Alcoholics Anonymous Experience: A Close-up View for Professionals.
        New York: McGraw-Hill.
Mead, G.H.
1964   "A pragmatic theory of truth," pp. 320-344 in Andrew J. Reck (ed.) George
        Herbert Mead: Selected Writings. Indianapolis, IN: Bobbs-Merrill. (1929)
1934   Mind, Self and Society. Chicago: University of Chicago Press.
1899   "The working hypothesis in social reform." American Journal of Sociology
        5: 369-371.
Mello, Nancy K.
1983   "A behavioral analysis of the reinforcing properties of alcohol and other drugs
        in man," pp. 133-198 in Benjamin Kissin and Henri Begleiter (eds.) The
        Biology of Alcoholism, Vol. 7: Biological Factors. New York: Plenum.
1972   "Behavioral studies of alcoholism," pp. 219-292 in Benjamin Kissin and Henri
        Begleiter (eds.) The Biology of Alcoholism, Vol. 2: Physiology and Behavior.
        New York: Plenum.
Menninger, Karl A.
1938   Man Against Himself. New York: Harcourt, Brace and World.
Merleau-Ponty, M.
1963   The Structure of Behavior (A. L. Fisher, trans.). Boston: Beacon. (originally
        published 1942)
Merryman, Richard
1984   Broken Promises, Mended Dreams. Boston: Little, Brown.
Mills, C. W.
1959   The Sociological Imagination. New York: Oxford University Press.
1940   "Situated actions and vocabularies of motive." American Sociological Review
        5: 904-913.
Mulford, Harold A.
1970   "Meeting the problems of alcohol abuse: a testable action plan for Iowa,"
        Cedar Rapids: Iowa Alcoholism Foundation.
1969   "Alcoholics, alcoholism, and problem drinkers: social objects in-the-making."
        Report to the National Center for Health Statistics, U.S. Department of
        Health, Education and Welfare (Contract PH. 86-65-91). (mimeo)
Mulford, Harold A. and Donald E. Miller
1964   "Measuring public acceptance of the alcoholic as a sick person." Quarterly
        Journal of Studies on Alcohol 25: 314-323.
Nathan, P. E., N. A. Titler, L. A. Lowenstein, P. Solomon, and A. M. Rossi
1970   "Behavioral analysis of chronic alcoholism." Archives of General Psychiatry
        22: 419-428.
Newsweek
1984a   "Getting straight: how Americans are breaking the grip of drugs and alcohol."
        (June 4): 62-69.
1984b   "Alcoholism and the recovering generation." (September 4): 71-80.

New York Times
   1983   "Alcohol abuse in the United States," (October 23): 1.
Neitzche, Friedrich
   1887   A Genealogy of Morals: Vol. 2 (William A. Hausemann, trans.). New York: Macmillian.
O'Neill, Eugene
   1955   Long Day's Journey into Night. New Haven, CT: Yale University Press.
Oscar-Berman, M.
   1984   "Central nervous system disorders," pp. 190-191 in Raymond J. Corsini (ed.) Encyclopedia of Psychology, Vol. 1. New York: John Wiley.
Parsons, Talcott
   1951   The Social System. New York: Free Press.
Pattison, E. Mansell, Mark B. Sobell, and Linda C. Sobell
   1977   Emerging Concepts of Alcohol Dependence. New York: Springer.
Pattison, E. Mansell
   1966   "A critique of alcoholism treatment concepts." Quarterly Journal of Studies on Alcohol 27: 49-71.
Pattison, E. Mansell, E. B. Headley, G. C. Gleser and L. A. Gottschalk
   1968   "Abstinence and normal drinking: an assessment of changes in drinking patterns in alcoholics after treatment." Quarterly Journal of Studies on Alcohol 29: 610-633.
Pendery, Mary L., Irving M. Maltzman, and L. Jolyon West
   1982   "Controlled drinking by alcoholics: new findings and a reevaluation of a major affirmative study." Science 217: 169-175.
Pernanen, Kai
   1976   "Alcohol and crimes of violence," pp. 351-444 in B. Kissin and H. Begleiter (eds.) The Biology of Alcoholism, Vol. 4: Social Aspects of Alcoholism. New York: Plenum.
Pittman, David
   1967   "International overview: social and cultural factors in drinking patterns, pathological and nonpathological," pp. 3-20 in David J. Pittman (ed.) Alcoholism. New York: Harper & Row.
Redd, William H., A. L. Porterfield, and Barbara L. Anderson
   1979   Behavior Modification: Behavioral Approaches to Human Problems. New York: Random House.
Roebuck, Julian B. and R. G. Kessler
   1972   The Etiology of Alcoholism: Constitutional, Psychological and Sociological Approaches. Springfield, IL: Charles C Thomas.
Robinson, David
   1979   Talking Out of Alcoholism: The Self-Help Process of Alcoholics Anonymous. Baltimore, MD: University Park Press.
Roman, Paul M. and Harrison M. Trice
   1976   "Alcohol abuse and work organization," pp. 445-519 in Benjamin Kissin and Henri Begleiter (eds.) The Biology of Alcoholism, Vol. 4: Social Aspects of Alcoholism. New York: Plenum.
Room, Robin
   1983   "Region and urbanization as factors in drinking practices and problems," pp. 555-604 in Benjamin Kissin and Henri Begleiter (eds.) The Biology of Alcoholism, Vol. 6: Psychosocial Factors. New York: Plenum.
   1982   "Alcohol, science and social control," pp. 371-384 in Edith L. Gomberg, Helene R. White, and John A. Carpenter (eds.) Alcohol, Science and Society Revisited. Ann Arbor: The University of Michigan Press.

Royce, James E.
1981 Alcoholic Problems and Alcoholism: A Comprehensive Survey. New York: Free Press.
Rubington, Earl
1977 "The role of the halfway house in the rehabilitation of alcoholics," pp. 351-384 in Benjamin Kissin and Henri Begleiter (eds.) The Biology of Alcoholism, Vol. 5: Treatment and Rehabilitation of the Chronic Alcoholic. New York: Plenum.
1973 Alcohol Problems and Social Control. Columbus, OH: Merrill.
Rudy, David
1986 Becoming an Alcoholic. Carbondale: Southern Illinois University.
Ryan, Christopher and Nelson Butters
1983 "Cognitive deficits in alcoholics," pp. 485-538 in Benjamin Kissin and Henri Begleiter (eds.) The Biology of Alcoholism, Vol. 7: Biological Factors. New York: Plenum.
Sagarin, E.
1969 Odd Man In: Societies of Deviants in America. Chicago: Quadrangle.
Sartre, Jean-Paul
1981 The Family Idiot, Gustave Flaubert Vol. I: 1821-1857. Chicago: University of Chicago Press. (originally published 1970)
1976 Critique of Dialectical Reason. London: NLP. (originally published 1960)
1956 Being and Nothingness. New York: Philosophical Library. (originally published 1943)
Scheff, Thomas J.
1979 Catharsis in Healing, Ritual and Drama. Berkeley: University of California Press.
Scheler, M.
1961 "Ressentiment," in L. A. Coser (ed.) [W. W. Holdeim, trans.] New York: Free Press. (originally published 1912)
Schuckit, Marc A. and Jane Duby
1983 "Alcoholism in women," pp. 215-242 in Benjamin Kissin and Henri Begleiter (eds.) The Biology of Alcoholism, Vol. 6: Psychosocial Factors. New York: Plenum.
Schutz, A.
1968 Collected Papers. Vol. III: Studies in Phenomenological Philosophy. (I. Schutz, ed.) The Hague: Martinus Nijhoff.
1967 The Phenomenology of the Social World. Evanston, IL: Northwestern University Press.
1964 Collected Papers. Vol. II: Studies in Social Theory. A. Brodersen (ed.) The Hague: Martinus Nijhoff.
1962 Collected Papers, Vol. I: The Problem of Social Reality. M. Natanson (ed.) The Hague: Martinus Nijhoff.
Schutz A. and T. Luckmann
1973 The Structures of the Life World. Evanston, IL: Northwestern University Press.
Searle, John
1970 Speech Acts. Cambridge, England: Cambridge University Press.
Scott, M. B. and S. M. Lyman.
1968 "Accounts." American Sociological Review 33: 46-62.

Shott, Susan
   1979   "Emotion and social life: a symbolic interactionist analysis." American Jour-
          nal of Sociology 84: 1317-1334.
Silkworth, William D.
   1976   "The doctor's opinion," pp. xxiii-xiv in Alcoholics Anonymous. New York:
          Alcoholics Anonymous World Services.
Skinner, B. F.
   1953   Science and Human Behavior. New York: Macmillan.
Smith, Bernard B.
   1957   "A friend looks at Alcoholics Anonymous," pp. 273-283 in Alcoholics
          Anonymous Comes of Age: A Brief History of A.A. New York: Alcoholics
          Anonymous World Services.
Sobell, Mark B. and Linda C. Sobell
   1978   Behavioral Treatment of Alcohol Problems: Individualized Therapy and Con-
          trolled Drinking. New York: Plenum.
Sobell, Linda C., Mark B. Sobell, and Elliot Ward
   1980   Evaluating Alcohol and Drug Abuse Treatment Effectiveness: Recent
          Advances. New York: Pergamon.
Solomon, Joel
   1983   "Psychiatric characteristics of alcoholics," pp. 67-112 in Benjamin Kissin and
          Henri Begleiter (eds.) The Biology of Alcoholism, Vol. 6: Psychosocial Fac-
          tors. New York: Plenum.
Spender, Stephen
   1984   "Introduction," pp. vii-xxiii in Malcolm Lowry, Under the Volcano. New
          York: New American Library. (originally published 1947)
Spinoza, Benedict
   1888   The Ethics (R.H.M. Elwes, trans.). London: George Bell and Sons.
Spradley, James P.
   1970   You Owe Yourself a Drunk: An Ethnography of Urban Nomads. Boston:
          Little, Brown.
Steinglass, Peter and Anne Robertson
   1983   "The alcoholic family," pp. 243-307 in Benjamin Kissin and Henri Begleiter
          (eds.) The Pathogenesis of Alcoholism, Vol. 6: Psychosocial Factors. New
          York: Plenum.
Stivers, Richard
   1976   A Hair of the Dog: Irish Drinking and American Stereotype. University Park:
          Pennsylvania State University Press.
Stone, Gregory P.
   1962   "Appearance and the self," pp. 86-118 in A. M. Rose (ed.) Human Nature
          and Social Process. Boston: Houghton Mifflin.
   1976   "Personal acts." Symbolic Interaction 1: 1-16.
Straus, Robert
   1974   Escape from Custody. New York: Harper & Row.
Strauss, Anselm
   1959   Mirrors and Masks: The Search for Identity. New York: Free Press.
Sullivan, H. S.
   1953   The Interpersonal Theory of Psychiatry. New York: W. W. Norton.
Sykes, G. M. and Matza, D.
   1959   "Techniques of neutralization: a theory of delinquency." American
          Sociological Review 22: 664-670.

Thorndike, E. L.
  1913 The Psychology of Learning: Educational Psychology, Vol. 2. New York: Columbia University, Teachers' College Press.
Thune, Carl E.
  1977 "Alcoholism, and the archetypical past: a phenomenological perspective on Alcoholics Anonymous." Quarterly Journal of Studies on Alcohol 38: 75-88.
Tiebout, Harry M.
  1954 "The ego factors in surrender in alcoholism." Quarterly Journal of Studies on Alcohol 15: 610-621.
  1953 "Surrender versus compliance in therapy." Quarterly Journal of Studies on Alcohol 14: 58-68.
  1949 "The act of surrender in the therapeutic process with special reference to alcoholism." Quarterly Journal of Studies on Alcohol 10:48-58.
  1944 "Therapeutic mechanisms in Alcoholics Anonymous." American Journal of Psychiatry 100: 468-473.
Time Magazine
  1985 "Cocktails' 85: America's new drinking habits." (May 20): 68-73, 76-78.
Travisano, Richard
  1981 "Alternation and conversion as qualitatively different transformations," pp. 237-248 in Gregory P. Stone and Harvey A. Farberman (eds.) Social Psychology Through Symbolic Interaction. New York: John Wiley.
Trice, Harrison M.
  1966 Alcoholism in America. New York: McGraw-Hill.
  1957 "A study of the process of affiliation with Alcoholics Anonymous." Quarterly Journal of Studies in Alcohol 18: 39-43.
Trice, Harrison, M. and Paul M. Roman
  1970 "Delabeling, relabeling and Alcoholics Anonymous." Social Problems 17: 468-480.
Ullman, Albert D.
  1958 "Sociocultural backgrounds conducive to alcoholism." Annals of the American Academy of Political and Social Science 315: 48-55.
United States Government Printing Office
  1976 Comprehensive Alcohol Abuse and Alcoholism Prevention, Treatment, and Rehabilitation Act Amendments of 1976. Washington, DC: Author.
Updike, John
  1984 "Modernist, postmodernist, what will they think of next?" New Yorker (September 10): 136-137, 140-142.
Urbina, S. P.
  1984 "Amnesia," pp. 56-57 in Raymond J. Corsini (ed.) Encyclopedia of Psychology, Vol. 1. New York: John Wiley.
Vaillant, George
  1983 The Natural History of Alcoholism: Causes, Patterns and Paths to Recovery. Cambridge, MA: Harvard University Press.
Vander Mey, Brenda J. Neff, and Ronald L. Neff
  1986 Incest as Child Abuse: Research and Implications. New York: Praeger.
Vogel-Sprott, M.
  1972 "Alcoholism and learning," pp. 485-509 in Benjamin Kissin and Henri Begleiter (eds.) The Biology of Alcoholism, Vol. 2: Physiology and Behavior. New York: Plenum.

Victor, M.
    1965   "Observations on the amnestic syndrome in man and its anatomical basis,"
            pp. 311-340 in M.A.B. Brazier (ed.) Brain Functions: Vol. 2. Berkeley: Univer-
            sity of California Press.
Wallace, John
    1982   "Alcoholism from the inside out: a phenomenological analysis," pp. 1-23
            in Nada J. Estes and M. Edith Heinemann (eds.) Alcoholism: Development,
            Consequences and Interventions. St. Louis, MO: Mosby.
Wallace, P. M.
    1984   "Aphasia," p. 80 in Raymond J. Corsini (ed.) Encyclopedia of Psychology,
            Vol. 1. New York: John Wiley.
Watson, J. B.
    1913   "Psychology as the behaviorist sees it." Psychological Review 20: 158-177.
Watts, Thomas D. and Roosevelt Wright, Jr.
    1983   Black Alcoholism: Toward a Comprehensive Understanding. Springfield, IL:
            Charles C Thomas.
Weber, M.
    1946   From Max Weber: Essays in Sociology. H. Gerth and C. W. Mills (eds.) New
            York: Oxford University Press.
Weinstein, E. A. and P. Deutschberger
    1962   "Some dimensions of altercasting." Sociometry 26: 454-466.
White, R. W.
    1956   The Abnormal Personality. New York: Ronald Press.
Whitney, Elizabeth D.
    1965   The Lonely Sickness. Boston: Beacon.
Wholey, Dennis [ed.]
    1984   The Courage to Change: Hope and Help for Alcoholics and Their Families.
            Personal Conversations with Dennis Wholey. Boston, MA: Houghton Mifflin.
Wilden, Anthony
    1968   "Lacan and the discourse of the other," pp. 86-222 in J. Lacan, Speech and
            Language in Psychoanalysis (A. Wilden, trans.) Baltimore, MD: Johns
            Hopkins University Press.
Williams, Allan F.
    1976   "The Alcoholic Personality," pp. 243-275 in Benjamin Kissin and Henri
            Begleiter (eds.) The Biology of Alcoholism, Vol. 4: Social Aspects of
            Alcoholism. New York: Plenum.
Wiseman, Jacqueline P.
    1970   Stations of the Lost: The Treatment of Skid Row Alcoholics. Englewood
            Cliffs, NJ: Prentice-Hall.
Woititz, Janet Geringer
    1983   Adult Children of Alcoholics. Rutgers, NJ: Health Communications.
Zuriff, G. E.
    1985   Behaviorism: A Conceptual Reconstruction. New York: Columbia Univer-
            sity Press.
Zwerling, Israel and Milton Rosenbaum
    1959   "Alcoholic addiction and personality," pp. 624-644 in S. Arieti (ed.) American
            Handbook of Psychiatry. New York: Basic Books.

NAME INDEX

SUBJECT INDEX

About the Author

Norman K. Denzin is Professor of Sociology and Humanities at the University of Illinois at Urbana-Champaign. He received a B.A. degree (1963) and a Ph.D. degree (1966) in sociology from the University of Iowa. Denzin's main research activities and interests have been in childhood socialization, the study of language, the self, interaction, interpretive theory, and phenomenology. He has been vice-president of the Society for the Study of Symbolic Interaction (1976-1977), and secretary of the Social Psychology Section of the American Sociological Association (1978-1980). Denzin is the author and editor of several books, including *Social Psychology* (1987, with A. Lindesmith and S. Strauss, 6th ed.), *Sociological Methods* (1978), *The Research Act* (1978), 2nd ed.), *Childhood Socialization* (1977), *Children and Their Caretakers* (1973), *The Values of Social Science* (1973), *The Mental Patient* (1968, with S. P. Spitzer), *On Understanding Emotion* (1984) *The Recovering Alcoholic* (1986), *Treating Alcoholism* (1987), and *Interpretive Interactionism* (1987). He is the editor of *Studies in Symbolic Interaction: A Research Annual* and the author of over fifty articles, which have appeared in such journals as *American Journal of Sociology, American Sociological Review, British Journal of Sociology, Semiotica, Social Forces, Social Problems,* and *Sociological Quarterly.*